Investigating *Shrek*

Investigating *Shrek*

Power, Identity, and Ideology

Edited by
Aurélie Lacassagne, Tim Nieguth, and François Dépelteau

INVESTIGATING *SHREK*
Copyright © Aurélie Lacassagne, Tim Nieguth, and François Dépelteau, 2011.

All rights reserved.

First published in 2011 by
PALGRAVE MACMILLAN®
in the United States—a division of St. Martin's Press LLC,
175 Fifth Avenue, New York, NY 10010.

Where this book is distributed in the UK, Europe and the rest of the World, this is by Palgrave Macmillan, a division of Macmillan Publishers Limited, registered in England, company number 785998, of Houndmills, Basingstoke, Hampshire RG21 6XS.

Palgrave Macmillan is the global academic imprint of the above companies and has companies and representatives throughout the world.

Palgrave® and Macmillan® are registered trademarks in the United States, the United Kingdom, Europe and other countries.

ISBN: 978-0-230-11415-9

Library of Congress Cataloging-in-Publication Data

Investigating Shrek : power, identity, and ideology / edited by Aurélie
    Lacassagne, Tim Nieguth, François Dépelteau.
      p. cm.
    Includes bibliographical references.
    Includes filmography.
    ISBN 978-0-230-11415-9 (hardback)
    1. Shrek (Motion picture) 2. Motion pictures—Political aspects—History and criticism. I. Nieguth, Tim, 1971– II. Lacassagne, Aurélie, 1978– III. Dépelteau, François, 1963– IV. Title.
    PN1997.2.S48I68 2011
    791.43'72—dc22   2011008777

A catalogue record of the book is available from the British Library.

Design by Integra Software Services

First edition: September 2011

10 9 8 7 6 5 4 3 2 1

Printed in the United States of America.

Contents

Acknowledgments — vii

Notes on Contributors — ix

1. Through the Looking Glass: *Shrek* in Perspective — 1
   Aurélie Lacassagne, Tim Nieguth, and François Dépelteau

Part I *Shrek* in the Classroom

2. Representing Political Regimes in the *Shrek* Trilogy — 15
   Aurélie Lacassagne
3. Big (and Green) Is Better: *Shrek* and Female Body Image — 27
   Mary Ryan
4. Green Consciousness: Earth-Based Myth and Meaning in *Shrek* — 39
   Jane Caputi
5. "Happiness Is Just a Teardrop Away": A Neo-Marxist Interpretation of *Shrek* — 59
   Alexander Spencer, Judith Renner, and Andreas Kruck

Part II *Shrek* in Context

6. The Mouse Is Dead, Long Live the Ogre: *Shrek* and the Boundaries of Transgression — 75
   Daniel Downes and June M. Madeley
7. Kantian Cosmopolitanism and the Dreamworkification of the Next Generation — 87
   Marianne Vardalos
8. *Shrek*: Simple Story or Nonhuman Transactor? — 103
   François Dépelteau

9 An Evolutionary Psychological Perspective on Shrek
   and Fiona   133
   Gayle Brewer

Part III Instead of a Conclusion

10 Potholes of Knowledge: The Politics of Studying *Shrek*   147
   Tim Nieguth

Filmography   163

Bibliography   165

Index   183

Acknowledgments

Putting together this volume has been an extraordinary adventure. Sometimes, the road we traveled was rocky, but more often, the ride was thoroughly enjoyable. Throughout our journey, we were lucky enough to enlist the support of many people; without them, we surely would not have reached our destination. We would like to take this opportunity to express our heartfelt gratitude to all of them.

Many of our friends and colleagues read parts of the manuscript and offered insights that helped us improve our arguments. All of them showed their support in other ways that were at least as important. At the risk of abbreviating what is, in fact, a long list, we are especially grateful to Thomas Gerbet, Jérôme Leclerc, and Éric Robitaille at Radio-Canada, Monique Benoit and Jean Dragon at Laurentian University, Jonathan Paquette at the University of Ottawa, and Yasmeen Abu-Laban, Natasja Treiberg, and Shauna Wilton at the University of Alberta. Thank you for believing in us, and in this project.

We are also thankful to our contributors, who have been prompt, professional, and a pleasure to work with throughout. Thank you for joining us on this adventure; it has been a privilege to travel with you.

Farideh Koohi-Kamali and Robyn Curtis at Palgrave Macmillan have shown exceptional enthusiasm for our project. Their support, efficiency, and diligence in shepherding the volume through the final editing and production process have been remarkable. We are also grateful to the anonymous reviewer at Palgrave for his or her keen insights and evident passion. They helped us tremendously in improving the manuscript and renewing our faith.

We are greatly indebted to Gina Webb, Wanda Gagné, and Robin Craig for their assistance in editing various parts of the volume.

Last, but certainly not least, we would like to thank our family members, the ones present and the ones gone—Dirk Nieguth, Elke Nieguth, and Heike Nieguth; Mario Beauchemin, Christian Couvrette,

Jean-Pierre Carrier, Tatiana Landini, and Ghislaine Berthiaume; Patricia, Dominique, Robert, Renée-Myriam, Betty, Jean-Benoit, Mathilde and Alexandre Lacassagne, Gérard Lévy, Paul and Laurette Quillet, Ludivine Allagnat, Julien Lizet, Sébastien Martin, Michel and Eliane Billart, Olivier Unger, Rob Coleman, and Richard and Moragh Dunning. They have made us who we are.

The book is dedicated to Marianne and Alexane, two very special little ogresses who provided the inspiration for our adventure. They cannot be blamed for what follows, but we sincerely hope that they will remain dreamers, no matter what people think, say, or do.

Notes on Contributors

GAYLE BREWER is senior lecturer in psychology at the University of Central Lancashire, England. Her primary research interests focus on the areas of physical attractiveness, body image, and sexual behavior. She has published a number of articles within an evolutionary psychology perspective.

JANE CAPUTI is professor of women's studies at Florida Atlantic University, USA. She is the author of several books, including *The Age of Sex Crime* (1987) and *Goddesses and Monsters: Women, Myth, Power, and Popular Culture* (2004), and the film *The Pornography of Everyday Life* (2006). She is widely recognized for her interpretations of popular culture, mythology, gender, and violence.

FRANÇOIS DÉPELTEAU is assistant professor of sociology at Laurentian University, Canada. His research interests focus on social movements and social theories. His publications include articles in *Sociological Theory* and contributions to several edited volumes. He is the author of a widely used textbook on social science methods, *La Démarche d'une recherche en sciences humaines*.

DANIEL DOWNES is associate professor of information and communication studies at the University of New Brunswick campus in Saint John, Canada. His research explores issues pertaining to cultural diversity, communication technologies, and the regulation of the new media economy. He has published articles on intellectual property and copyright, new media regulation, and the changing nature of the audience. In 2005, he published *Interactive Realism: The Poetics of Cyberspace* with McGill-Queen's University Press.

ANDREAS KRUCK is a teaching and research associate in international relations and global governance at Ludwig Maximilians University of Munich, Germany. In his PhD project he analyzes the reallocation of political authority to transnational private actors. His broader research interests include the links between global governance and multilateralism and the function of credit ratings in the financial system of international political economy.

AURÉLIE LACASSAGNE is associate professor of political science at Laurentian University, Canada. Her research centers mainly on immigration and popular culture studies. Her publications include articles in the *Canadian Political Science Review* and the *Journal of Marketing and Communication* as well as a coedited book entitled *Belarus, l'état de l'exception*. She is a collaborator in a major research initiative on the inclusion of visible minorities and immigrants in Ontario's cities.

JUNE M. MADELEY is assistant professor of information and communication studies at the University of New Brunswick campus in Saint John, Canada. She is interested in the content, production, and reception of various communications media and applies a focus on class, gender, ethnicity, and racialization to her work. Her current research centers on gender and the audiences of manga (Japanese comics). She is also currently working on analyses of science fiction and fantasy fandom.

TIM NIEGUTH is associate professor of political science at Laurentian University, Canada. His research centers on nationalism, secession, and the politics of popular culture. His publications include articles in the *Canadian Journal of Political Science, Space and Polity,* and *Nations and Nationalism*. He is currently conducting research on globalization and online games, science fiction and American nationalism, and the connection between Euroscepticism and popular culture in Britain.

JUDITH RENNER is a PhD candidate and research fellow at the Geschwister-Scholl-Institute for Political Science at the Ludwig-Maximilians-University Munich, Germany. Her research interests focus on discourse theory, peace and conflict, and international norms. Her most recent article, " 'I'm Sorry for Apologizing': Czech and German Apologies and their Perlocutionary Effects," is to appear in the *Review of International Studies*.

MARY RYAN is a doctoral student of English literature at Mary Immaculate College, Limerick, Ireland. Her thesis focuses on the connection between feminist theory and contemporary Irish women's writing, including Irish chick lit novels. She has published papers on feminist theory, women's literature, and popular culture.

ALEXANDER SPENCER is assistant professor at the Geschwister-Scholl-Institute for Political Science, Ludwig-Maximilians-University of Munich, Germany. His research focuses on constructivist IR theory, terrorism, and popular culture. He has written a number of articles on terrorism and has published a book with Palgrave Macmillan in 2010 titled *The Tabloid Terrorist. The Predicative Construction of New Terrorism in the Media.*

MARIANNE VARDALOS is assistant professor of sociology at the Laurentian University campus in Barrie, Canada. Her research interests focus on cultural studies, political economy, globalization, and the social construction of identity and subjectivity. She is a founder of The Human Condition Conference Series and the author of *Invading Goa: New Tourism or Old Imperialism?*

CHAPTER 1

Through the Looking Glass: *Shrek* in Perspective

Aurélie Lacassagne, Tim Nieguth, and François Dépelteau

This book began to lead a life of its own well before it appeared in print. The plan for the book was hatched one memorable evening in a basement where we had once again taken refuge from the harsh realities of a Northern Ontario winter. At one point, the conversation turned to our growing interest in the relationship between popular culture, power, identity, and social theory. Since two of us have small children who adore *Shrek* and had in consequence been exposed to repeated viewings of the original three movies in the franchise, the green ogre quite naturally became the focal point of our discussion. Idle musings at first, our reflections on the significance of *Shrek* soon led one of us to suggest that we seriously consider a book-length study on the subject.

Thusly born on a dark and stormy night in due observance of a time-honored cliché (as befits a project that is, after all, concerned with a modern fairy tale), the book was off to an auspicious start. One of us sent a call for papers to several mailing lists and websites in social sciences, soliciting scholarly analyses of Shrek, Fiona, Donkey, and the other members of the ogre's cabal. At that point, we had not yet written our own papers. It was, in other words, business as usual—until a journalist from one of the local newspapers happened upon the call for papers. This was when events took an unexpected turn. News about our nonexistent book made it to the first page of *The Sudbury Star* in the form of a relatively long article, relegating a report on a local concert by Bryan Adams to the second page. We were surprised and somewhat amused: after all, it is not often that social scientists beat pop stars in the media (even in the local media)! We took for granted that public interest in our project would be short lived and would go no further than this article. We were mistaken.

Soon after the publication of the initial article, other journalists (from local, regional, and national media outlets) began to call, requesting for interviews. They were undeterred by our insistence that the book, far from being a reality, was only a project at that point in time, and a project in its earliest stages at that. For almost two weeks, not a day would go by without requests for an interview. Taken somewhat aback by the strong media echo, we ultimately gave roughly a dozen interviews on the book project (and the social implications of *Shrek* more generally), some of which were rebroadcast internationally.

Nor was interest in the project limited to the media. Hoping for a momentary reprieve from the media's attention, one of us had been preparing a lecture on Ulrich Beck for a sociology course on environmental risks. Upon entering the classroom, this editor was surprised to find at least half of the students engaged in an animated debate about this hyperreal book on *Shrek*. His hope for a respite from *Shrek* somewhat dimmed, the editor valiantly tried to ignore the students' conversation and proceeded to announce the (serious) topic of the day: the management of environmental risks in a capitalist society. Unimpressed, the students immediately interrupted him to turn the discussion back to the matter that obviously preoccupied them:

> FIRST STUDENT   Did you write a book on Shrek?
> EDITOR   Well, I am one of the three editors. The book still does not exist, just a call for papers at this point. But today, I want to talk about environmental issues in the risk society. We will study the thesis of Ulrich Beck...
> SECOND STUDENT   [INTERRUPTING]
>   This is an interesting topic.
> EDITOR   Beck is interesting? You mean the risk society is an interesting topic? Well, I am happy that...
> SECOND STUDENT   [INTERRUPTING]
>   Oh yeah, of course... That one too...

Unsurprisingly, not everybody was this enthusiastic about our book project (see Chapter 10 of this volume for a detailed discussion). The initial article published in *The Sudbury Star*, for instance, soon attracted negative comments from members of the public, who described the project as a waste of time and funds. Likewise, some of our colleagues were less than impressed with the project, since they considered *Shrek* an unfit object for "serious" social scientific study.

In light of these developments, it became impossible to deny that we were dealing with a bigger topic than we had initially thought. Of course, we already knew that the movies had attracted millions of viewers, both at the time of their initial theatrical release and later in the form of movie rentals and sales. Since their first appearance on screen, the green ogre and his companions have emerged as an economically significant and highly lucrative franchise. As Table 1.1 illustrates, the costs involved in the production of the *Shrek* trilogy and the box office revenue the three movies have earned to date are considerable: the former amounts to 280 million U.S. dollars, while the latter hovers around 2.2 billion U.S. dollars.

Of course, ticket sales are not the only sources of revenue tapped by the *Shrek* franchise. Thus, by 2005, VHS and DVD sales of *Shrek* and *Shrek 2* alone had already reached 1.6 billion U.S. dollars ("DreamWorks' Shrek Franchise Delivers a Record-Setting $1.6 Billion in Consumer Home Entertainment Spending," 2005). DreamWorks' fortunes—and the livelihood of its employees—have, in good measure, hinged on the continued stream of revenue from the *Shrek* franchise. Regardless of whether one agrees or disagrees with the conclusion that the green ogre and company may offer important insights into contemporary culture and society, then, it is undeniable that the *Shrek* franchise has, at a minimum, had a significant economic impact.

When we embarked on this project, we were also aware that at least one neoconservative group in the United States had denounced the green ogre as part of a gay and lesbian conspiracy—a somewhat dubious distinction the *Shrek* franchise shared with the *Teletubbies* and

Table 1.1 *Shrek* trilogy: production costs and box office revenue in million U.S. dollars

Movie	Production budget	Box office revenue
Shrek	50	484.4
Shrek 2	70	919.8
Shrek the Third	160	799.0
Total	280	2, 203.2

Source: Nash Information Services (1997–2009).

Harry Potter. We had not anticipated that the premature announcement of this book—a book that did not yet exist—would so deeply upset some taxpayers. And we had not expected that, in the middle of a significant economic and environmental crisis, many students would be more attracted by an intellectual analysis of *Shrek* than, for instance, an analysis of the very real risks posed by soil contamination in their hometown. Astonished at the response our project had elicited, we became all the more convinced that *Shrek* deserved serious attention. Apparently, the green ogre was a more important social actor than we had given him credit for. In different ways, the chapters contained in this volume support this suspicion.

From the Written to the Visual Text: A Will to Politicize

Before providing an overview of the contents of this volume, we wish to briefly turn our attention to the history of the *Shrek* franchise. More specifically, we are interested in the narrative changes that accompany the transformation of *Shrek!*, the original book by William Steig, into the movie trilogy *Shrek*. A discussion of this transformation process can serve to highlight some of the inescapably political aspects of *Shrek* (inescapable, because they are the very root of the franchise), and can simultaneously provide a useful background for the chapters that follow. In essence, we wish to suggest that the *Shrek* franchise offers both a reflection and a critique of some of the cultural conventions that characterize modernity. As we do so, we should emphasize that the book focuses exclusively on the original three movies in the *Shrek* franchise. These movies form a coherent trilogy that is characterized by a high level of thematic unity and that follows an identifiable narrative structure. In contrast, the fourth installment in the series, entitled *Shrek Forever After* and released in 2010, represents a significant thematic and narrative departure from the original trilogy. Consequently, we chose not to include it in our analysis.

To begin at the beginning (if there is such a thing), *Shrek!* originated as a book written and illustrated in 1990 by William Steig. Steig was a well-known cartoonist for *The New Yorker* before launching a career as one of the most successful children's books authors of the last few decades. In his books, Steig created an original universe inhabited by talking animals, wonder, nature, and dreams, largely inspired by his own readings of classical fairy tales as a young boy (Hedblad, 2000). *Shrek!* fits this general mould in some ways, but also represents a significant departure from it: at heart, it is a rather fierce and gruesome story of an awful ogre who marries an awful ogress. There are few animals, apart from some snakes and (already) a donkey. There are no dreams in this story, only the ogre's terrible nightmare of children kissing and hugging him in the midst of a lovely landscape filled with flowers:

> He dreamed he was in a field of flowers where children frolicked and birds warbled. Some of the children kept hugging and kissing him, and there was nothing he could do to make them stop. He woke up in a daze, babbling like a baby: "It was only a bad dream...a horrible dream!" (Steig, 1990: p. 13)

This particular story of Steig's thus simultaneously represents a departure from the conventions of the classical fairy tale. To be sure, several traditional fairy-tale elements are present in Steig's *Shrek!*: we encounter a witch, a dragon, a knight, a castle, a talking animal, an ogre, and a princess. But the narrative deviates in a number of crucial ways from the pattern established by Andersen, the Grimm brothers, and other key authors in the fairy-tale genre: the hero (or antihero) is an ogre; the princess is ugly; the ogre and princess do get married, but "lived horribly ever after" (Steig, 1990: p. 25). There is no wonder, and if there is magic, it tends toward the blackish kind.

It is instructive to contrast Steig's version of the *Shrek* story with the one developed in the movie trilogy. As Sibley observes, the transformation of a written text into a visual text and the reappropriation of an artwork by other artists constitute

> a process that cannot be accomplished without change: the requirement of a film, opera, musical, ballet or radio play will always require some measure of extrapolation or a degree of compression; there will, invariably, be additions (...), and, in all likelihood, there will be many deletions. (Sibley, cited in Mathijs (ed.), 2006: p. xvi)

In transitioning from the book to the movie trilogy, we find substantial changes in the *Shrek* franchise: the cast of characters changes, as do the basic narrative and sociopolitical content. Unsurprisingly, the movie trilogy contains a much more substantial cast of characters than Steig's *Shrek!*, a short book of 25 pages. The trilogy keeps some of the central characters from the book but changes their roles. For instance, as is the case in the book, Shrek encounters a peasant during his adventures; unlike the book, this peasant is part of a mob intent on killing the ogre. Similarly, in the book as well as in the movies, Shrek defeats a dragon; but in the book, the character of the dragon remains undeveloped, whereas in the movie trilogy, she becomes a helper to the hero. Finally, Steig's version of Donkey embarks with Shrek on his quest for the princess. Unlike the movie trilogy, though, Donkey's role ends there; although garrulous, he remains rather passive.

In part, these changes are owed to the dramaturgical necessities of feature-length movies—not least the necessity of developing a lead character capable of sustaining such movies. Hopkins, discussing the transformation of the book into the movie trilogy, makes the following observation concerning the challenges inherent in that transformation:

> Certainly, the unique irreverence of the book would have to be preserved. At the same time, however, Shrek as a character does not exactly grow or develop in a way capable of sustaining an entire feature-length motion picture. It was obvious the creators would have to delve within the character of the ogre himself and discover the very human hopes, fears, conflicts and dreams of a classic movie hero. As Adamson [Andrew Adamson, the director of *Shrek* and *Shrek 2*] put it, it was a task of "deconstructing traditional fairy tales and reconstructing a new fairy tale." (2004: p. 14)

That de- and reconstruction process involved a politicization of the text that operates at several levels. Steig's book was "nasty, brutish and short"; it was very much a postmodern, thoroughly amoral story, quite different in this respect from the classical canon of children's literature. The *Shrek* trilogy is a decidedly modern story. Formally, it obeys the classical structure of a fairy tale to a much greater degree than Steig's book. For one thing, the trilogy has a moral. This moral is at once conventional and revolutionary: roughly, it suggests that, if the marginalized members of society band together and fight, the good can triumph over the bad. Good/bad, powerful/powerless, civilized/savage—the movies appear to incorporate many of the dichotomies that are commonly found in popular culture.

That being the case, one might be tempted to apply a structuralist framework to an interpretation of the movies. Such applications have yielded interesting results in other areas of popular culture. Will Wright, for instance, used a structuralist approach to study Hollywood Westerns in his seminal book entitled *Sixguns and Society* (1975). He argued that the Western genre works with a number of binary oppositions that can be used to group individual characters based on their relation to social action and the institutions of society. Wright (1975: p. 49) listed these dichotomies as follows:

INSIDE SOCIETY	OUTSIDE SOCIETY
Good	Bad
Strong	Weak
Civilization	Wilderness

In essence, Wright suggests that a classical Western movie "is the story of a hero who is somehow estranged from his society but on whose ability rests the fate of that society. The villains threatened the society until the hero acts to protect and save it. Thus, for analysis, we can reduce each story to three sets of characters: the hero, the society, and the villains" (1975: p. 40). In addition, Wright explained that the plot of a classical Western was marked by a standard sequence that contained 16 key events:

1. The hero enters a social group.
2. The hero is unknown to the society.
3. The hero is revealed to have an exceptional ability.
4. The society recognizes a difference between themselves and the hero; the hero is given a special status.
5. The society does not completely accept the hero.
6. There is a conflict of interests between the villains and the society.
7. The villains are stronger than the society; the society is weak.
8. There is a strong friendship or [respect] between the hero and a villain.
9. The villains threaten the society.
10. The hero avoids involvement in the conflict.
11. The villains endanger a friend of the hero's.
12. The hero fights the villains.
13. The hero defeats the villains.
14. The society is safe.
15. The society accepts the hero.
16. The hero loses or gives up his special status.

(Wright, 1975: pp. 142–3)

The parallels between this classical Western plot and the entries in the *Shrek* trilogy seem striking: after all, the first movie starts out with an ogre living in complete isolation from society who only decides to enter society when it intrudes on his splendid isolation. He encounters a situation where society is dominated by a villainous dictator, Lord Farquaad; Shrek attempts to stay out of the conflict between society and the villain, but is forced to become involved. A few heroic acts later, the villain is defeated and society is safe.

Resisting the temptation of declaring *Shrek* a post-Western fairy tale, we would instead point out that the sort of structuralist analysis charted by Wright and others is ultimately of limited value for grappling with the complexities of the *Shrek* trilogy. This is for two reasons: first, the narrative employed in the *Shrek* movies is not as linear as the ones one might, following Wright, consider to be typical of classical Westerns. For instance, in *Shrek,* the day is saved, and the villain defeated, not by the hero, but by a dragon—typically regarded as an archetypal Other in classical fairy tales. The trilogy's hero (or antihero) himself is thoroughly ambivalent about entering society, assuming the role of a hero, and defending those who have been excluded by society.

The sort of binary oppositions underpinning Wright's analysis are likewise unhelpful when applied to *Shrek*: in contrast to classical Westerns (and classical fairy tales), many of the trilogy's key characters or sets of characters cannot be assigned to either the "good" or the "evil" category in any straightforward fashion. For one thing, the *Shrek* trilogy resists attempts to reduce the complexity of social groups. Society's outsiders, for instance, are represented by two sets of characters: magical creatures who are good (such as the three pigs and Pinocchio) and magical creatures and other people who are bad (including Captain Hook, the talking trees, and other regulars at the seedy Poison Apple Tavern). In addition, the behavior and personality of specific individuals often tend toward ambivalence: sometimes they are good, sometimes they are bad; sometimes they are civilized, sometimes they are wild. As noted earlier, this ambivalence is characteristic of Shrek himself. In this sense, he does represent the complexities of individual actors, actors who are embedded in ongoing, multifaceted, and contradictory negotiations about how to behave (be a coward or a hero; be on the right side or not) and how to properly interact with others. As Hopkins puts it, "Shrek's most formidable opponent is himself" (2004: p. 124). This is a deliberate choice on the part of the trilogy's writers: Hopkins outlines in some detail how the writers changed the script numerous times in an attempt to keep Shrek emotional, in crisis, and unsure of his ability to be loved.

In Steig's book, Shrek is not ambivalent; he knows what kind of life he wants to live and does not question this choice. His parents kick him out of their house, and he does not challenge their decision. A witch instructs him to meet and marry the ugly princess, and he obediently follows those instructions. In the films, Shrek's character assumes greater depth; the ogre "faces his innermost demons of identity and insecurity" (Hopkins, 2004: p. 60). Arguably, the character is deepened in a way that is politically and socially highly relevant, by pointing up the complexities, inequities, and contradictions inherent in an individual's social positions. The same is true for the trilogy's considerable emphasis on the politics of gender, race, identity, and the body. The movies are a rich source for problematizing processes of otherization. In the first movie, for instance, the magical creatures are expelled from the Kingdom of Farquaad because Lord Farquaad does not believe that they fit into the "perfect world" he wishes to create. Shrek, as an ogre, is rejected by society because his body is otherized. Fiona is locked in a remote castle because she has an ambivalent body (which transforms into that of an ogress at night). In *Shrek 2,* we learn that the king of Far Far Away is forced to hide his real body (that of a frog). Individuals who transgress against gender norms—such as Pinocchio, the wolf, and the barmaid at the Poison Apple Tavern—are excluded from society and exist on its margins.

Consequently, it can be argued (and, as we will see, hotly debated) that *Shrek,* similar to other recent children's movies, challenges the classical conception of fairy tales and myths. Classical fairy tales and myths may "communicate a conceptual order to the members of that society" (Wright, 1975: p. 17), but one possible contention is that *Shrek* is too subversive for that purpose. Or, to be more precise, the conceptual order of our contemporary world is so chaotic that the conceptual order communicated by *Shrek* reveals its contradictions. On this reading, *Shrek* therefore might be seen as a call for a new social order in which everybody is part of the community, an inclusive community that does not marginalize groups or individuals on the basis of otherization. The moral of this new fairy tale would be, as mentioned earlier, that the excluded can become part of the established. Needless to say, not everyone agrees with this reading of *Shrek* as an emancipatory text. This includes the authors of some of the texts assembled in this volume. In fact, we are delighted to say that the contributions to this volume take very different sides in a lively debate over the nature and social significance of *Shrek.*

Overview and Plan of the Book

The book pursues two different, yet intertwined objectives. The first is to present *Shrek* as pedagogical tool that could be usefully employed in a number of different disciplines. In this sense, the current volume follows the trail blazed by several recent volumes on popular culture and social science, not least Daniel H. Nexon and Iver B. Neumann's collection of essays, *Harry Potter and International Relations* (2006), or Cynthia Weber's introduction to *International Relations Theory* (2009). The pedagogical uses of *Shrek* are the focus of the volume's first part, entitled "*Shrek* in the Classroom." Chapters in this section primarily use *Shrek* to illustrate different theoretical or conceptual frameworks.

Thus, Aurélie Lacassagne approaches *Shrek* from a political science angle. She argues that the *Shrek* trilogy represents three political regimes: individual anarchism, totalitarianism, and liberal democracy (Chapter 2). Lacassagne shows that the movies criticize implicitly or explicitly the three regimes and reject them as acceptable models. According to Lacassagne, "one feature common to all three regimes is the logic of exclusion of a certain segment of the society in question" (p. 25). In this sense, *Shrek* is pushing for a more inclusive society. From a sociological perspective, Mary Ryan connects the relationship between Fiona and Shrek to the contestation of the "myth of beauty" so forcefully denounced by Wolf and others (Chapter 3). This myth "works by encouraging women that they should not settle for their natural looks but should strive to achieve the unattainable model of 'perfection'" (p. 36). For Ryan, the *Shrek* trilogy has "potentially feminist aspects, specifically in terms of female body image" (p. 28).

In Chapter 4, Jane Caputi connects Shrek—the *green* ogre—to the valorization of a new "green consciousness" and a condemnation of the master culture of patriarchal society. From this perspective, *Shrek* is seen "as a contemporary retelling of ancient chthonic or earth-based myth" (p. 44), stressing environmental consciousness, egalitarianism, and the feminine principle. Alexander Spencer, Judith Renner, and Andreas Kruck expose a critical approach to *Shrek* (Chapter 5). They suggest that the movie trilogy draws on tropes that strongly resonate with Marxist theory and the reality of the class struggle, but ultimately serves the interest of capitalism by underlining the role of the media as an instrument of class rule.

The second section of the volume, entitled "*Shrek* in Context," pursues a somewhat different objective. Chapters in this section are concerned with outlining some of the ways in which *Shrek* is actively bound up with various aspects of social reality—such as capitalism, power relations, inequality, rule and resistance. In Chapter 6, for example, Daniel Downes and June M. Madeley argue that *Shrek* is ultimately banal: it refuses to engage in fundamental social critique and chooses instead to emphasize individual choice and acceptance of one's lot in life. Marianne Vardalos provides a similar argument in Chapter 7, relying on the Frankfurt School. Her chapter contests any connection made between *DreamWorks Animation* and subversive stories pushing for social change. In her eyes, *Shrek* reinforces rather than challenges the status quo. Vardalos suggests that *Shrek* is part of a process of DreamWorkification, "a process of producing the worldview supportive of neoliberalism and a process of ensuring that the neoliberal doxa and no other, penetrates every corner of the earth" (p. 91).

Chapter 8 takes a stance that, in many respects, challenges the perspective of the two previous chapters. Outlining a relational (or transactional) approach to *Shrek*, François Dépelteau interprets the latter as a legacy and an active part of new social movements such as the women's movement, gay and lesbian movements, and environmental movements. Dépelteau argues that the trilogy cannot be analyzed through the framework offered by critical theories, such as Chomsky's "manufactured consent" thesis. In this view, the *Shrek* movies cannot be reduced to marketing and entertainment strategies that alienate or try to divert the attention of "ordinary" people from real social and political issues. In order to appreciate the significance of the green ogre, one has to look at the complexity of a large web of transactions.

Finally, Gayle Brewer (Chapter 9) applies the tenets of evolutionary psychology to Shrek. She suggests that the ogre's adventures reflect the fact that "some psychological mechanisms (such as jealousy) have also evolved in their current form because they addressed specific problems of survival or reproduction across evolutionary history" (p. 133). For instance, Shrek is attracted to Fiona because her body shape evokes fertility and maternity even when she has transformed into an ogress. Clearly, this reading takes us in a very different direction from interpretations that see critical feminist content in *Shrek*.

In different ways, these chapters help us understand why some of our students may have appeared to be more interested in a book on *Shrek* than in Ulrich Beck's risk society. They know the green ogre; he is a deeply entrenched part of their cultural environment. The assembled chapters also help us understand why the mere mention of a book project on *Shrek* aroused such strong sentiments among our colleagues and in the wider public. For better or worse, *Shrek* is about our shared social reality and about some of the key issues that divide us. Taking these observations as a starting point, Tim Nieguth, in the volume's final chapter, analyzes the reactions to our book project with an eye toward their implications for a politics of knowledge. He suggests that the book project may have evoked such a strong response precisely because it did not yet exist, thus offering a screen onto which observers could project their own assumptions, ideas, and desires about the nature of social science and valuable knowledge.

Thanks to the variety of—sometimes clashing—interpretations of *Shrek* offered by our contributors, we believe that this book could assist readers in making up their own minds about the green ogre and his companions. We hope that it does so in a way that is entertaining as well as informative. For whatever else the *Shrek* universe may be, and whatever our own take on its social and political messages, it is also entertainment on a grand scale.

PART I

Shrek *in the Classroom*

CHAPTER 2

Representing Political Regimes in the *Shrek* Trilogy

Aurélie Lacassagne

The trilogy *Shrek* has been among the most successful animated movies at the box office in the history of cinema. DreamWorks, the production company, decided to make the green ogre a worldwide cultural product, by designing hundreds of products related to the monster. The profits of the franchise are estimated at 1.4 billion dollars ("Interview," 2007). Just the first movie, *Shrek*, made a total box office of 479.2 million dollars (Hopkins, 2004: p. 33). This fact could clearly lead to insights pertaining to the political economy of film. This chapter, however, will focus on the narratives of the movies. We are interested in these narratives (in our case visual representations) and their interplay with power politics, especially race and gender conflicts. Insofar as movies constitute partly social reality, how can we interpret these visual texts? Our contention is that popular culture, including children's movies, constitutes and represents the social world. Therefore, proposing an interpretation of these movies as texts also offers an interpretation and a representation of the world. Children (and in our case adults also) are more than just socialized by movies; the films as texts directly affect their representation of the world and participate in the constitution of the social world. As the early writers on cultural studies, such as Hall (1997), showed, popular culture is a site of struggles between the hegemonic discourse and resistance to it. The immanent divisions of our capitalist societies (in terms of class, race, and gender) are, at the same time, produced, reproduced, and contested through popular culture.

Will Wright illustrates our statement by using the example of Burke's version of *Venus and Adonis*, in which he

> interprets the characters of a narrative as representing social types acting out a drama of social order. In this way, interaction—such as conflict or sexual attraction—is never simply interaction between individuals but always involves the social principles that the characters represent. Thus, a fight in a narrative would not simply be a conflict of men but a conflict of principles—good versus evil, rich versus poor, black versus white. (1975: p. 19)

The narratives being very rich, we will focus on representations of political regimes. Indeed, the movie series depicts a number of regime types: a liberal capitalist democracy, in the form of Far Far Away; totalitarianism as instantiated in the Kingdom of Farquaad; and finally, an individualist anarchist space—Shrek's swamp. All of these regimes are disrupted by rebellions led by groups excluded from the established social order. The three political regimes identified are all territorially based. The space is segregated into an inside and an outside. This spatial segregation is associated with a social segregation. In international relations literature, Andrew Linklater (1990) speaks about this "tension" between "men" and "citizens." Citizens of a particular spatially defined political community are entitled to specific rights, while outsiders are deprived of those very rights. But even within the community of citizens, appears the logic of "established" and "outsiders," to speak in Eliasian terms (Elias and Scotson, 1994). This logic often relies upon exclusion based on perceptions of gender, race, class, ethnicity, and bodies. This chapter explores how these logics of exclusion are constructed. It is divided into three sections, each describing a particular political regime.

Individual Anarchism

The first few scenes of the first movie, *Shrek,* open with the ogre living by himself in his swamp. The space is clearly delimited by the "décor" of the swamp; but the ogre goes further and territorially marks his space with signs to signify to the others that this territory belongs to him and that no one can trespass. Two images can come to one's mind while watching this scene. First, the absence of authority: Shrek lives alone in his swamp and he is the sole master of his life. It refers to individualist anarchism. Second, for anyone familiar with French literature and political philosophy, Shrek evokes images of the myth of *le bon sauvage* (the noble savage) depicted by Montaigne (1595/1960) in his *Essays* and Rousseau (1754/1983) in his *Discourse on the Origin of Inequality Among Men*.

Individualist anarchism encompasses various conceptions. It is not the point here to refer to a particular conception of this philosophy but to make the point that, Shrek living in his swamp matches with the spirit of individualist anarchism. There is no state, no society. Nothing seems to prevent Shrek from fulfilling his self-interest. Shrek also appears very reluctant to engage in any form of social relations. One can say that he is an egoist. He represents more the tradition of Max Stirner than William Godwin. Shrek looks fully in control of himself—of his mind and body. Even if one can see a sort of melancholia, he seems satisfied and happy, enjoying the calm of his swamp and the easiness of his life. He eats whatever he finds around him and has arranged his shelter to his taste. He does not appear to have intellectual or spiritual concerns. As long as he can live alone in his swamp, he fully accepts the body he has; his physical appearance becomes an issue only when he enters into social transactions. These control and acceptance of his body are two key elements for the story itself as well as for his portrayal as an egoistic individualist anarchist:

> Not till one has fallen in love with his *corporeal* self, and takes a pleasure in himself as a living flesh-and-blood person—but it is in mature years, in the man, that we find it so—not till then has one a personal or *egoistic* interest, i.e., an interest not only of our spirit, for instance, but of total satisfaction, satisfaction of the whole chap, a *selfish* interest. (Stirner, 1964: p. 295)

Shrek seems to represent this egoist adult with none of the material and spiritual constraints described by Stirner. He is fully satisfied.

But as stated earlier, for someone brought up with French literature, Shrek also triggers memories of the myth of the noble savage. When Montaigne speaks about the Indians, he underlines the fact that they live in harmony with nature:

> Now to return to my subject, I think there is nothing barbarous and savage in that nation, from what I have been told, except that each man calls barbarism whatever is not his own practice; for indeed it seems we have no other test of truth and reason than the example and pattern of the opinions and customs of the country we live in. There is always the perfect religion, the perfect government, the perfect and accomplished

manners in all things. Those people are wild, just as we call wild the fruits that Nature has produced by herself and in her normal course; whereas really it is those that we have changed artificially and led astray from the common order, that we should rather call wild. The former retain alive and vigorous their genuine, their most useful and natural, virtues and properties, which have debased in the latter in adapting them to gratify our corrupted taste. And yet for all that, the savor and delicacy of some uncultivated fruits of those countries is quite excellent, even to our taste, as that of our own. (Montaigne, 1595/1960: p. 210)

Montaigne goes on to describe how their shelters are made with materials from their natural surroundings, how their food is made, and what they hunt and gather. He depicts a perfect world, an idealized world. For Montaigne, society is a form of corruption of the man living in harmony with his natural surroundings. Rousseau, a century and a half later, would echo this idea:

O man, whatever may be your country, and whatever opinions you may hold, listen to me: Here is your history, as I believe I have read it, not in books by your fellow men, who are liars, but in Nature, who never lies. Everything that comes from her will be true; if there is falsehood, it will be mine, added unintentionally. The times of which I am going to speak are very remote: How greatly you have changed from what you once were! It is, so to speak, the life of your species that I shall describe to you, on the basis of the qualities that you have received. Your upbringing, education, and habits may have corrupted those qualities, but they have not been able to destroy them. There is, I feel, an age at which each individual man would like to stop: you will seek the age at which you would have liked your species to stop. (Rousseau, 1754/1983: p. 145)

He continues:

When I strip that being, thus constituted, of all the supernatural gifts he may have received, and of all the artificial faculties that he could have acquired only by long progress; when I consider him, in short, as he must have come from the hands of nature, I see an animal less strong than some, less agile that others, but on the whole, the most advantageously constituted of all. I see him sitting under an oak tree, quenching his thirst at the nearest stream, finding his bed at the foot of the same tree that supplied him with his meal; and thus all his needs are satisfied. (Rousseau, 1754/1983: pp. 146–7)

And indeed, Shrek is reluctant to enter into the social world because he equates it with problems. When his swamp gets invaded by the magical creatures that Farquaad dumped there, he mentions very clearly that he wants to be alone, "in peace"; solitude means for him peace of mind. And it is egoism that leads him to speak with Farquaad about the issue: his trip to Duloc (the name of the kingdom ruled by Farquaad) and his quest to rescue the princess are motivated by his selfish interest to get rid of the magical creatures and live alone, in peace, in his swamp. In the course of his adventures, he will develop a more altruistic behavior. Yet, he remains overly skeptical about the benefits of living within a society. His actions are mainly motivated by his will to go back and live in his swamp with his true love, Fiona. The fact that in *Shrek the Third*, he refuses to become king and does everything he can to find another heir, represents very well his rejection of the society, independent of the way it may be organized.

Totalitarianism

We interpret the kingdom of Duloc as analogous to a totalitarian state. It is our contention that this kingdom does not represent an authoritarian dictatorship, but indeed the very special category of totalitarianism. One needs to go back to the five elements of totalitarianism as described by Hannah Arendt. The first element underlined by Arendt (2004: pp. 407–22) is a classless society that allows for the mobilization of the masses, which follow the leader without any doubt. Each scene in which the people of Duloc appear reveals that the town is not a gathering of individuals but indeed an undifferentiated mass. There is no specific way to distinguish one character from another. Visually, all characters look the same and all act in the same manner as a mass, as one body. They shout, move, and applaud as a single entity. Here, the similarities with the propaganda films of the Nazi regime are striking.

This idea is linked to the second element, that is, the atomization of individuals within a society (Arendt, 2004: pp. 422–24) and the total loyalty of these atomized individuals to the leader. Arendt explains: "Such loyalty can be expected only from the completely isolated human being who, without any other social ties to family, friend, comrades, or even mere acquaintances, derives his sense of having a place in the world only from his belonging to a movement, his membership in the party" (2004: p. 429). The mass of Duloc is represented in different scenes (in the arena, in the church) as completely subjugated by orders. One character hands posters to order the people to laugh or to applaud. The people of Duloc do not possess individual agency or collective agency; they systematically obey the orders in a mechanical fashion.

The third element is a sort of consequence of the previous two: there is no more a distinction between the private sphere and the public sphere. As Arendt (2004: p. 431) puts it: "Totalitarianism is never content to rule by external means, through the state and a machinery of violence; thanks to its peculiar ideology and the role assigned to it in this apparatus of coercion, totalitarianism has discovered a means of dominating and terrorizing human beings from within." And further: "Their [National Socialism and Bolshevism] idea of domination was something that no state and no mere apparatus of violence can ever achieve, but only a movement that is constantly kept in motion: namely, the permanent domination of each single individual in each and every sphere of life" (Arendt, 2004: p. 432). There is no scene in which one can see the people of Duloc in their private sphere. Their movements, actions, and words are always fully controlled by the state. They are all dressed in the same manner. Another indicative feature is the architecture of Duloc. In nontotalitarian societies, people organize their private spaces (their gardens, their homes) in distinctive ways. This is a way of expressing individuality. In Duloc, however, one can see a perfect example of a totalitarian architecture: there are very large avenues (nowhere to hide), similar houses, and symmetrically displayed flower beds. There is no one patch of color or one type of flower that could show that this space is organized, arranged by individuals. Duloc reminded me of Minsk. The Belarusian capital was completely destroyed during the Second World War and rebuilt in a Stalinist fashion. Its architecture is quite similar to Duloc's, except that it is even uglier; but one experiences the same sense of oppression just because of the architectural arrangements. And to reinforce this idea there is the enormous tower of the Duloc castle (like in Minsk there is the monument to the 1945 victory on the *plochiat' pobedi* (Liberty Square)). Apart from the obvious phallic symbolism, it is a clear representation of the absolute power of the leader. Several times, one can witness that Lord Farquaad has the right to life and death for any of his subjects. The first room the viewer is introduced to in the castle is the long hallway leading to the torture room, where indeed a masked brutish executioner is torturing Gingerbread. The character of Farquaad represents a clear analogy with Hitler. The rather short size of Farquaad (pointed out several times) is an obvious mockery of Hitler's own size. Another biographical common point is the "low" social background of both. The fact that Hitler came from a low social background and the impact this had in the development of Nazism have been widely documented. Farquaad must marry a princess to become a king because he is not of royal origin.

The fourth element is the use of totalitarian propaganda and terror. Arendt (2004: p. 450) wrote: "Wherever totalitarianism possesses absolute control, it replaces propaganda with indoctrination and uses violence not so much to frighten people (...) as to realize constantly its ideological doctrines and its practical lies." She continued: "Propaganda, in other words, is one, and possibly the most important, instrument of totalitarianism for dealing with the nontotalitarian world; terror, on the contrary, is the very essence of its form of government" (Arendt, 2004: p. 453). Every aspect of the life in Duloc is violent, and people behave toward violence again in a mechanistic way; they have no reflexivity. Farquaad calls the knights in the arena and explains to them that they will have to fight possibly to the death to see who is the best fighter. Then, the "winner" will be sent to combat a dragon and bring back the princess to Lord Farquaad. Not one knight challenges this crazy idea. The risk of losing one's life for the Lord and his kingdom is taken for granted and fully internalized. Worse, it is an honor, as Farquaad points out. And the public is happy; it is delighted at the prospect of the bloody combat. When Shrek enters and Farquaad orders to kill the ogre, there is a complete delectation of the fight between Shrek and the knights; there is no self-restraint, no self-control. Norbert Elias and Eric Dunning (1986) in their study of sport showed that this is the very purpose of the development of sports and their regulations: to create a regulated space where people can express some degree of violence in order to compensate for the increasing self-restraint on violence in everyday life. But in the case of the people of Duloc, it is not certain whether there are moments in their life in which violence is not expressed. Another scene involving the people of Duloc shows that the peasants have gathered to capture and kill the ogre. There is no discussion as to why they should kill him (the discussion is on the methods...). This specific scene can also quite clearly be read as analogous to the pogroms. Several visual elements make the allegory pretty clear: the scene takes place at night; they go in a group to attack an isolated individual; they have pitchforks and other farmers' tools to be used as weapons. This is how pogroms are imagined in the collective memory of Europeans. Another scene represents the inhabitants of Duloc obeying the order to bring their magical creatures to the authorities so that they can be "removed." Again, no one challenges the order or questions the guards; the people of Duloc are so docile—as were citizens, gendarmes, and civil servants in Europe when the Nazi authorities decided to "remove" Jews and other "unfit" people from Europe.

The fifth element is the totalitarian will to create a new man and a new society—be it the *Volksgemeinschaft* (racially defined national community) of Hitler or the "communist promise of a classless society" (Arendt, 2004: pp. 473–74). This is probably the most distinctive and peculiar feature of totalitarianism. And it is clearly identifiable in Duloc. The whole *Shrek* story starts with the will of Lord Farquaad to get rid of the magical and fairy-tale creatures from his world in order to build a "perfect world." They do not fit in, like the Jews, Gypsies, disabled, and homosexuals did not fit in. Every single action in Duloc must fit into the ideal of the perfect world. This is brilliantly explained when one arrives at Duloc and goes to the information desk. There, one can pull a knob and a song (worth quoting wholly) starts:

> Welcome to Duloc, such a perfect town
> Here we have some rules, let us lay them down
> Don't make waves, stay in line
> And we'll get along fine
> Duloc is a perfect place
> Keep your feet off the grass
> Shine your shoes, wipe your . . . face
> Duloc is, Duloc is
> Duloc is a perfect place.
> (Elliott et al., 2001)

This song is sung by a school choir comprising wooden boys and girls, all absolutely physically similar. They sing and dance in unison and in line. The teacher is the conductor and on her score that she unfolds, one can read "rules." Farquaad is obsessed with creating and maintaining his perfect world, which implies the expulsion of those who, in his eyes, do not fit into this perfect world.

Liberal Democracy

Far Far Away is the kingdom of Harold, Fiona's father. Politically, this kingdom seems to represent a democratic monarchy. We do not actually have a visual text that clearly indicates the democratic character of the kingdom, but neither do we have visual texts indicating that the kingdom is ruled in an authoritarian fashion. Nevertheless, several scenes support the idea that Far Far Away is a democratic polity. For instance, when King Harold is asked by the Fairy Godmother to get rid of Shrek, he does not use his oppression forces (his army or secret services); he calls on Puss in Boots to take care of this task. Harold is obliged to disguise himself and secretly asks Puss in Boots to carry out this illegal mission. Now, these are certainly not actions that respect the rule of law, but if Far Far Away were a dictatorship, Harold would not be obliged to take all these precautions. Only in a democratic state does one need to do these types of dirty jobs in a secretive fashion. A second example can be seen in the way the society functions. The subjects look as if they enjoy complete freedom in their movements and in the expression of their individuality (they are wearing different clothes, their physical appearance differs, and they are engaged in different professions). But the people of Far Far Away are nevertheless alienated by their extreme consumerism. The function of Far Far Away is to serve as a clear and assumed denunciation of the capitalist consumerist society.

> Far Far Away came to resemble more and more the familiar mecca of conspicuous consumption we all know and love: broad, immaculate streets lined with Palm trees, star-map stands, carriage limos, and oversized shop windows crammed with every conceivable luxury. However, this was more than just clever visual satire. The perception of Beverly Hills—its emphasis on glamour and glitter, appearance over reality—was perfect for intensifying the Shrekian themes of identity and self-doubt. After all, it is the Fairy Godmother who dominates this land of milk and honey, and it is her insidious influence that can be found on every street corner and store sign. It is in this world of image and unreality that Shrek, as on ogre and an outcast, must struggle to survive and ultimately triumph. (Hopkins, 2004: p. 66)

When producer Katzenberg saw the first drawings of Far Far Away, he demanded that the very characteristics of Beverly Hills be more accentuated. He wanted the analogy to be understood by anybody (Hopkins, 2004: p. 66). As explained in the extract, this peculiar description of a consumerist society accentuates Shrek's identity issues. What matters in Far Far Away is your appearance and self-confidence. The politics of bodies at play in this kingdom is paramount in the structuration of social—and political—relations. You are successful and powerful if you fit into the canon of beauty. Politically, the fact that the kingdom seems to be a democratic polity does not mean that phenomena of exclusion are not present. Fiona, the heir to the kingdom, was sent to and locked up in a castle for most of her life because she transformed into an ogress at night. King Harold was a frog and entered into an immoral contract with the Fairy Godmother; She gave him a proper human body, but he promised his daughter to the Fairy Godmother's son. Thus, he abandoned his real political power to the evil Fairy Godmother, and later to Prince Charming, the complete idiot who then served the function of the false hero (Propp, 1968).

Another group was excluded from the kingdom: all the fairy-tale characters that were not beautiful, that did not fit into the frame of acceptable body appearance—Captain Hook, the talking trees, the one-eyed man, one of Cinderella's stepsisters, Snow White's stepmother, and other villains to use Propp's classification (Propp, 1968). Because they were not beautiful, they were considered as bad. And indeed, their exclusion from the society transformed them into resentful people, ready for violence, full of hate, at the mercy of anyone who would give them back their social status and inverse the logic of distinction. We see that Prince Charming uses their exclusion and their status as outcasts to form a social movement and seize political power. Yet, at the end of *Shrek the Third*, the moral of the future king, Arthur, is that one's physical appearance should not matter; one can be ugly and good, and everyone indistinctively of their bodies can be part of a more inclusive society. The last element that should be noted about the social inclusion and exclusion game in Far Far Away is that some villains are accepted within the society. Two are particularly worth noting: the first, Cinderella's stepsister, who has become friends with Fiona and the other princesses, and the second, the Wolfe, who is part of Shrek's close friends group along with Pinocchio, Gingerbread, and the three pigs. But in both these cases, politics is at play: the politics of body is overruled by the politics of gender. Indeed, both characters are transgender (Pinocchio is also transgender; he wears pink sexy underwear). Thus, Far Far Away is permissive about gender issues but not about body issues. Clearly, the message is as follows: no matter how permissive and open a society is, there always seems to be some exclusion at play. And in a consumerist society, exclusion is based on physical appearance, thus transforming bodies into mere consumption items, into fetishized objects. Far Far Away is a sign in Baudrillard's sense (1981)—the identity of the individuals is built through their frenetic activity of consumption. It is a spectacle in Debord's sense (2006)—social relations in the kingdom exist only through the images projected by the individuals. If we see Far Far Away as a spectacle, then we are not far from a form of totalitarianism, which explains why Shrek rejects both Duloc and Far Far Away. He does not want to share the weltanschauung of Far Far Away.

Conclusion

We have described how three different political regimes are represented and can be interpreted in the *Shrek* trilogy. These regimes are necessarily places of struggles. Indeed, one feature common to all three regimes is the logic of exclusion of a certain segment of the society in question. Those logics of exclusion beget roots for resistance and social movements hoping to bring about political change. We unfortunately do not have the space here to offer a description of the different social movements that are emerging to fight these logics of exclusion. Therefore, we could say that the movies carry an important political message: different political regimes, even a democracy, are based on spatial and social exclusion. Yet, we could hope for the development of a polity that will be all inclusive, a cosmopolitan community. The movies resonate with the vibrant call of Andrew Linklater (1998) to transform the political community, to transcend our identity with particularist communities (whose boundaries are based on class, space, gender, ethnicity, and race) and become citizens of a new cosmopolitan community of humankind. In fact, the movies are very Kantian. The message is delivered as a Kantian moral at the end of *Shrek the Third* (2007) when the future king, Arthur, explains that everybody can change and that everybody would be accepted in his kingdom.

CHAPTER 3

Big (and Green) Is Better: *Shrek* and Female Body Image

Mary Ryan

Once upon a time, in a land near by, there were fairy tales. Brave princes slew dragons and saved fair damsels. Princesses and scullery maids waited for brave knights and true love. The good were pretty, the evil ugly, the morals absolute. And lo, it was good.
("Is Shrek Bad for Kids?," 2007)

But not in this story!

We are, of course, talking about the *Shrek* trilogy, the critically acclaimed animated movies that have been thoroughly enjoyed by both children and adults alike while they have explicitly challenged everything we have ever known about fairy tales: "Forget handsome princes, damsels in distress and living happily ever after—*Shrek*'s stars are an ugly beast and an ugly princess, whose best friend is a donkey 'with issues', who all live 'ugly ever after'" (O'Neill, 2001: para. 2). Granted, the first film in the trilogy (2001) does *begin* like a traditional fairy tale, as the opening scene shows "the film's hero in the outhouse reading a generic fairy tale about a princess locked in a tower awaiting her 'true love's first kiss'" (Takolander and McCooey, 2005: para. 9). Shrek himself also seems aware of how to play along with the conventions of traditional fairy tales, such as when he arrives at the castle where Fiona has been trapped and knows instinctively where to find her:

SHREK
[PUTTING ON A HELMET] The princess will be up the stairs in the highest room in the tallest tower.

DONKEY
What makes you think she'll be there?
SHREK
I read it in a book once.
(Elliott et al., 2001; caps and boldface added)

The opening scene is where *Shrek*'s similarities with the traditional fairy tale ends, however, as the scene continues with a green hand tearing out a page of the book and the sound of a toilet flushing as we are led to believe that Shrek has used the page as toilet paper. The message this scene presents seems all too clear: "*Shrek* shits on the traditional fairy tale. Literally" (O'Neill, 2001: para. 3).

In considering *Shrek* as a type of anti – fairy tale, this chapter intends to discuss how this anti – fairy tale perspective has resulted in the trilogy having potentially feminist aspects, specifically in terms of female body image. The way that the films present a discussion about the contemporary woman's obsession with beauty and image, and the way that they potentially portray more positive role models in terms of image, is seen primarily through the character of Princess Fiona, largely because her entire image and her *perceptions* of her own image change as the first movie in the trilogy progresses. When we first encounter Fiona, she is "a single, beautiful, stick-figured Charlie's Angel" (Takolander and McCooey, 2005: para. 6). She is initially playing the role of the traditional fairy-tale heroine, trapped in the castle tower, eagerly awaiting her rescue and her "true love's first kiss" by her knight in shining armor. Viewers soon learn, however, that Fiona is, in actuality, far from the typical fairy-tale heroine. When her wish comes true and she is rescued from the castle by Shrek, she struggles against his rescue attempts and makes demands on him. This is closely followed by an encounter with Robin Hood and his Merry Men, where Fiona displays her martial arts skills by fighting off the whole group, leaving her rescuers, Shrek and Donkey, looking on openmouthed. One reviewer (2001) declared that Fiona is "no shrinking violet. She belches, kickboxes, blows up frogs with a straw, [and] steals birds' eggs for breakfast" (O'Neill, 2001: para. 5). A far cry from the "damsels in distress" whom we commonly see in fairy tales!

A further area that highlights Fiona's differences from other fairy-tale heroines is her appearance. The perfect, model-like Fiona we first see is, in fact, only her temporary appearance; a "disguise," perhaps. We later learn that Fiona is actually an ogre, just like Shrek, who she initially claimed to be disgusted by. Fiona later explains that "she was cursed as a child and turns into an ogre every night, which is why she was locked away in the castle, and that only a kiss from her true love will return her to her proper form." Although Fiona is originally embarrassed and disgusted by her ogre form, by the end of the film she realizes that Shrek loves her exactly for who she is; her confidence in herself grows enormously, thus sending positive messages about self-confidence to women of all ages.

Much feminist theory has focused on the beauty myth and the way society is causing women to have a strained and even damaging relationship with their own body image, because of "our contemporary aesthetic ideal for women, an ideal whose obsessive pursuit has become the central torment of many women's lives" (Bordo, 1993b: p. 2364). Sue Thornham (1998: p. 213), for instance, discusses how much of this "concern was with media representations as false *images* of women, stereotypes which damage women's self-perceptions and limit their social roles." The problem with such stereotypes of the female body is that they do not provide a realistic or an easily attainable image for other women to aspire to; indeed, they suggest that women are "supposed" to look a certain way and that their natural appearance will never meet the standards of (patriarchal) society. That is, under the beauty myth, a woman never feels that she can be considered beautiful *for who she is,* but rather is "trapped in the confines of the structured definition of what beauty should comprise" (Weissman, 1999: p. 24). As a result, "unless they [i.e., women] meet a certain criteria of beauty, they are considered to be nonexistent in society" (Weissman, 1999: p. 31). As Suzanna Danuta Walters (1995: p. 56) explains further:

> Women are urged to think of their bodies as "things" that need to be molded, shaped, and remade into a male conception of female perfection. The fragmentation of the female body into parts that should be "improved" or "worked on" often results in women having a self-hating relationship with their bodies.

This idea of how women are "supposed" to look is portrayed in the first *Shrek* film (2001) when Fiona is discussing how, as a princess, she is expected by society to look a certain way, and so she must always hide her natural appearance from the world:

FIONA
I can't just marry whoever I want. Take a good look at me, Donkey. I mean, really, who can ever love a beast so hideous and ugly? "Princess" and "ugly" don't go together. That's why I can't stay here with Shrek.
(Elliott et al., 2001; boldface added)

Walters' notion of the *male* vision of female beauty has been repeated by many other theorists, as men are often viewed as "one of the most imminent and powerful reasons that women yearn to be beautiful" (Weissman, 1999: p. 22). One reason for this is the concept of the *male gaze,* which centers around the idea that, in contemporary society, women are situated as images that are subjected to the controlling gaze of the spectator, who is always assumed to be male (Mulvey, 1975). Therefore, as women are conscious that they must always assume the role of "a sight for the pleasures of men, constructed and driven by the ideals and desires of men" (Weissman, 1999: p. 21), they are constantly aware of how they look and always feel that their look needs to be "improved":

> The western visual culture depends on the relationship between the image and the viewer. It is the expected role of the man to assume the controlling position in society, and demonstrate the continuous production of the male gaze. It is of crucial importance how a woman appears to a man, and the appreciation of herself is granted only by her acceptance from the dominant male. She now begins to graciously stand in the light of the eyes of men, and allow their watchful glance to measure and calculate her worth. (Weissman, 1999: p. 20)

Because of the impact of the male gaze, women often genuinely believe that men judge and "choose" them purely on the basis of their looks and so they feel in competition with other women over their appearances:

> When women are reduced to the embodied equivalent of objects competing for shelf space in some consumer-based economy where men choose the newest, shiniest, thinnest, blondest models, a profound mistrust of "lesser brands" or envy of "designer models" develops. (Umminger, 2006: p. 246)

An example of how beauty and image cause competition and jealousy between women is seen in *Shrek the Third* (2007) when we witness the various fairy-tale heroines bickering about their looks and making sarcastic comments to each other with the aim of reducing one another's self-esteem:

> **SLEEPING BEAUTY**
> Everything's always about you, isn't it? It's not like your attitude is helping, Snow.

SNOW WHITE
Well may be it just bothers you that I was voted fairest in the land.

RAPUNZEL
You mean in that rigged election?

SNOW WHITE
Oh, give me a break [GESTURING TOWARD HAIR] "Rapunzel, Rapunzel, let down thy golden *extensions*!"
(Price et al., 2007; caps and boldface added)

Shrek also presents a clear example of the male gaze, and of the notion of men "choosing" women on the basis of their looks, regardless of a woman's own wishes regarding the situation. In the following scene, Lord Farquaad's magic mirror is displaying pictures of a number of fairy-tale heroines, in a type of *Blind Date* – style scenario. The idea is that Lord Farquaad has the choice of who he will marry, and as the women get no say in the matter, they become the equivalent of objects that Lord Farquaad can keep or discard as he desires:

FARQUAAD
Evening. Mirror, mirror on the wall. Is this not the most perfect kingdom of them all?

MIRROR
Well, technically you're not a king.

FARQUAAD
Uh, Thelonius. [THELONIUS HOLDS UP A HAND MIRROR AND SMASHES IT WITH HIS FIST.] You were saying?

MIRROR
What I mean is you're not a king yet. But you can become one. All you have to do is marry a princess.

FARQUAAD
Go on.

MIRROR
[CHUCKLES NERVOUSLY] So, just sit back and relax, my lord, because it's time for you to meet today's eligible bachelorettes. And here they are! Bachelorette number one is a mentally abused shut-in from a kingdom far, far away. She likes sushi and hot tubbing anytime. Her hobbies include cooking and cleaning for her two evil sisters. Please welcome Cinderella [SHOWS PICTURE OF CINDERELLA]. Bachelorette number two is a cape-wearing girl from the land of fancy. Although she lives with seven other men, she's not easy. Just kiss her dead, frozen lips and find

out what a live wire she is. Come on. Give it up for Snow White! [SHOWS PICTURE OF SNOW WHITE] And last, but certainly not last, bachelorette number three is a fiery redhead from a dragon-guarded castle surrounded by hot boiling lava! But don't let that cool you off. She's a loaded pistol who likes pina coladas and getting caught in the rain. Yours for the rescuing, Princess Fiona! [SHOWS PICTURE OF PRINCESS FIONA] So will it be bachelorette number one, bachelorette number two or bachelorette number three?

GUARDS
Two! Two! Three! Three! Two! Two! Three!

FARQUAAD
Three? One? Three?

THELONIUS
Three! [HOLDS UP 2 FINGERS] Pick number three, my lord!

FARQUAAD
Okay, okay, uh, number three!

MIRROR
Lord Farquaad, you've chosen Princess Fiona.
(Elliott et al., 2001; caps and boldface added)

Shrek 2 (2004) further reiterates this situation as the Fairy Godmother is providing Fiona with numerous wishes that she could grant her. The worrying thing is that most of these wishes involve the Fairy Godmother informing Fiona that she will change her appearance in order for her to obtain her Prince Charming, as if that is the only concern that a young woman should have. This perspective maintains the beauty myth's lie that women need to look a certain way in order to be thought attractive:

FAIRY GODMOTHER
I'll make you fancy, I'll make you great, the kind of girl a prince would date! [...] Banish your blemishes, tooth decay, cellulite thighs will fade away [...] Nip and tuck, here and there to land that prince with the perfect hair, lipstick liners, shadows blush, to get that prince with the sexy tush.
(Adamson et al., 2004; boldface added)

Situations such as this portray a strong cynicism about men in general, as they seem to imply that *all* men judge women on their looks alone, although it may be argued that this is what the beauty myth wants women to believe in order to maintain control over women:

Men, it appears, are far too superficial and shallow ever to love a woman for her imperfect self. In these fictional worlds no man is strong or deep enough to love an overweight woman, not publicly at any rate. Thus all the characters remain trapped (or willingly ensnared) by a culture that values surface first, substance second. (Umminger, 2006: p. 249)

It is worth noting, however, that theorists such as Naomi Wolf (1991) have blamed the beauty myth, instead of men, on this situation. Wolf states how the beauty myth makes women *believe* that men are judging them on their looks so much that women no longer trust that men could love them for who they are; women are thus kept under the control of the patriarchal society that forces them to continuously work on their image, reducing any confidence that they may have:

> He loves her, physically, because she is who she is. In our culture, though, the woman is forced to throw his gift back in his face: That is supposed to be less valuable than for him to rate her as a top-notch art object. If his loving her "the way she is" were considered more exciting than his assigning her a four-star rating, the woman could feel secure, desirable, irreplaceable—but then she wouldn't need to buy so many products. She would like herself too much. She would like other women too much. She would raise her voice. (Wolf, 1991: p. 171)

Shrek attempts to challenge the beauty myth by showing a woman who is actually *more* relaxed and confident when she is told by her true love that she is beautiful in her natural form. When Fiona is in her "human" form, she seems more aware of her looks, self-conscious of how she appears to others. She frets that her natural looks will be discovered and that she will not meet societal standards; she even stops to fix her hair in the middle of a fight scene! Fiona's confidence in herself is restored when her curse is broken and she realizes that she must remain in ogre form. It is at this time that Shrek finally told Fiona that she is beautiful:

SHREK
[GOING OVER TO HER] Fiona? Fiona. Are you all right?

FIONA
[STANDING UP, SHE'S STILL AN OGRE] Well, yes. But I don't understand. I'm supposed to be beautiful.

SHREK
But you *are* beautiful. [THEY SMILE AT EACH OTHER.]
(Elliott et al., 2001; caps and boldface added)

It is at this point that Fiona's attitude toward her appearance changes. She seems more comfortable and confident about her own appearance, able to relax and enjoy life rather than always being preoccupied with her appearance. In her ogre form, Fiona also appears to be a more sexual and maternal being, almost as if she feels more *womanly* than when she was trying too hard to be stereotypically attractive. As an additional example, Fiona's fears threaten to surface once again later on in the trilogy when her friends remark on how the supposed after effects of childbirth, such as stretch marks, may cause her husband to fall out of love with her:

> **FIONA**
> So what are Shrek and I supposed to do?
>
> **RAPUNZEL**
> Well, now you'll have plenty of time to work on your marriage.
>
> **FIONA**
> Gee thanks Rapunzel, and what's that supposed to mean?
>
> **RAPUNZEL**
> Oh, come on now, Fiona. You know what happens. [CINDERELLA PRODS BEAUTY.]
>
> **SLEEPING BEAUTY**
> [WAKING] Huh? You're tired all the time . . .
>
> **SNOW WHITE**
> You'll start letting yourself go . . .
>
> **GINGERBREAD MAN**
> Stretch marks!
>
> **RAPUNZEL**
> Say goodbye to romance.
>
> (Price et al., 2007; caps and boldface added)

However, Fiona's concerns are proven false as, once again, she is assured of Shrek's undying love for her and her confidence and happiness return.

To counteract these debilitating effects of the beauty myth, Wolf encourages women to look around and realize that men *are* loving women who they see as perfect in their natural state, without having to resort to drastic, and dangerous, measures to achieve a nonexistent level of perfection:

> The idea that adult women, with their fully developed array of sexual characteristics, are inadequate to stimulate and gratify heterosexual male

desire, and that "beauty" is what will complete them, is the beauty myth's Big Lie. All around us, men are contradicting it. The fact is that the myth's version of sexuality is by definition just not true: Most men who are at this moment being aroused by women, flirting with them, in love with them, dreaming about them, having crushes on them, or making love to them, are doing so to women who look exactly like who they are. (Wolf, 1991: pp. 177–78)

In *Shrek,* this point is reaffirmed, as discussed earlier, as it is only when Fiona is in her ogre form that Shrek finally sees and admits that Fiona is beautiful; even though she always felt that she was grotesque when she looked like that, it is in her natural form that Shrek finds her most beautiful, and Fiona finally learns that there is no one standard or ideal of what is considered "beautiful," despite what society had previously led her to believe. As it is Shrek who finally makes Fiona believe that she is naturally beautiful, without having to resort to extreme methods to maintain the looks that she feels are most acceptable in society, it may be argued that, in a sense, it is, in fact, Shrek, a man, "who saves Fiona from her patriarchal delusions" regarding beauty and image (Takolander and McCooey, 2005: para. 31). At another point in the film, Shrek makes another positive statement about image. In a conversation with Donkey, he "complains that people make assumptions about his personality on the basis of his appearance" (Takolander and McCooey, 2005: para. 33); this is followed by his statement that ogres have layers, a lot like onions. Thus, *Shrek* may be said to be promoting "the revolutionary idea that beauty is more than skin deep" (Takolander and McCooey, 2005: para. 33), planting the positive idea in viewers' minds that a strong personality will shine through, regardless of one's looks. Fiona further reinforces this point in the following "charming" scene:

[SHREK BELCHES.]

DONKEY
Shrek!

SHREK
What? It's a compliment. Better out than in, I always say. [LAUGHS]

DONKEY
Well, it's no way to behave in front of a princess. [FIONA BELCHES]

FIONA
Thanks.

DONKEY
She's as nasty as you are.

SHREK
[CHUCKLES] You know, you're not exactly what I expected.

FIONA
Well, maybe you shouldn't judge people before you get to know them.
(Elliott et al., 2001; caps and boldface added)

Feminist theory regarding the female body has also focused on the dieting and slimming industries; that is, how women put their lives in danger trying to achieve "perfection" and why women feel the need to put their bodies through such dangerous ordeals. One possible cause for the increasing amount of women with eating disorders and similar body-related illnesses is the concept of "role models" in popular culture. Contemporary media places a great emphasis on the female body, and after being continually bombarded with images of women's bodies, women tend to view other women in the media as having the ideal body shape (regardless of the increasing awareness of, for instance, photos in magazines being airbrushed or otherwise doctored) and strive to obtain the same figure and features:

> Role models are normally those who inspire others to excel in their chosen field; but this homage that manifests itself as imitation does nothing to dismantle the association of female success with a very rigid definition of femininity. Worse still, it does nothing to reassure young girls about their bodies; perversely, starvation becomes a message of empowerment to these young people as they make the association between stardom and skinniness. (Whelehan, 2000: p. 49)

Weissman (1999: pp. 35–6) reaffirms these concerns as she states how "the way that women relate to these cultural ideals, achieving a match to the 'perfect' standard of an image [. . .] illuminates the damaging path to acceptance that they begin to follow." The beauty myth works by encouraging women that they should not settle for their natural looks but should strive to achieve the unattainable model of "perfection," despite the risks to their bodies in the process, almost implying that there is an ultimate cure for perceived "ugliness" (Wolf, 1991: p. 223). In her search for this "cure," a woman who is, for instance, starving herself to achieve her perfect figure ends up, from the perspective of a male-dominated society, as "the perfect woman. She is weak, sexless, and voiceless, and can only with difficulty focus on a world beyond her plate. The woman has been killed off in her" (Wolf, 1991: p. 197). Wolf asks why contemporary society feels "the need to defend itself by evading the fact of real women, our faces and voices and bodies, and reducing the meaning of women to these formulaic and endlessly reproduced 'beautiful' images" (1991: p. 18). What, after all, is so wrong with women reveling in their own natural beauty? Wolf wonders if the stories that women hear from a young age—films, books, fairy tales—are, even unintentionally, responsible for enforcing the idea that "stories [only] happen to 'beautiful' women, whether they are interesting or not. And, interesting or not, stories do not happen to women who are not 'beautiful'" (1991: p. 61). If this is the case, then, from a young age, women were led to believe that, unless they are considered stereotypically "beautiful" (and, it is important to ask, who sets the standard as to what is "beautiful"?) there will always be something lacking from their lives.

Shrek 2 (2004) shows how it is not only women who feel this lack of self-confidence and feel that they must meet societal standards of beauty. In a strange turn of events, when Shrek and Fiona go to visit Fiona's parents, Shrek is now the one who feels self-conscious about his image:

SHREK
I mean, don't you think they might be a bit... shocked to see you like this?
FIONA
[CHUCKLES] Well, they might be a bit surprised. But they're my parents, Shrek. They love me. And don't worry. They'll love you, too.
SHREK
Yeah, right.
(Adamson et al., 2004; caps and boldface added)

Shrek becomes convinced that Fiona would be happier if he were to fit the role of the stereotypically handsome Prince Charming, and in a moment of desperation, he steals a potion from the Fairy Godmother that is guaranteed to make him look "perfect." It is only toward the end of the film that Shrek understands that Fiona loves the ogre that she married and will continue to love him no matter how he looks, or perhaps even *because* of how he looks:

FIONA'S FATHER
You might find you like this new Shrek.

FIONA
But it's the old one I fell in love with, Dad. I'd give anything to have him back.

(Adamson et al., 2004; **boldface added**)

Toward the end of *The Beauty Myth* (1991), Wolf comes to the following realization about contemporary society:

> The larger world never gives girls the message that their bodies are valuable simply because they are inside them. Until our culture tells young girls that they are welcome in any shape—that women are valuable to it with or without the excuse of "beauty"—girls will continue to starve. (Wolf, 1991: p. 205)

Movies such as *Shrek* arguably have the potential to be one form of popular culture that *does* tell women that they are welcome in any shape, regardless of apparent "beauty." Critics have stated that one of the "most apparently radical aspects of *Shrek* is its rejection of the discourse of beauty found in fairy tales [...] Fiona's ugliness would appear to be the most liberatingly subversive feature of the film. Fiona is 'allowed' to be ugly" (Takolander and McCooey, 2005: para. 32). In portraying a heroine who is far from society's expected standards of what is considered "beautiful," and yet who is still shown as happy, healthy, and loved, *Shrek* is sending a positive message to viewers that beauty is, indeed, in the eye of the beholder and that confidence and personality are what will ultimately shine through and make someone attractive. If young girls (and, indeed, young boys) grow up with that mentality, perhaps women's relationships to their bodies will finally change for the better. Wolf ends her book with the following vision for the future:

> A generation ago, Germaine Greer wondered about women: "What *will* you do?" What women did was brought about a quarter century of cataclysmic social revolution. The next phase of our movement forward as individual women, as women together, and as tenants of our bodies and this planet, depends now on what we decide to see when we look in the mirror. What *will* we see? (Wolf, 1991: p. 291)

If the positive messages that movies such as *Shrek* send out to contemporary girls and women about their bodies are any indication, then we, as women, will perhaps finally be able to look in the mirror and smile at our reflection, recognizing the natural beauty inherent in each one of us—even if we are chubby green ogresses!

CHAPTER 4

Green Consciousness: Earth-Based Myth and Meaning in *Shrek**

Jane Caputi

According to the 2005 Millennium Ecosystem Assessment, a report compiled by 1,300 leading scientists from 95 countries, pollution and exploitative practices are damaging the planet at a rapid rate and to the point that the "ability of the planet's ecosystems to sustain future generations can no longer be taken for granted" (Connor, 2005). The planet, in response to this abuse, will no longer be so readily providing such "services" as purification of air and water, protection from natural disasters, and provision of foods and medicines. While practices of the richest nations, greedy for excess energy, food, water, and raw materials, are at the root of the problem, it is the poor who suffer and will continue to suffer the worst effects. The study urges dratsic and immediate changes in consumption; an emphasis on local regulation of resources; a better education; new technologies; and higher costs to be borne by those who exploit ecosystems.

This state of crisis is as much a crisis of consciousness, of mind, heart, and spirit, as it is a material one (Gottlieb, 2004b: p. 12), and it is of great concern for education and educators. Beginning most significantly with Aldo Leopold (1947), ecological thinkers have stressed the dire need for a sweeping transformation of consciousness at all levels. In brief, ordinary citizens need an ecological education. This education for sustainability can be imparted in specific classes, but, optimally, ecological issues, values, and worldviews should be spread throughout the curriculum. This chapter employs perspectives drawn from women and gender studies, religious studies, popular culture, and environmental studies: *Shrek* could be used as an effective text in classes in any of these fields. My analysis of *Shrek* intends to provide not only a different interpretive frame, but also argues that the film illustrates the basic principles of what we can think of as an ecological or a green consciousness.

By *Green consciousness* I mean an ecological worldview or consciousness that diverges widely from the mainstream conceptions that have allowed environmental devastations as a supposedly inevitable part of human progress. Green consciousness is not a wholly new worldview, but one that is based in many ancient and still current principles and wisdoms, many of which are elaborated in oral traditions as well as environmentalist and feminist philosophy, nature writing, fiction, poetry, art, and music.[1] Green consciousness is a holistic worldview, and one that offers alternative conceptions of human and nonhuman subjectivity, of humans' relationships with each other and with nonhuman nature. And Green consciousness is not a totally unfamiliar worldview, even to those of us in the industrialized West who have little familiarity with environmentalism, for its principles continue to pervade our popular culture, including such recent films as the trilogy *The Lord of the Rings* (2001, 2002, 2003), *The Matrix* (1999), and *Shrek*. My focus here will be on the original film *Shrek,* but before turning to a direct discussion of it, I would like to first sketch out some of the core precepts of this ecological or "Green consciousness."

Much of Green consciousness is allied with feminist critiques of the historical social structure known as *patriarchy*,[2] and its paradigmatic orientation, what Susan Griffin (1989) has characterized as a "split culture" and Val Plumwood (1993) as a "master" consciousness. Master consciousness understands *power* not as capacity or potential but as power over/domination; it imposes (and then naturalizes) oppressive hierarchies—of sex, gender, ethnicity, sexual orientation, and so on. This type of power is predicated upon a core splitting apart of what are underlying unities, including masculine from feminine, subject from "other," human from animal, order from chaos, sex from spirit, mind from body, humanity from nature, and life from death. These psychical fissionings are, in their way, as destructive as the splitting of atoms. For example, the schisming that makes a "master" separate from and dominant over a "slave" denies the underlying interconnection and dependence of all life. The "master" presumes, wrongly, that one can lord it over others without ultimately debasing oneself, that one can pollute, exploit, or dump on others, including human and nonhuman others, without also ultimately polluting, exploiting, or objectifying oneself (Plumwood, 1993).

In the overall splitting that characterizes master consciousness, men are aligned with culture/order and women with nature/chaos, and nature is understood as something that must be mastered, tamed, controlled. Concomitantly, elite groups deem those they subjugate to be "closer to nature," more savage, less civilized. Those "savages," like the nonhuman world itself, are subjected to abuse and the exploitation of their "services." They are enslaved, often literally. Women, of all classes, much like the Earth, are expected to provide generative, sexual, caretaking, and nurturing services on demand and for free. The word *service*, which appeared so prominently in the Millennium Ecosystem Report, significantly, derives from the Latin *servus*, meaning slave.

Green consciousness proposes another model altogether. First of all, it recognizes that there are "vast forces not of man's making that shape and channel the nature and direction of life" (Carson, 1998: p. 193). Such forces cannot be enslaved. The services these forces provide are neither controllable nor "free," but are gifts contingent upon human respect and reciprocity. Numerous ancient and still vibrant world traditions guide humans to "give back" to the Earth, to honor necessary obligations to the Earth and nature. It is our responsibility to nurture the Earth and the elemental, and to feed and serve what we can understand as the Green, the life force, as it feeds and serves us. We do this with responsible ordering of our interactions with nonhuman nature, as well as by offering praise, song, dance, and prayer, which we can understand as *energetic* communication with the life force. We also give back through our simple life processes, including sexual exuberance as well as excretion, respiration, and final expiration through which we feed the primal source, for example, by replenishing the soil as our waste and bodies decompose.[3]

Green consciousness understands, again along with Rachel Carson (1998: p. 193), that all of life is a "unified force." Green consciousness raises awareness of the profound consequences of each and every action due to the underlying interrelatedness of all that exists. Buddhist teacher Thich Nhat Hanh (1988: pp. 3–5) suggests that we recognize not only our individual being but also the reality of our *inter-being* with all of life, past, present, and future. As such Green consciousness turns us away from domination and toward relationships of sustainable and loving reciprocity. Carson simultaneously reminds us that the unified force of life is "composed of an infinite number and variety of separate lives." To diminish that variety is a grave error. Monocultures are antithetical to life. Diversity, biological and cultural, is one of the greatest gifts of the Earth (Shiva, 1997; Bagemihl, 1999).

Green consciousness displaces elite human beings from a self-appointed place at the top of a hierarchy that posits some other humans and all other life forms as less valuable. Master consciousness would have us believe that "humanity" (often a code word for the privileged) possesses "some divinely mandated dominion over all creation" and thereby owns "all living things, along with the very earth, air, and water in which they live" (Carroll, 1999). Green consciousness understands that women and men and all types of humans are equally natural and naturally equal, and that all generate culture. Furthermore, while master consciousness holds that only humans are ensouled and conscious, the Green worldview recognizes consciousness as an attribute of all beings, not just human beings.

Green consciousness refuses the master culture's habitual and hierarchical mind/body split (Bordo, 1993a). It recognizes that consciousness is sourced in and shaped by biology (Sjöö and Mor, 1991: p. 423; Finch, 2004). It understands nature as a generative, creative principle that encompasses *all* of the life force, including sex and death (Plumwood, 1993). Natural death is not evil and bodies and sexualities (including non-procreative sexualities) are basically intelligent and good, not originally sinful or in need of control (Caputi, 2005b).

Many of us think of popular culture as, at best, mere entertainment and, at worst, the source of negative stereotypes and crass commercialism in support of the status quo. To be sure, much popular culture fits this bill. But some popular culture continues to serve as a continuation of ancient and/or alternative oral traditions, including these principles of Green consciousness. Some instances of popular culture (particularly some horror, science fiction, and children's stories) continue to transmit ways of knowing and being, including Green ways of knowing and being that have been officially discredited, trivialized, and forgotten. *Popular*, after all, comes from a Latin word meaning *people*. A most valuable index to what people commonly know, value, fear, remember, and believe can be found there. Oddly enough, it also is a place where things usually unspoken, things that go against established canons, can be spoken, albeit usually symbolically (Caputi, 2004).

The Story

> If there were Druids whose temples were the oak groves, my temple is the swamp.
>
> Henry David Thoreau (cited in Hurd, 2001: unpaged epigraph)

The symbolically resonant story of the film *Shrek* (Andrew Adamson, Vicky Jenson, 2001) concerns a large, green, swamp-dwelling ogre, whose unique personality is as capacious as his frame. The film opens as Shrek ruminates in his outhouse, reading a fairy tale: "Once upon a time, there was a lovely princess. But she had an enchantment upon her of a fearful sort which could only be broken by love's first kiss. She was locked away in a castle guarded by a terrible fire-breathing dragon. Many brave knights had attempted to free her from this dreadful prison, but none prevailed. She waited in the dragon's keep, in the highest room of the tallest tower, for her true love, and true love's first kiss." Shrek scoffs at the romanticism of the tale and cynically tears off a page to use as toilet paper. Next, we see Shrek enjoying a mud bath, issuing a few farts into the ooze, and savoring a meal and a martini in his exceptionally cozy cottage in the base of a tree. Right away, we are led to realize that Shrek is at home in his body, comfortable with those features of the body (e.g., defecation) and the Earth (the swampy, muddy wetlands) that too often elicit only shame, suspicion, disdain, and distancing from the "master" culture. Due to humanity's misplaced fears, and Shrek's own fears of his feelings, Shrek has become isolated in his swampland home. Lonely and somewhat embittered, he is emotionally immature and has no relationships with others.

Shrek's existence is about to be mightily disrupted. The local tyrant, Lord Farquaad, lives atop a risible phallic tower and keeps his would-be kingdom in rule-bound tidiness, physical as well as psychical. To this end, he adopts a strategy of "ethnic cleansing," rounding up all the fairy-tale beings and dumping them in the swamp, much to Shrek's chagrin. One of these beings, a talking donkey, is not so much like a fairy-tale character as he is like the central figure in the second-century novel *The Golden Ass* by Apuleius (1994) (a devotee of the Green Goddess Isis). Donkey persists in accompanying Shrek, first as an unwelcome sidekick and later an essential friend. The cowardly and conniving Farquaad tells Shrek that he can have the swamp back for himself if he goes and rescues a princess for him (the one from the fairy tale Shrek was reading in the outhouse). Farquaad's only interest in the Princess is to possess her—as a sexual object and as something to enhance his status. This red-haired Princess Fiona, resplendent in a verdant dress, is guarded by a fire-breathing dragon—a female dragon who falls in love with Donkey while he and Shrek manage to escape with the Princess. Fiona at first thinks Shrek, disguised by a helmet, is her knight but he reveals himself as an ogre and tells her that his job is only to transport her to Farquaad. Fiona at first seems to be a fairly standard issue feminine-type, but soon shows that she has a great deal of fire, spunk, and strength.

And this princess is keeping a powerful secret. At night she turns into a green-skinned ogre, the hidden source of her potency but, due to conventional expectations, also a cause of shame. Fiona has always known that the first kiss of her true love will restore her to her true form, so she figures that Farquaad can solve her dilemma and make her a pretty princess for the rest of her life. On the journey to his tower, she and Shrek fall in love but the usual misunderstandings ensue. They separate as she is met by a party of Farquaad's men and she goes off with them to prepare for the wedding. Still, love does triumph. Dragon finds Donkey, this latter realizes that he is as smitten with her as she with him. The two gather up Shrek and set out atop the flying Dragon to stop the Princess from marrying Farquaad. As they disrupt the proceedings, the sun sets, and the Princess turns into her ogre self. Farquaad is disgusted, but Dragon continues to save the day by simply swallowing Farquaad. As Shrek and Fiona share her first kiss of true love, she is swept into the air and covered with a cloud. Viewers anticipate her transformation back into the pretty princess. But instead she emerges as her ogre self. Fiona is at first flabbergasted but then realizes how wonderful this is as Shrek tells her that he finds her beautiful. The film ends with their wedding, a fabulous song and dance party. All the fairy-tale beings cavort with Shrek, Fiona, Donkey, and Dragon in the swampland. Donkey takes center stage and sings, "I'm a Believer."

Shrek, however delightful and comic, also can be appreciated, through the lens of Green consciousness, as a contemporary retelling of an ancient chthonic or earth-based myth, specifically around its imagination of greenness, its respect for the feminine principle and Goddess traditions, its refusal of hierarchy and split consciousness, its endorsement of the happy body and communal ecstasy, and its ringing celebration of diversity. Let's begin with its imaginative transmission of ancient, and contemporary, understandings of the power of the Green.

Greening Power

> The Green can best be described as a transcendent state of harmony with all of nature in which the "knower" is united with the "known." The energy of all living vegetation forms the Green, which extends as far as plant life reaches. It is a restorative, healing place where there is compassion and love for all. One who enters the Green feels he is slipping into a cool and comfortable place where all cares dissolve into the safe and nurturing bosom of the Mother of All Life.
> (Greenberg, 1992: p. 125)

Shrek and the Princess (in both of her manifestations) are gloriously green, sharing in a tradition of popular culture characters, including Poison Ivy of the Batman series as well as the *Star Wars* series' Yoda, and all the other "little green men," of science fiction. There is also, of course, the iconic green Witch in the original *The Wizard of Oz* and her revival as an animal-rights and anti-fascist heroine in Gregory Maguire's (1995) Oz-revisionary novel *Wicked*. The quote with which I open this section is from a DC comics publication, which provides background information about the concepts and characters in "the DC universe." Although comic books are not generally regarded as an important contributor to theological discourse, the qualities ascribed to "The Green" reflect an ancient understanding linking greenness with the sacredness of nature and with a mystical awareness of the consciousness that encompasses all life and all beings, one that refuses an epistemology based upon domination and oppositional objectification, but, instead, unites the "knower with the known."

Nowadays, *green* is the color most commonly associated with ecological concerns, but its symbolic associations extend much farther back in world mythology and mystical traditions. Typically, green is the sacred symbol of nature, of growing things, and of life itself. In ancient Egypt, "to do 'green things' was a euphemism for positive, life-producing behavior" (Wilkinson, 1994: p. 108). The color green was associated with the Goddesses Hathor and Isis; Isis was known as the "'Queen of Earth', the 'Green Goddess, whose green color is like unto the greenness of the earth', 'Creator of green things'" (Baring and Cashford, 1991: p. 237). She and her brother Osiris frequently appeared with green visage and skin tone. *Wadjet,* "the green one," was the name of the protective serpent Goddess of Lower Egypt (Wilkinson, 1994: p. 108). Similar divine figures include the European pagan Green Goddess and Green Man, the Greek Demeter ("the green one") and Persephone, the Aztec Xochiquertzal, Hindu's Green Vishnu, Buddhism's Green Tara, and Gauguin's image of the Green Christ. These deities all are rooted in distinct traditions and I do not claim identical meanings of greeness for each, but possibly, for all them, the green coloring indicates, as Miranda Shaw (2006) suggests in reference to Green Tara, "an association with nature, trees, and vegetation... [and the] magical and religious properties connected with plant life." These include sustenance, transformation, and renewal. These metaphysical forces are manifested physically in photosynthesis, the process enabled by chlorophyll, the green pigment that enables plants to convert sunlight into food, the process that is the basic source of earthly life.

A mystical vision of the Green as the elemental and divine life force, the spirit of nature and of the land, also prevails throughout common world folk, poetic, and popular traditions. Green is the color most associated with fairies (Briggs, 1976: p. 108), who also wear a red cap (rather like the red-haired and green-dressed Fiona). There also are green leprechauns, green sea nymphs, elves and gnomes, foundling green children (Briggs, 1976: pp. 200–1), and green giants. In numerous traditional images, as in a window at Chartres Cathedral where he has green skin and huge green eyes (Chevalier and Gheerbrant, 1994: p. 455), Satan himself is green and even grassy. This motif (like his horns and tail) indicates his origins as a nature deity.

Islamic cultures have a legendary figure, Khisr, the Green Man, who represents the mean in human relations, midway between the High and the Low (Chevalier and Gheerbrant, 1994: p. 452), suggesting an alternative to oppositional consciousness. A distinctive spiritual tradition associating divinity with the Green also can be found in Catholicism in the work of the twelfth-century mystic Hildegard of Bingen (1985), who spoke of greening power, which she called *viriditas* (from the Latin), as a principle of divinity manifesting in nature. *Viriditas* is the source of fruitfulness, moistness, and growth. Hildegard's theology refused the splitting characteristic of master consciousness. As Beverly Lomer (2005: p. 762) argues: "For Hildegard, Viriditas was the ultimate expression of sacred fertility, and it abrogates the dualism between the spiritual and the natural/fecund/Earth/feminine.... most clearly manifested through the divine motherhood of Mary." Significantly, Hildegard consistently spoke of the Virgin Mary in ways that recalled the ancient traditions of Earth, nature, and Goddess worship, calling Mary the "greenest branch" and the "author of life" (Lomer, 2005).

And, as I will take up in more detail later in this chapter, while green is the color of living things, life, hope, strength, and longevity, it simultaneously is the color also of slime, putrefaction, disease, death, and decay. This is because this mystical understanding of the Green is grounded in a chthonian or earth mythos, and thus, ineluctably, has an ambivalent character, a complementary, not an oppositional, dualism (Geffcken, 1926: p. 573). Green symbolizes both life and death because these are the two necessary and interrelated sides of earthly existence. Perhaps the most essential feature of Green consciousness is the acceptance of death as a part of life.

The Happy Body

> A society based in body hate destroys itself and causes harm to all of Grandmother's grandchildren.
>
> (Allen, 1990: p. 53)

The film *Shrek* is based upon a children's picture book by *The New Yorker* cartoonist William Steig (1990), who began writing and illustrating children's books at the age of 60. Steig's work, purportedly for children, but really for all of us, features the common themes of finding happiness through "romantic love, friendship, creativity, and a feeling of oneness with nature" (*Newsday,* 1984). Steig describes the philosophy underlying his work as being that "people are basically good and beautiful, and that neurosis is the biggest obstacle to peace and happiness" (*Newsday,* 1984). Jonathon Cott discerns that in Steig's characterizations, "a happy consciousness is a function of a happy body and incapable of existing independently of a fulfilled sense of life" (cited in *Newsday,* 1984).

In numerous interviews, Steig reveals that he bases much of his philosophy on the thought of his friend and doctor, Wilhelm Reich, the radical psychoanalyst who believed that a happy consciousness is a function of a happy body and a free sexuality. Throughout *The Mass Psychology of Fascism* and other works, Reich (1970) argued that there were profound connections between spiritual and sexual repressions and political oppression and that it was through such repressions that people in Western civilization were conditioned to unquestioningly follow authoritarian, sadistic, and genocidal regimes.[4]

The unhappy body is the result of the mind/body splitting that characterizes master consciousness. In this paradigm, that which is *not* body—mind, soul, spirit, or will—is seen as the true self, closest to "God," the most high and noble aspect of humanity. Concomitantly, the body is rendered as the most low, a source of shame, a troubling reminder of our supposedly gross and dirty animal, Earthy (and even Satanic) natures, and a source of appetites that can defeat our triumph-seeking will (Bordo, 1993a). Body-negative messages are communicated to us in a great variety of ways: religions that present the flesh as the antithesis of spirit and as the source of sin and the cause of shame; the consumerist culture where human appetites and desires are distorted and manipulated for profit; racism, which falsely adores some bodies and just as falsely negates others; and sexism, which creates unrealistic beauty standards for women based in youth, slenderness, and willingness to conform. Fear, denial, and denigration of the body profoundly influence not only individual unhappiness but provide a conceptual basis for oppression as elites define themselves as clean and pure and define others (e.g., women, dark-skinned people) indelibly associated with the "grossities" of matter—dirt, sex, elimination, and death (Dworkin, 1987: p. 173). In the same way, body-loathing leads to environmental devastation. For Earth and the elements are the source of our bodies, the original matter; dirt is our very substance (Caputi, 2005a). The word *human* is from the Latin *humus*, meaning earth or dirt. In the words of Paula Gunn Allen (1990: p. 56), our body is our "most precious talisman" connecting us to the Earth.

The large and chubby Shrek (and, ultimately, Fiona) are immediately and obviously associated with the happy body. *Shrek* has become such a beloved popular phenomenon because the film's narrative so clearly recognizes and reveres those loveable and enjoyable aspects of ourselves that our culture rejects, deeming them ugly and fearsome. (The word *Shrek* means *monster* in Yiddish and is related to concepts of terror and fear.) The cumulative cultural opprobrium causes us to hide, isolate, and repress those aspects of our being that are pejoratively understood as our "natural" selves. In a society that tries (futilely) to conquer nature, disciplines the body, demands uniformity, and worships speed, transcendence, order, and immortality, Shrek, the natural, one-of-a-kind, ambling, and very round self, ends up being lonely indeed.

The site of Shrek's home is most significant. It is a swamp, a wetland, that part of the ecosystem where water remains at the surface of the land. Wetlands so frequently are drained, filled in, and paved over to allow human commerce and habitation. But in so doing, humans destroy one of nature's most precious places. Though they might be smelly, thick with growth, and moist (rather like some tabooed parts of our bodies), swamps are necessary, providing habitat for the most beauteous birds and creatures as well as spawning and fishing grounds. Wetlands act as natural sponges, soaking up excess water from storms and preventing catastrophic flooding.[5] And wetlands provide those essential natural *services* of providing and filtering water, prevention of soil erosion, and preservation of biological diversity. But we don't always properly value them because swamps epitomize "the low" in a world that worships "the high." Wetlands, moreover, are "marginal" spaces (Hurd, 2001: p. 5) in a world that prefers tidy categories; they are both land and water, edgy places of obvious decay and renewal where things "are often on the brink of becoming something else," where things don't always "fit the current definitions of normal" (Hurd, 2001: p. 7), where borders become blurry and what at first seems separate soon seems to be one. Swamps, Barbara Hurd (2001: p. 11) further suggests, are analogous to the half-waking, half-sleeping hypnagogic state, "a time rich in [the] dreams and fantasy" that profoundly nourish and express our imaginations.

Shrek's swamp is vividly contrasted with the egotistical Lord Farquaad's supposedly perfect, really sterile, monoculture, and monochromatic city, from which he bans all the fairy-tale beings. These beings provide fodder for much of the film's humor, but that is not their only function in the story. They symbolize what truly is magic—color, imagination, wonder, difference, uniqueness, queerness (which is gloriously clear in the 2008 Broadway show *Shrek the Musical*), and the creative process itself—all that is repressed and straightened by the patriarchal moralistic, the repressive, and the authoritarian (Sjöö and Mor, 1991: p. 427).

As many of their scholars and interpreters have noted, fairy tales have long been a primary source of Green or Earth-based wisdom traditions. Folklore scholar Harold Bayley (1996: p. 190) avers that ancient fairy tales themselves issued "from the soil." Key features of these tales (Zipes, 1999: p. 5) include not only the powers of the imagination, but also the efficacy of a good heart, the ensoullment, consciousness, and intelligence of all creatures (animals speak in fairy tales), the need for humans to maintain respectful relations with creatures, a reverence for nature and an honoring of the ability to recognize and read its wondrous signs despite lack of social power, wealth, or formal education. Fairy tales encourage belief in the miraculous processes of life, luck, and transformation. They teach that we can actualize "possibilities for overcoming the obstacles that prevent other characters or creatures from living in a peaceful and pleasurable way" (Zipes, 1999: p. 6) and suggest that we truly can live, as the saying goes, "happily ever after." Although the isolated, alienated, and abusive Shrek starts off rejecting the fairy tale, he ultimately himself becomes a participant in one, achieving his own transformation and subsequent happy ending.

Key to his emotional rescue is his friendship with Donkey, the talking ass. Shrek, voiced by Mike Myers, has a Scottish accent. Donkey, voiced by Eddie Murphy, has an unmistakably African-American style of speech. This conventional pairing of white hero and darker sidekick is a problematic aspect of *Shrek*. First of all, the pairing is a common one reflecting racist hierarchies. Moreover, Donkey (who apparently has no other name[6]) is characterized in ways that draw upon stereotypic "coon" associations (Pilgrim, 2000)—the African-American man as a figure of comic relief, one who is vulgar, shiftless, cowardly, and dominated by women. These racist representations are projections, telling us nothing about African-Americans but, instead, pointing to traits whites fear or reject in themselves, constructing that dualism in order to maintain a view of themselves as more "properly" gendered, rational, civilized, and superior.

The characteristics associated with the coon stereotype again point to the ways that racism is mired in patterns of dualistic master consciousness that result in and justify abuse of nature. So too, do the symbolic meanings of the ass or donkey. This animal represents "nature," dualistically understood as opposed to "spirit," and is "the symbol of the sexual organs, the libido, human instinct and of life confined to the earthly plane of the senses" (Chevalier and Gheerbrant, 1996: p. 52). The double meaning of *ass* as the buttocks reminds us as well that Donkey represents the fundamental human body, with the kind of humor and wisdom that is grounded in the body.

Thus, in cultures ruled by a mind/body split, the instinctual, sexual, animal, bodily, and sensual are degraded and projected upon those cast in the role of a sexual, gendered, or ethnic "other." While renouncing the racist "coon" stereotype, we can simultaneously re-embrace what the frank and humorous Donkey represents—the invaluable and often life-saving body brain, what scientists call the "enteric nervous system," the "gut knowledge" that ideally works in balanced harmony with "brain knowledge" (Brown, 2005). It is Donkey who is able to induce the emotionally shutdown Shrek to be able to experience and express feelings of love and friendship; it is Donkey who demands respect and equality from Shrek; and it is Donkey who *first* sees, and accepts, Fiona in her ogre form. In all of these ways, Donkey speaks for and enacts the Green consciousness that seeks to heal the mind/body split and access holistic, earthy, emotional, and frequently riotous carnal wisdom rather than the disembodied and objective cognition so prized by master consciousness.

Of course, viewers still might question the believability of the transformation of Shrek from abuser to respectful friend and lover. In the beginning, Shrek has an explosive temper and is verbally abusive to Fiona as well as to Donkey. In one scene, Shrek pushes Fiona with such force that she careens out of the frame. And this is played for laughs! Fiona is unhurt only because she is, of course still secretly, an ogre. Significantly, the film does not incorporate a scene where Fiona gets to speak her mind, demanding accountability from Shrek for his verbal and physical violence.

By film's end, Shrek has changed—and in a far more believable and complex way than other originally abusive heroes—for example, those lurking behind princely facades in the male leads of *Pretty Woman* (1990) and Disney's *Beauty and the Beast* (1991) (Caputi, 2004). Still, the film's stereotypically comic rendering of male violence against a female partner remains disturbing. Nonetheless, we soon learn that Fiona is every bit as formidable as Shrek, and that, love, coupled necessarily with respect, is her due, resulting in happiness all round.

Respecting the Feminine Principle

> What greater praise can I give you than to call you green? Green, rooted in light, shining like the sun that pours riches on the wheeling earth; incomprehensible green, divinely mysterious green, comforting arms of divine green protecting us in their powerful circle.
> Hildegard of Bingen, twelfth century, praise song to the Virgin
> (cited in Monaghan, 1999: p. 123)

Vandana Shiva (1988: pp. 38–43), the global environmental theorist and activist, writes explicitly of the "feminine principle" in nature as the intelligent, active, originating, fructifying, and diverse force, in which both women and men participate. Generally, world mythologies symbolize this principle variously as Goddess, Mother Earth, or Mother Nature. It is beyond my scope here to discuss the differing ways Nature as a feminine principle has been understood (Starbuck, 1926; Shiva, 1988; Tuana, 1993; Newman, 2003; Roach, 2005; Caputi, forthcoming 2012). Suffice it to say that the religions that derive from the Abrahamic tradition (Judaism, Christianity, and Islam) feature a purely male divinity. This male God, as he is generally pictured and understood, is firmly associated with the heavens, and is understood as designing nature, making and eventually even destroying the Earth (Daly, 1984).

Original generative Goddesses are identified strongly with the Earth and, as in Sumerian myth, commonly take the form of a dragon or serpent. But as patriarchal social structures became established (from the fourth millennium B.C. (Lerner, 1986: p. 7), these Goddesses were said to be monsters, emblems of evil, and were righteously destroyed by Gods and heroes (Caputi, 2004). This iconography remains current. A statue in front of the United Nations in New York presents the classic heroic trope: a knight slaying a dragon. The sculpture (by Zora Tsereteli) is titled "Good Defeats Evil." Much mainstream metaphor, religious and otherwise, continues to malign the dragon or serpent as the quintessential emblem of evil. But older, green and gynocentric (female-centered) myth tells us that the serpent/dragon is no symbol of evil, but of the feminine principle, earthy wisdom, and the sinuous and quickening life force itself. With this understanding we can recognize the older and Greener story underlying all those familiar ones about maidens supposedly held captive by nasty dragons. From the perspective of Green consciousness, the dragon is *not* threatening or holding her captive. Rather, the dragon is her double, her emanation, and represents the underlying potency of the feminine principle.[7] By slaying the dragon, the hero kills off "Goddess," a principle understood by feminist philosophers Mary Daly (1978) and Luce Irigaray (1993), as autonomous female being and becoming.

In the standard patriarchal myths, the hero kills the dragon and is then able to "rescue," that is capture, the woman and make her his servant/wife. The narrative of *Shrek,* of course, gloriously reverses this hoary trope. This time, the dragon is female, but she is not slain to save the day. Rather, it is Dragon who ultimately intervenes to bring about the happy ending. Through this portrayal, *Shrek* reverses patriarchal myth that identifies evil, sometimes overtly and sometimes more subtly, with the feminine principle and implicitly with nature and with the Earth. And it does so in one other respect as well. The other key female figure is the dual-natured Princess, by daytime human and "beautiful" and by night an "ugly" ogre. This configuration also has exceptional resonance with ancient Earth-based or chthonic myth.

In such myth from numerous cultures, chthonic (earth) deities "nearly always appear in a dual aspect—one friendly and beneficent, the other dark and sinister, just as the divine pair Demeter and Persephone symbolize, on the one hand, the kindly earth yielding food for man and, on the other, the gloomy depths of Hades" (Geffcken, 1926: pp. 573–75). This pattern is replicated worldwide. For example, Erzulie (sometimes conflated with Oshun) a Goddess of the African Diaspora, is sometimes loving, beautiful, gentle, and ministering. At other times, she is an older woman and terrible to look at" (Hurston, 1983: p. 147). In this mode, she can be "insensitive, capricious, and voluble, and she can even become nasty and treacherous; in these darker apparitions, we also see her as an old carrion-eating witch and as the orisha of death" (Benito-Rojo, 1988: p. 14).

It is this complementary dualistic nature of nature—whose twin and necessarily inseparable gifts are both life and death, light and dark, order and chaos—that chthonic deities represent. Patriarchal rewritings of egalitarian myth deliberately changed such complementary dualism into hierarchical opposition, splitting the divine essence, separating Goddess from God, making God wholly male, and then recasting Goddess as dreadful dragon, ugly monster, witch or whore. The Aztec experience, as described by Gloria Anzaldúa (1987: pp. 27–8) is exemplary: "The male-dominated *Azteca-Mexica* culture drove the powerful female deities underground by giving them monstrous attributes... thus splitting the female Self and the female deities. They divided her who had been complete, who possessed both upper (light) and underworld (dark) aspects.... into chaste virgins and... *putas,* into Beauties and the Beasts."[8] In such binary thinking, one part is not simply different from its counterpart, though with some underlying relation (Collins, 1998). Rather, it is seen as inherently opposed to the other, for example human feelings cannot be incorporated into thought because feeling supposedly blocks or retards thought. Binary thinking also underlies all types of oppression where one group is defined as the norm and another is defined as the "other." Green Consciousness departs from this model as it is based in a complementary dual pattern, reflecting the necessities of honoring and balancing the high and the low, feminine and masculine, light and dark, increase and decrease, life and death. It recognizes the need to honor the body and not just the spirit, including the functions of the body such as eating, desiring, defecating, growing round, being hairy, getting old—all of which are particularly taboo for women—for human bodies reflect cosmic processes of life, growth and decay and as we eat and grow strong one day, another day our bodies will provide food to other creatures.

This complementary dual pattern is evidenced in the narrative of *Shrek*, a film one of my students suggested should really be called *Fiona*,[9] since the story perhaps might really belong to her. Fiona has two sides, an ogre and a princess, a beast *and* a beauty. The story resolves as Fiona is allowed to integrate into consciousness (the daylight) that powerful part of her inner core that was previously hidden. Still, it always was that green core that had functioned as her power source, for example, driving her when she handily overcomes Monsieur Hood, a would-be rescuer, who really is a captor. Fiona's voice also is remarkably potent, causing a small bird to blow up when she hits a high note as they sing a duet. Adapting to the situation, the Princess takes the eggs for breakfast. While this scene, which is played for laughs, might disturb some viewers, who read it as disrespectful to animals, I would suggest that we consider several factors before rendering judgment. The eggs had no chance of survival without the parent bird; and all living beings need to eat. It is also worthwhile to compare the practical and powerful Fiona with the conventional Disneyfied princess who sings only sweetly, radiates a purely passive beauty, and possesses no bodily appetites or needs at all. This representation of an impotent feminine principle is the projection of a master consciousness where nature (and women) are mere handmaidens (or, if out of control, troublesome witches) to omnipotent Gods and men. Fiona, like Shrek, begins by being ashamed of her ogre side, but, by film's end, finds that she can be happy and proud as she integrates and assumes the form of her physically and psychically large, powerful, and very green self.

When the world is ruled by the likes of the fascist Farquaad, the Ogre is either covered up or cast out, said to be the monster, the "other," the very face of fear. The "Keep Out" sign that Shrek paints at the beginning of the film bears his own supposedly ugly and fearsome visage. The archetypally frightful face, of course, belongs to Medusa, the Greek Goddess/monster with hair of snakes, she of the powerful voice and eye, and she whose visage was said to be so horrific that all who beheld her would be turned to stone. In patriarchal myth, Medusa, like other dragon and serpent-identified chthonic Goddesses, is righteously killed by a "hero."

In a celebrated essay, the philosopher Hélène Cixous (1981) looks upon the face of Medusa and affirms that she is not ugly and fearful at all. Rather, she calls upon us to openly gaze at her face, so that we can see that she is "beautiful and laughing" (p. 264). From the perspective of Green consciousness, the chthonic Medusa,[10] like Fiona, the Princess/Ogre and like Shrek himself, symbolize what for our health and happiness we need to stop fearing and instead face and embrace—our uniqueness, our diversity, our feelings, our bodily powers and wisdom, our connection to others, and our kinship with all of Earthly life and the Earth itself. *Shrek's* storyline, in fine keeping with the principles of Green consciousness, reminds us to love these aspects of ourselves and others, and to remember that when we do, we can overcome isolation, alienation and shame, and experience a happiness that is otherwise closed to us.

"Then I Saw Her Face"

Throughout the world, the colonization of diverse peoples was, at its root, a forced subjugation of ecological concepts of nature and of the Earth as the repository of all forms, latencies and powers of creation, the ground and cause of the world. The symbolism of Terra Mater, the earth in the form of the Great Mother, creative and protective, has been a shared but diverse symbol across space and time, and ecology movements in the West today are inspired in large part by the recovery of the concept of Gaia, the earth goddess.

(Shiva, 1988: pp. 41–2)

In *The Great Cosmic Mother: Remembering the Religion of the Earth*, Barbara Mor and Monica Sjöö (1991) characterize the patriarchal historical period of the last 5,000-7,000 years as a time of domination and increasing environmental devastation, due to a mass forgetting of a crucial wisdom that humans have known since time immemorial, "the primal consciousness of oneness between all living things" (p. 424). Master consciousness, founded upon splitting, forecloses the possibility of union, fusion, ecstasy, which, Sjöö and Mor suggest, is actually humans' original state of being. To ritually recognize and conjure ecstasy, they write, Earth-based religions celebrated a sacred dance, which allowed participants to return to this state of "original communion" and to generate "sheer evolutionary" energy (Sjöö and Mor, 1991: p. 429).

Shrek ends with the marriage of Fiona and Shrek and an ecstatic dance party including the whole crowd of fairy-tale beings. Donkey takes the stage and sings "I'm a Believer." This final scene has an uncanny mythic resonance with *The Golden Ass*, the second century novel written by Apuleius, a believer and initiate in the Mysteries of the Green Goddess Isis. The novel's central figure, Lucius, has been turned into an ass as a necessary step in his initiation; he must die, even in the sense of being human, before being spiritually reborn. At the culmination of his trials, he prays to the green goddess Isis, at the ocean's edge, with a full moon rising, and with "tears running down my hairy face." Suddenly, he sees her face: "The apparition of a woman began to rise from the middle of the sea with so lovely a face that the gods themselves would have fallen down in adoration of it" (cited in Baring and Cashford, 1991: p. 271).

Let's now jump back to the film's *finale* as Donkey, the contemporary talking ass, sings: "I thought love was only truly in fairy tales, and for someone else but not for me. Love was out to get me. That's the way it seemed. Disappointment haunted all my dreams. Then I saw her face, now I'm a believer."[11] The reference to "her face" recalls not only the previously suppressed ogre face of Fiona, but also the long repressed face of the Green Goddess or Nature.

To maintain their power, dominant groups create and maintain a system of self-serving beliefs, but such ideologies, if they are radically *disbelieved*, begin to lose their power. *Shrek* is an act of faith in a belief system that reverences Nature, which embraces the Green, the body, the feminine principle, and the powers of the imagination. *Shrek* values the humble and not the egomaniacal and it honors the living world in all of its diversity, not only of species but also the uniqueness of individuals. This contemporary mythic story puts forth the possibility of a world based in equality, love, tolerance, respect for the Green, and of course, happiness.

Notes

*This chapter is a slightly revised version of Caputi, Jane (2007). "Green Consciousness: Earth-Based Myth and Meaning in Shrek," *Ethics and the Environment*, vol. 12, no. 2: 23–44.

1. Many of the works cited throughout this piece are relevant here, as are many of the popular songs of Nina Simone, Joni Mitchell, Sinead O'Connor, and Tori Amos (to mention just a few of the artists I have successfully used in a class when I teach on "Green Consciousness." I also ask students to make a "Green scrapbook," analyzing elements of Green consciousness that they find in popular culture, and they regale me with relevant examples from popular music. A sampling of other sources includes Leopold (1968 (1949)); Gottlieb (2004a); Caputi (1993); Hogan (1995, 1998); Lopez (1986); Nasr (2004);

Shiva (1988); Zohar (1990). A sample syllabus for my course on Green Consciousness is available at the Plowshares website, http://www.plowsharesproject.org/php/resources/participating.syllabi.php.
2. I take some of my phrasing here from an earlier piece (Caputi, 2001).
3. Some feminists would not use the word *patriarchy* because they argue that it is a limited concept and does not take into account oppressions other than those of sex. For example, in her excellent feminist response to David Abram, Ann Zavalkoff (2004, p. 122) takes issue with radical feminists who speak of *patriarchy*, arguing that this overlooks "the connections which exist between sexism, racism, heterosexism, classism, and all other forms of oppression, whereby these systems are mutually supporting and sustaining." Yet, to the contrary, most feminists who rely upon the concept of *patriarchy* do not overlook these interlocking oppressions at all. Rather, they point to that paradigm at one that is at the heart of patriarchy, defined by historian Gerda Lerner (1997, pp. 146–47) in this way: "Patriarchy is a hierarchical, militaristic social organization in which resources, property, status and privilege are allocated to persons in accordance with culturally defined gender roles.... Patriarchy is a system of dominance based on the 'invention' that arbitrary differences among people can be used to construct categories by which the unequal distribution of resources and power by small elites over large and diverse populations can be justified, explained and made acceptable to those exploited." Again, according in Lerner (1986, pp. 8–9), at the beginning of patriarchy as a social formation, during the time of the archaic states, men first defined women as "other" (1986, p. 15) and appropriated women's sexual and reproductive capacities. This practice of domination over women led to the institutionalization of slavery, private property, and organized force to maintain these. Sexual oppression is the origin of hierarchy and oppression and the primary model for the series of interlocking oppressions that constitute patriarchy, including those of race and class. For further elaboration see Lerner (1997, pp. 146–98). See also Sjöö and Mor (1991), pp. 229–432.
4. Sjöö and Mor (1991, pp. 17–18) offer a feminist interpretation of Reich, finding great values in his theories on the connections between political oppression and spiritual and sexual oppression. They do note, however, that he continued to enact a form of sexual oppression by advocating only heterosexual sex.
5. Wetlands are regularly destroyed though what we might think of as everyday "unintelligent design"—reckless development, poor planning, and the kind of arrogance that leads some to imagine they can tame rivers, like the Mississippi. Such destruction of wetlands contributed heavily to the disastrous results of Hurricane Katrina in New Orleans, 2005 (Editorial, 2005; Ingham, 2005).
6. I thank Paula Willoquet, an early reader of this paper, who urged me to consider the racism associated with the character of Donkey as did Renata Menezes Camara, who pointed out that Donkey never has a name.
7. Robert Graves (1966, p. 363) writes: "It is wrong to suggest that the hero rescues the chained virgin from a male sea-beast. The sea-beast is female—the Goddess Tiamat or Rahab.... it has even been suggested that in the original

icon, the Goddess's chains were really necklaces, bracelets and anklets, while the sea-beast was her emanation."
8. I first developed these ideas and used some of the language and references in Caputi (2004, pp. 13–14).
9. Thanks to Alex Chery for this insight.
10. Medusa's chthonic nature is evident not only in her association with snakes, but also because it was believed that the blood drawn from one side of her body would heal, and blood drawn from the other side would kill.
11. "I'm a Believer," was written by Neil Diamond and the song first became a hit when sung by the Monkees in 1966.

CHAPTER 5

"Happiness Is Just a Teardrop Away": A Neo-Marxist Interpretation of *Shrek*

Alexander Spencer, Judith Renner, and Andreas Kruck

Cartoons have always been a part of politics. Yet while the use of caricatures in newspapers and of cartoons such as Mickey Mouse and Bugs Bunny as propaganda tools is fairly well established (Smoodin, 1994; Bell et al., 1995; Giroux, 1999), the socializing effect of animated movies has only recently been considered worthy of attention in political science. It is only with the so called cultural turn that the analysis of cultural phenomena such as films has become widely accepted as genuine scientific research (Weldes, 2006; Grayson et al., 2009). The central notion in much of this research is that movies not only reflect aspects of politics but actively take part in the construction of the world as we know it (Weldes, 2003; Weber, 2006). There are now quite a number of studies that examine the depiction and constitution of politics in "children's films" such as *Harry Potter* (Nexon and Neumann, 2006) but also animated movies such as *The Incredibles* (Dunn, 2006), *Toy Story, A Bug's Life,* or *Rescue Heroes: The Movie* (Doucet, 2005).

The film tetralogy *Shrek* is particularly interesting in this respect as it not only reflects a vast range of political, social, and economic aspects but actively partakes in the construction of the political, social, and economic world. However, while a number of authors have examined the role of gender and sexuality (Unger and Sunderland, 2007; Marshall and Sensoy, 2009) or of identity (Brabham, 2006; Pimentel and Velázquez,

2009) in the *Shrek* movies, little has been said about the role of class. This chapter wants to address this gap by providing a neo-Marxist reading of *Shrek 2* and thereby offering a double perspective on the content as well as the socializing effect of the movie on its (young) audience. We argue, in the first three parts of the chapter, that neo-Marxist thoughts on bourgeois domination, oppressed proletarian masses, and class struggle permeate the film as it raises revolutionary themes sympathetic to the plights and aspirations of the "fairytale proletariat." In the movie the capitalist class, personified by the Fairy Godmother, seeks to dominate political decision makers (King Harold). Its power is based on the exploitation of the proletariat (nonhuman fairy-tale characters) and on a consumerist illusion of happiness that is manufactured industrially (potion factory) and reproduced by the media (the Medieval Entertainment Channel). In the film the media is presented as a crucial pillar of capitalist rule. It contributes to bourgeois rule through the recreation of the powerful consumerist ideology of happiness and through its general alignment with the capitalist system. As the final part of the chapter shows, rather than calling for a class revolution in the "real" world, the film ultimately serves to stabilize the capitalist system by falling victim to the capitalist ideology reproduced by the media. Just as the "fairytale proletariat" is blinded and deceived by the glamorous Hollywood-style happy ending of *Shrek 2*, the audience is tricked by the rebellious anti-Disney appearance as the seemingly revolutionary message is turned into an affirmation of the media as an ideological apparatus of the bourgeois state.

(Neo-)Marxist Themes and Ideas in *Shrek 2*

In the following subsections, we analyze selected aspects of the film *Shrek 2* from a neo-Marxist perspective. While we argue that Marxist, and in particular neo-Marxist, thought offers itself as a heuristic framework for a reading of both the contents and the socializing effects of the movie, we certainly do not purport to reconstruct and consistently apply one coherent neo-Marxist theory to the film. Rather, we draw on different ideas and approaches from classical Marxist, and particularly neo-Marxist, thought that we deem useful for our analysis. More precisely, we focus on the neo-Marxist themes of class relations, the superiority of economic power in the relationship between business and politics, and the creation of an illusionary but powerful ideology of "happy ever after."

The Working Class, the Bourgeoisie, and the Capitalist System

One central aspect of any kind of Marxist theoretical understanding is the notion of different social classes defined by their relationship to the means of production. Social class is caused by the fundamental economic structure of work and property. Throughout the film it becomes obvious that the world in which Shrek lives is made up of two very different social classes: the nonhuman fairy-tale proletariat with run down cloths and the predominantly human-like, good looking, and nicely dressed bourgeoisie. The proletariat in *Shrek* consists of both peasants from the countryside, such as Shrek and Donkey and later Pinocchio, Gingy, and the Three Little Pigs, who leave their swamp for the city, and already alienated but unconscious town proletariat, such as Puss in Boots, Hook, the Talking Trees, and the Ugly Step Sister, who spend their time drinking, gambling, and fighting with each other in the Seedy Poisoned Apple Tavern. At the beginning of the movie the proletariat is blissfully unaware of its enslavement to the capitalist system and there is no solidarity between the working classes. For example, Puss in Boots is paid by the king, at that stage an ally of the bourgeoisie, to kill Shrek and with him the revolutionary vanguard. However, at the end of the film the fairy-tale working classes unite into a revolutionary mass. Here, for example, the working class masses are represented by the giant gingerbread man Mongo, who destroys the Fairy Godmother advertising billboard as a representation of the capitalist system on the way to storming the castle/Bastille.

In stark contrast to the natural swamp from which Shrek and his friends come, the city of Far Far Away represents a swamp of capitalist consumption modeled on Beverly Hills. Just like in Los Angeles, the film depicts wide roads lined with palm trees; large, expensive houses; streets bustling with stretch limousines or rather stretch carriages; and vendors selling star-maps that tell visitors where the rich, famous, and beautiful human fairy-tale characters such as Rapunzel live. Like in Hollywood, the city is overlooked by a huge white "Far Far Away" sign and there are streets such as Saxon Fifth Avenue (Sax Fifth Avenue) or Romeo Drive (Rodeo Drive) full of luxurious shops such as Versarchery (Versace) and Armani Armoury (Armani) or clothes stores such as Olde Knavery (Old Navy) and typical consumerist franchises such as Burger Prince (Burger King) or Farbucks Coffee (Starbucks) (Evely, 2005). The climax of this consumerist society is a large, brightly lit, and animated billboard advertising the products of the Fairy Godmother.

In a seductive, model-like pose with an expensive dress, she offers her services: "For all your Happy ever afters." As John Hopkins (2004: p. 66) argues: Far Far Away is a "mecca of conspicuous consumption" and "it is the Fairy Godmother who dominates this land of milk and honey, and it is her insidious influence that can be found on every street corner and store sign."

The most obvious indicator of the bourgeois domination of the capitalist system in Far Far Away is the scene in the movie in which Shrek visits the Potion Factory owned by the Fairy Godmother. In order to gain access to the factory Shrek tells the Elf, a white-collar worker, at the reception that he is from the union: "We represent the workers in all magical industries, both evil and benign [...]. Are you feeling at all degraded or oppressed?" (Adamson et al., 2004). After the Elf lets Shrek in, the audience gets an insight into the conditions under which the fairy-tale proletariat is exploited by the bourgeoisie through their control over the means of production. In the huge industrial complex of the Potion Factory the working class has to surrender its surplus labor to capitalist profit. The industrialized means of mass production and the monotonous assembly line work have alienated the proletariatfrom the product (potions) and from their coworkers. In the factory, the workers—both white (elves) and blue collar (strange small creatures in protective clothing)—all look the same. They do not recognize each other as Shrek is able to sneak into the factory using one of the workers' protective clothing, which is much too small and only covers his head. The clothes and masks have robbed the workers of their individuality; they have become one mass, oppressed and exploited by the bourgeoisie epitomized by the Fairy Godmother. As Christine Evely (2005: p. 62) points out: "Despite her grandmotherly appearance, this sinister character runs a vast empire, in which downtrodden factory workers tirelessly manufacture powerful potions, spells and hexes."

Business and Politics: The Superiority of Economic Power

While the Marxist motif of bourgeois domination over the proletarians is a key component in the depiction of politics in *Shrek 2*, the film makes it very clear that the Fairy Godmother's rule extends beyond her exploited and alienated factory workers. In fact, she also reigns over the political class of Far Far Away, which becomes most obvious in her relationship with King Harold. In depicting the king's dependence, subservience, and moral corruptibility in the face of the Fairy Godmother's demands, *Shrek 2* pervasively refers to (neo-)Marxist ideas, emphasizing the superiority of economic power and the dependency of politics on business.

Classical, "fundamentalist" Marxism has made the point that political institutions constitute merely a superstructure that arises from, and is ultimately subordinate to, the economic base, *id est* the totality of the relations of production of a society (Marx, 1977). The political superstructure not only has its origin in the economic base, but also reflects the prevalent economic mode of production and the interests of the ruling class. While later approaches have attributed somewhat more autonomy to political institutions, neo-Marxist thought continues to privilege the power of capital and "regard economic power as the main form of political power" (Linklater, 2001: p. 136). Politics is seen as structurally dependent on capital. Thus, government is effectively compelled to serve the long-term interest of the capitalist class; in this view, business has a veto power over public policy (Rupert, 2007: p. 155).

The film strikingly picks up these neo-Marxist notions. This is perhaps most obvious in an early encounter between King Harold and the Fairy Godmother. The Fairy Godmother arrives at the royal balcony to take King Harold on a ride in her flying carriage and remind him of his promise to take care that Fiona will marry the Fairy Godmother's son, Prince Charming. This (involuntary) meeting between the king and the Fairy Godmother, that is, the main political and economic powers of Far Far Away, depicts a relationship of dependency: politics, represented by the king, seems to be dependent on, and subordinate to, business, epitomized by the Fairy Godmother. This is very evident in the assertiveness and the taken-for-grantedness with which the Fairy Godmother seeks to put Prince Charming into top political positions (as the husband of the king's daughter). There can be no doubt that the handsome dream prince, who is the shining product and naïve accomplice of a flourishing entertainment industry, would merely be the puppet of his mighty mother (business), thus tightening her grip on political power in the kingdom. "Mommy can handle this" (Adamson et al., 2004), the Fairy Godmother tells him, and in fact, the Fairy Godmother, that is, business, seems to be ultimately in control of what is going on in this kingdom. The Fairy Godmother's extremely self-assured and commanding demeanor and King Harold's subservience clearly indicate that the Fairy Godmother usually gets her way and pushes through her dictates. The superior power of business, the lamentable weakness of politics, and the prevalence of latent structural violence are even physically displayed in the king's meager appearance of being squeezed in-between two aggressive musclemen who serve as the Fairy Godmother's guards.

The Fairy Godmother's remark that a marriage between Fiona and Prince Charming would be "... what's best. Not only for your daughter... but also for your kingdom" (Adamson et al., 2004) implies a hardly concealed threat. The Fairy Godmother can take away not only the king's human- (rather than frog-) like outer appearance (which is the basis for his social status and his chance to live up to socially entrenched, economy-defined notions of "happiness") but consequently also his political power. Business controls the state, as only the Fairy Godmother can maintain the "happiness" and the rule of the king, who under the dictates of the prevalent, media-induced idea-system in Far Far Away can be king only when he is human—rather than a frog (or an ogre for that matter).

The king is terrified after this encounter and determined to give in to the Fairy Godmother's demands. Interestingly, under the pressure of business, politics is not only weakened and corrupted, it also turns into a corrupting force itself. King Harold goes to the pub The Poisoned Apple, where the stranded city proletariat meets, and hires Puss in Boots as a hit man to kill Shrek and ensure that Fiona will marry Prince Charming. While first and foremost the king is concerned with preserving his own reign, he also acts as a collaborator, in fact as an instrument of the superior capitalist class, betraying his people and even sowing the seeds of treachery among the inhabitants of Far Far Away. From a Marxist point of view, this is not expressive of a deformation of an individual character. Rather, in Far Far Away, the state as an instrument of the capitalist class (in an unholy alliance with the media) systematically stabilizes and enforces the ruling capitalist system. This is also evidenced by the display of state repression in a reality TV program on the Medieval Entertainment Channel where anonymous knights in armour violently oppress and put Shrek and his comrades into jail, revealing both the iron grip of the capitalist system and the complicity of the state with the powerful entertainment industry.

To be sure, politics seems to (re-)discover morality from time to time. At a later visit to the pub after the planned murder of Shrek has failed, the king tries to resist further demands by the Fairy Godmother; but, under the renewed threat that she will take away his beauty, happiness, and power, he turns out to be too weak to resist and backs down to become complicit in the Fairy Godmother's new scheme. Tellingly, when the king finally does stand firm against the plans of the Fairy Godmother and enters into an alliance with (parts of) the fairy-tale proletariat at the very end of the movie, he is turned into a frog *id est* a moral but, given the prevalent social idea-system, ridiculous and powerless creature unable to further run a kingdom (as we learn at the very beginning of *Shrek the Third*).

The Social Ideology of "Happy Ever After"

The third neo-Marxist theme running through the story of *Shrek 2* is that of ideology as a manifestation and a means of reproduction of (economic) power. Specifically, in the movie, the dominance and power of the business sector personified by the Fairy Godmother materialize in the authoritative social ideology of "happy ever after." Throughout the movie, "happy ever after" is presented as a particular ideological narrative that portrays a consumerist and an illusionary kind of happiness as a desirable social good. It thereby confirms the role of the Fairy Godmother as an authoritative figure that controls the lives and "happiness" of the other characters and simultaneously denies the possibility of happiness to Shrek and the other swamp inhabitants.

Ideology plays a particular role in the neo-Marxist theory of Louis Althusser (1977), who considers ideology as an important function of the existing social power relations. Althusser conceives of ideology in terms of neither a mere social illusion nor a strategic instrument of powerful actors, but rather as a dominant social discourse that comprises social images, myths, ideas, and practices that form a "well-organised system of beliefs which serves to reinforce or reproduce the existing set of social relations" (Smith, 1984: p. 130). As such, ideologies stabilize the existing "social formations" or social power relations and provide individuals with the possibility of adopting certain identities by positioning themselves in relation to this social structure. As Althusser puts it: ideology "is indispensable in any society if men are to be formed, transformed and equipped to respond to the demands of their conditions of existence" (Althusser, quoted in Smith, 1984: p. 134). While ideology interpellates the identities of both classes, the powerful and the oppressed, it nevertheless stands in the service of the ruling class as it reproduces and stabilizes its power while simultaneously keeping the oppressed down. For Althusser, ideology is therefore part of the existing power structure and is transported in and through social institutions such as the church, the educational system, the information system, or popular culture, which are all understood as parts of the "Ideological State Apparatus" (ISA) (Althusser, 1977: p. 119).

In *Shrek 2*, the dominant social ideology manifests itself in the "happy ever after" narrative that runs through the movie as a recurrent theme. This ideology establishes a consumerist and superficial understanding of happiness that stresses the importance of a stereotypical happy illusion over "real," heart-felt, individual happiness. Happiness is nothing one can find or define for oneself. Rather, it is an ideologically prescribed social good that stresses consumption, wealth, beauty, and love as important prerequisites. The consumerist character of the "happy ever after" ideology is well illustrated by the Fairy Godmother's song and her first encounter with Fiona. In her song, the Fairy Godmother introduces herself as the central expert and provider of happiness:

> Your fallen tears have called me
> So, here comes my sweet remedy
> I know what every princess needs
> For her to live life happily....
> (Adamson et al., 2004)

While she is singing, numerous goods materialize in Fiona's room: cash, clothes, expensive furniture, music instruments, and a cute white puppy. A handsome young man also appears and lasciviously dances around Fiona. The speed with which more and more items arrive and circulate in the room suggests an excessive and almost morbid kind of consumption that is associated with modern understandings of "happiness."

Apart from consumption, fairy-tale illusions of eternal love and beauty are important features of the happiness ideology. "Happy ever after" is the fairy-tale love story of a beautiful princess and a handsome prince who, after marrying, live "happily ever after." The power of this ideology and its grip even on Fiona is disclosed, for example, by her diary entries that reveal that from her early childhood on she has been socialized with the "happy ever after" narrative:

> Mom says that when I'm old enough,
>
> my Prince Charming will rescue me
> from my tower
>
> and bring me back to my family,

and we'll all live
happily ever after.
Mrs. Fiona Charming.
(Adamson et al., 2004)

In other words, this diary entry draws the stereotypical picture of happy endings well known from the stories, for example, of Cinderella and Snow White. Importantly, the "happy ever after" narrative is a love story of two *human* characters; no ogres or other nonhuman fairy-tale characters are part of the plot. Instead, it is suggested that a beautiful human identity is a central feature and a prerequisite of happiness. The happiness ideology has profoundly permeated the society of Far Far Away and has shaped these human characters' expectations in regard to Fiona's future husband and life. When Fiona and Shrek arrive at the royal castle of Far Far Away, everything has been arranged to create the perfect "happy ever after" illusion: the whole royal household has assembled, the fanfare horns are ringing, a group of white doves is released into the sky, and the envoy announces "the long-awaited return of the beautiful princess Fiona and her new husband" (Adamson et al., 2004). However, as soon as Fiona and Shrek embark from their carriage and their ogre identity becomes obvious, the fanfare horns fall silent, the crowd is shocked, and one of the doves crashes into the wall and dies.

Shrek 2 presents the happiness ideology not as a harmless dream or as a nice social illusion; rather it seems to depict the "happy ever after" narrative in an Althusserian sense, as part of the social power structure that reproduces the existing social formation and interpellates the identities of subjects. In regard to the latter, the happiness ideology has an impact on the self-perception of the individual characters and forces them to reinterpret their identities in relation to the "happy ever after" narrative. This repositioning becomes particularly obvious in the development of Shrek's self-perception. In the beginning of the movie, Shrek is convinced of his and Fiona's happiness and both enjoy their honeymoon and life in the swamp. However, when they come to Far Far Away and Shrek is exposed to the happiness ideology, he increasingly believes that he, as an ogre, is unable to make Fiona happy because, as the Fairy Godmother makes clear, "ogres don't live happily ever after" (Adamson et al., 2004). In the course of the movie, the powerful happiness ideology begins to interpellate Shrek, and alone with Donkey and Puss in Boots, he becomes more and more convinced that for Fiona to be happy he would have to change into a Prince Charming: "Maybe Fiona would've been better off if I were some sort of Prince Charming. (...) Well, it's not like I wouldn't change if I could. I just... I just wish I could make her happy" (Adamson et al., 2004). Eventually, the ideology drives him to the Fairy Godmother's Potion Factory, where he tries to steal the "handsome potion" in order to become human and to be able to make Fiona happy.

Apart from shaping the identities of the movie characters, the "happy ever after" ideology is also essential for the reproduction of the Fairy Godmother's power, as it establishes her as the sole person who defines and provides (or denies) happiness. As long as happiness is accepted as a desirable social good and identified with the illusion of "happy ever after," the Fairy Godmother retains social control as she alone can provide the unreal "happy ever after" illusion through her magic and her potions. She produces "love potions" and "handsome potions" and has even turned King Harold from a frog into a man. The Fairy Godmother thereby enables him to find happiness with his wife, Lillian, and rule the kingdom of Far Far Away, while at the same time being increasingly able to dominate and exploit him. On her business cards the Fairy Godmother promises the industrial production of happiness as required through the imprint "happiness—just a teardrop away" and reinforces her and her business's role as the producer of the happiness illusion.

At the end of the movie, the power of the happiness ideology is severely put into question, as Fiona and Shrek prefer their ogre identities over their human ones. To the audience they eventually seem to have freed themselves from the grip of the "happy ever after" narrative and are now able to define their own happiness. However, as will be argued in the last section of this chapter, this emancipation is rather an illusion that reproduces an ideology of happy ending with consequences this time for the "real world."

Shrek 2 and the Socialization of the Masses: A neo-Marxist View

So far, we have focused on the depiction of politics *in* the film *Shrek 2*, arguing that the film strongly echoes themes and motifs from neo-Marxist thought. However, more recent research in political science has gone beyond the notion that movies merely pick up or reflect aspects of politics. Instead, a growing number of constructivist scholars have made the point that movies actively take part in the construction of the social and political world (Doucet, 2005). From that perspective, movies not only depict "political realities" but *are* highly political themselves in that they socialize their audience into certain sets of norms and ideas pertaining to the constitution of society and political power relations. Depicting and shaping politics are thus considered to be inextricably intertwined functions. This concluding section therefore addresses the politics *of* the movie *Shrek 2* and analyzes the film's socializing effect on its (young) audience from a neo-Marxist stance. Essentially, we argue that despite its seemingly unconventional and critical posture, *Shrek 2* is politically rather conservative as it ultimately celebrates and stabilizes the very consumerist entertainment ideology that it purports to ridicule and denounce. This becomes most obvious in the glamorous, Hollywood-style happy ending of *Shrek 2* and in the huge marketing industry surrounding the *Shrek* movies. At the end of the day, not only the movie's protagonists but also its audiences are tricked as the seemingly subversive, if not revolutionary, message of the film is actually turned into an affirmative appraisal of prevalent consumerist-capitalist ideas that legitimize and stabilize the existing system of class inequalities.

(Neo-)Marxist media theorists have a lot to say that is of relevance for a critical reading of the movie *Shrek 2*. (Neo-)Marxists have traditionally ascribed quite some power to the mass media (both print and audiovisual media) in terms of "renewing, amplifying and extending the existing predispositions that constitute the dominant culture" (Curran et al., 1982: p. 14). According to classical Marxists, the mass media serve to produce "false consciousness" in the working classes (Chandler, 2000: p. 6). Classical Marxists conceive of the media as part of the superstructure of society, which is inevitably governed according to the interests of the ruling class (Curran et al., 1982: p. 22). As Marx and Engels argue: "[t]he class which has the means of material production at its disposal has control at the same time over the means of mental production, so that thereby, generally speaking, the ideas of those who lack the means of mental production are subject to it" (Marx and Engels, cited in Curran et al., 1982: p. 22). The mass media are locked into the dominant power structure through ownership, legal regulation, structures of prevailing modes of production, et cetera. They spread the ideas and worldviews of the ruling class while denying or de-legitimizing alternative ideas (Chandler, 2000: p. 5) and "thus reproduce the viewpoints of dominant institutions not as one among a number of alternative perspectives, but as the central and 'obvious' or 'natural' perspective" (Curran et al., 1982: p. 21).

Neo-Marxists such as Louis Althusser (1977) have rejected the simplistic, fundamentalist Marxist notion of "false consciousness" and the view that media products are "monolithic expressions of ruling class values" (Chandler, 2000: p. 7). However, while neo-Marxists have claimed relative autonomy for the mass media and conceived of the mass media as "a field of ideological struggle" (Woollacott, 1982: p. 110), they agree with classical Marxists that the mass media overall contribute to the stabilization of the capitalist system as they tend to reproduce dominant ideologies (Chandler, 2000: p. 7). Media professionals are themselves socialized into, and internalize, norms of the dominant culture and disseminate interpretive frameworks that legitimize the existing social system and favor the interests of the ruling class (Gurevitch et al., 1982: p. 1; Linklater, 2001: p. 133).

As noted, Louis Althusser (1977) conceptualizes the process of mass socialization by the media as a mechanism of "interpellation" in which "subjects" are constituted as the effects of pre-given material and ideological structures (Chandler, 2000: p. 10). The mass media are conceived as "ideological state apparatuses" (similar to, for example, schools) conferring social identities and understandings of social realities upon individual consumers (Lapsley and Westlake, 1988: p. 8). They thus contribute to define the terms in which their audience thinks about the world (Bennett, 1982: p. 44). They usually do so in a way that those who are subordinated by the prevalent economic and political system accept this system as "common sense" and "natural" rather than revolt against it (Chandler, 2000: p. 17).

A lot of these ideas seem applicable to the movie *Shrek 2*. First of all, the enormous commercial exploitation of the *Shrek* movies, in fact the whole media empire built around the movies, should give us pause. *Shrek 2* features an all-star Hollywood cast, including Mike Myers (Shrek), Cameron Diaz (Fiona), Eddie Murphy (Donkey), Antonio Banderas (Puss in Boots), Julie Andrews (Queen Lillian), John Cleese (King Harold), and Jennifer Saunders (Fairy Godmother). *Shrek* won an Oscar for best animated feature in 2002. As of 2010, the four *Shrek* movies have a worldwide gross total of 2.9 billion U.S. dollars. *Shrek 2* has been the most successful of the *Shrek* films. *Shrek 2* was the top-grossing movie of 2004 worldwide and ranks among the five top-grossing movies in U.S. box office history. Even the (less successful) fourth film, *Shrek Forever After*, which was released in 2010, has earned almost 700 million U.S. dollars (as of August 2010). On top of that, there is a huge variety of *Shrek* merchandise including dolls, stuffed toys, post cards, posters, Halloween dresses, and computer games. In sum, the *Shrek* franchise is an "indisputable media monster" (Marshall and Sensoy, 2009: p. 151).

The outright commercialization of the *Shrek* movies represents a striking contradiction to their seemingly critical impetus: *Shrek* is a (highly profitable) product for the entertainment of the masses. What is parodied and (at least in parts) denounced in the movies, that is, an abounding consumerist media industry, is thus replicated and reproduced in the real world. From a neo-Marxist point of view, it is only logical that *such a trilogy*, which is produced within a media entertainment and a broader social system based on capitalist structures of production and ideologies, will both reflect and reproduce dominant ideas and worldviews rather than work toward radical transformation. The commercialization of the *Shrek* movies (including their box office and merchandising success) demonstrates impressively how much the *Shrek* franchise is based on and simultaneously supports the prevalent capitalist logic of revenue maximization.

But we need not even go beyond the content of *Shrek 2* to doubt the apparently critical, antiestablishment posture of the movie. A closer look at the ending of *the film* reveals several aspects expressive of an ultimately affirmative rather than revolutionary stance of *Shrek 2*. At first sight, the ending of the movie seems to offer a subversive punch line. Fiona consciously decides to be an ogre rather than a supposedly "handsome" human being. There appears to be a great deal of disenchantment among Fiona, Shrek's friends, and the royal family with the "industrial happiness ideal" that had been prevalent in Far Far Away and a determination to leave it behind as there emerges an alliance against the Fairy Godmother; her son, Prince Charming; and their claim to power.

But on a closer look the seemingly subversive ending all but loses its revolutionary bite. Instead, there is exuberant joy and happiness celebrated and orchestrated in a rather conventional Hollywood-style happy ending. Puss in Boots calls: "Hey! Isn't [*sic!*] we supposed to be having a fiesta?" (Adamson et al., 2004)—and no one seems to disagree. The fairy-tale proletariat celebrates, harmony is omnipresent, and the monarchy remains intact; there is no more need for critical questions. The protagonists are blinded by the glamorous shining light of a consumerist entertainment ideology that is still firmly in place and will keep them subordinated and disempowered.

While the populace—Mongo, the de-individualized, giant gingerbread man who did not do for a proper hero of the movie—lies in the ditch, the revolutionary, antiestablishment emotions ignited through large parts of the movie falter as the protagonists effectively resign into and align with the established Hollywood-like capitalist system of meaning and power (re-)production. Contentment reigns; no need for a broad social revolution. Interestingly, the same affirmative rather than subversive twist is also very obvious in the conclusion of *Shrek the Third*. In the final monologue of the new king, Arthur, the American Dream, that is, the capitalist myth of success for (potentially) all, is restated and reproduced as Arthur underlines that there is no barrier to what "you" (namely, the young audience of the movies) can achieve besides your own hesitation or lack of effort.

Not only the fairy-tale proletariat in the movie buys the trick, but we as spectators are strongly tempted do so, too. The audience is led to view *Shrek 2* as an unconventional and critical "anti-Disney, anti-Hollywood" movie, but actually the spectators are duped as the film falls back on the reproduction of dominant norms and ideals of the status quo of consumerist individual happiness. When the movie has ended, we (as an audience) are happy with how things unfolded in the film; there are no more hard feelings, no need for greater critical questions related to the dominant political and economic system we live in; we are satisfied rather than angry. The ideology of the entertainment society has been all but solidified. Those who watch the bonus material included in the *Shrek 2* DVD are further amused as the protagonists enthusiastically take part in a "Far Far Away Idol" show featuring Simon Cowell: happy in ignorance, aided by the media and this movie. Thus, the trilogy does not undermine the conventional system of meaning and power (re-)production but rather works within the logic, and contributes (willingly or unwillingly) to the stabilization, of the dominant capitalist system and its ideological instruments of rule.

PART II

Shrek *in Context*

CHAPTER 6

The Mouse Is Dead, Long Live the Ogre: *Shrek* and the Boundaries of Transgression

Daniel Downes and June M. Madeley

"You're not supposed to be an ogre"—Fiona, in *Shrek* (2001)
"They Lived Horribly Ever After"—*Shrek!*
(Steig, 1990, p. 25)

Introduction

The DreamWorks vehicle *Shrek* (2001) offered the promise of turning audience expectation on its head—a tangible challenge to the Disney colonization of animated fairy tales, and the resurgence of animation as social satire. The *Shrek* movies are sometimes discussed for their satirical treatment of gender, race, and political power structures. They are also hailed for containing subtle innuendo obvious to grownups, but obscure to young spectators—entertainment for the whole family! Much of the comedy arises from deliberate undermining of social and narrative expectations: an ogre saves the princess, and Prince Charming is not only a jerk, but also the bad guy from whom the princess needs to be saved. This sort of role switching stands out as a key trope in the *Shrek* films and is something that has been highlighted in press and scholarly reviews. A fairy tale, is "not supposed to be this way," as Princess Fiona complains a number of times in the first film. However, as will be shown, authors and performers have played with the conventions of the fairy tale for almost as long as the form has existed.

It is tempting to think about *Shrek* just in terms of textual analysis, but popular culture is best understood by unpacking the tension between culture and cultural industries of which *Shrek* provides a contemporary example and its source material, the common well of fairy tales, provides one of the first.

It is our contention that Shrek, as both character and franchise, abdicates the responsibility of social critique in favor of a banal message about individual choice and satisfaction with one's social station. The producers similarly abdicate the burden of social satire. Instead the *Shrek* franchise demonstrates a set of industrial practices motivated by product differentiation, cross-marketing, and industrial competition as well as a historically consistent interpretation of the role of fairy tales as source material in popular culture.

Fairy Tales, Pedagogy, and Genre

Shrek is critically acclaimed for its subversive content; challenges to gender, genre, and narrative expectations; and "return" to a kind of cinematic sophistication characteristic of classic Hollywood films—mass appeal in an age of audience fragmentation (Mitchell, 2001: p. E1). Ultimately, the success of the first film built a lucrative franchise for the budding new studio DreamWorks. The subversive content consists primarily of innuendo meant to be enjoyed by adults and to be above the heads of the younger spectators. *Shrek* targeted a broad audience, a "Disney-sized audience" (Maltin, 1987: p. 350). *Shrek* has received much acclaim for the sort of transgressive content that is laden with grown-up humor, challenges to gender depictions in classic fairy tales— Disney fairy tales in particular (Marshall and Sensoy, 2009: p. 152). It has also been criticized for the way it reinforces gender roles. Further, such critical responses are often based upon a problematically functionalist understanding of what roles media texts play in society. Let's look at these points separately: (1) *Shrek* as pedagogical text and (2) *Shrek* and the fairy tale genre.

Henry Giroux (2004) makes much of the pedagogical function of film. In particular, Giroux is concerned with the ways film teaches the rules of social behavior. He argues that animated films are "teaching machines" and that the entertainment industry is a producer of culture (p. 164. See also Kellner, 2003; Marshall and Sensoy, 2009). This is a bit simplistic. Media functionalism goes back to the political scientist Harold Lasswell (1948), who claimed that the media as *institutions* performed a number of functions in mass society that were previously the purview of family, church, and community elders (surveillance of the environment, correlation of information, transmission of cultural heritage, and added a decade later by the sociologist R. Wright, entertainment). Further, fairy tales have explicitly engaged in moral instruction, social critique, and entertainment at various times in the past. Whereas Giroux looks at the function of the texts themselves, Lasswell looks at the media as institutions. We need to look at the *Shrek* franchise as a series of texts as well as part of the institution of fairy tales, particularly once the fairy tale comes in contact with mass, popular culture.

Marshall and Sensoy (2009) narrow the pedagogical function of media. They argue that *Shrek* is less subversive than it is supportive of mainstream (heterosexist) readings of feminine social and moral education. In part they base this reading on the fact that the scripts (in particular *Shrek 2*, 2004) are written by men. More interesting is the fact that they cite the relative ambiguity of "girl power" in both challenging and reinforcing feminine social stereotypes (Marshall and Sensoy, 2009: p. 157).

Ignoring this obvious reading of *Shrek* as a failed subversive text, the films can be understood as *playing with the boundaries* of genre categories and expectations much more convincingly than they can be positioned as subversive media artifacts or indeed as a successful challenge to those genre categories and expectations. In fact, this reading points to the robust nature of the fairy tale as (1) a social critique, (2) a pedagogical tool, and (3) an example of the cross-marketing and cross-categorical potential of the fairy tale as popular culture. This is a phenomenon the entertainment industries redefined as "synergy" in the 1990s.

Genre is a complex and useful analytical category. Drawing on Keith Negus's (1999) work on genre in popular music, we can understand the term as a set of at least four overlapping concepts. Genre is, first, a tool for the classification or categorization of different texts according to similarities in structure, subject matter, et cetera. Second, genre can be understood by paying attention to the expectations an audience has of the category. Understood in this way, genre determines "what is *supposed* to happen." Third, genre boundaries are the places where the category is transgressed and policed by a kind of establishment, by critics, and by the audience itself. Here, any transgressions are deliberate on the part of the creators of the cultural text. Finally (and of less value to the present discussion), Negus discusses genre culture made up of the people who identify with particular forms of cultural production (in his case of music).

Anne Martin (2006) traces some pertinent elements in the evolution of the fairy tale that enable us to identify some recurring themes in the relationship between the genre and its evolution, and ultimately, its parody in the *Shrek* films. As a literary form the fairy tale was a sixteenth-century construction derived from and inspired by folktales that became "the conduits for veiled critiques of the court, of contemporary manners, and of the patriarchal social system" (Martin 2006: p. 18). The French author Charles Perrault softened the social critique and claimed that his books aimed to please and to entertain, ultimately identifying the books with a young audience.

During the Enlightenment, English audiences rejected the fairy tale as frivolous. This claim can also be seen as a bit of sour grapes since the fairy tale was "constructed" in eighteenth-century England rather than recovered from a vanishing tradition of oral storytelling. Indeed, most of the canon was "translated" through the appropriation of Perrault's tales and the Grimms' (see Harries, 2001: particularly Chapter 3). It was during the Enlightenment that the form was recast as an important element in moral education—particularly for girls and for the middle class. As Martin observes, the didacticism in *Beauty and the Beast* "is directed toward its feminine readers, apparently to further the cause of arranged marriages, but in a pleasing and relatively subtle way" (2006: p. 20).

With the popularity of chap books in the late eighteenth century, fairy tales were the vehicle for an early form of cross-marketing that remained an important component of popular culture for the next 200 years. During the nineteenth century, the fairy tale was a complicated site of meaning. It could be seen as threatening to the social order through the gender confusion and class-jumping fantasies of the fairy as pantomime, while at the same time reinforcing new commercial and metropolitan ideals characteristic of nineteenth-century British city life (Martin, 2006: pp. 23–32). According to Martin, pantomimes "are influenced by contemporary consumer realities, being not only staged and marketed in the major commercial centers of Britain, but often depicting the experience of the modern metropolis and its stores" (Martin, 2006: p. 31). The *Shrek* films continue this tradition with elaborate product references (Rodeo Drive, Baskin-Robbins, Old Navy, and Starbucks).

Martin goes on to emphasize how the potential rebelliousness of the pantomime is contained within the theatrical form itself: "[w]hile the harliquinade 'satirically and crazily reflected [the] real world and simultaneously laughed at it'... the panto ends comically with a reassertion of community and of society, containing the critique within the space of the theatre" (Martin, 2006: p. 32).

One particularly powerful strategy used in fairy tales to enable social commentary is narrative distancing and framing ("Once upon a time," "Long ago in a galaxy far, far away," etc). This strategy allows space for readers to eschew the transgressive implications of the story. As a transgressive genre, fairy tales share this narrative strategy with animated cartoons.

Animation and the "transgressive" Fairy Tale

Cartoons (particularly the ones of the golden age of Hollywood, featuring characters like Betty Boop, Bugs Bunny, and Popeye) established a number of elements that have become standard comic tropes (flexible boundaries between the narrative world and the entertainment industry, transgression of gender/racial/species characteristics, breaking the "fourth wall," and mockery of contemporary social conventions). They also drew extensively on the fairy tale for subject matter: Disney's first 2-reel *Three Little Pigs* (1936); Fleischer's technically innovative *Popeye the Sailor Meets Sinbad the Sailor* (1936), *Popeye the Sailor Meets Ali-Baba's Forty Thieves* (1937), and *Aladdin and His Wonderful Lamp* (1939)—all featured Popeye; and Warner Brothers' adaptations of Red Riding Hood (*Red Hot Riding Hood,*1943) and Snow White (*Coal Black and the Sebben Dwarfs,* 1934), which all speak to the range in style, taste, and cultural sensitivity of the genre. In many of these films the cartoon includes social commentary, if not outright social critique.

Cartoon shorts were allowed in all their transgressive grandeur because they were ancillary to the main feature of the evening. In fact, the Warner Brothers animation team was isolated from the main studio to such a degree that it was allowed to pursue whatever narrative or artistic ideas it liked—as long as the films were made on time and on budget. Indeed, the lesson to be learned from the relationship of the short and the main feature is that chaos need not equal rebellion (a lesson learned well by the makers of the *Shrek* films).

During the golden age of the American animated short (1928-1960), a number of common social and ideological attitudes were shared by all of the animation studios, although perhaps best exemplified by Disney.

First, a new mass/popular culture, of which animation was a primary feature, eroded the differences between uplifting bourgeois entertainment and rowdier working-class pastimes. According to Steven Watts (1997), the "emergence of commercialized entertainment in the early 1900s—vaudeville, professional sports, amusement parks, urban music clubs, radio, phonograph records—helped blur class distinctions. The American love affair with the movie represented the apex of this new ethos" (pp. 32–3). Disney's early films were part of this general cultural alignment, and as Watts observes, not without criticism for their "lack of decency" (Watts, 1997: p. 35).

Second, Disney's golden age films are characterized by a sentimental populism and an equally sentimental modernism—conflicting views of the success of the little guy over adversity, a nostalgic view of a small-town past, and the modernist sensibilities of the technological innovations in art, culture, and mass entertainment. Disney cross-markets early, ends up on Broadway—ties back to fairy tales and pantomimes. Disney's films "continue to occupy a central position in the fairy-tale market, the stories are an increasingly important part of commodity culture, whether at the cinema or at home through sin-off products" (Martin, 2006: p. 33).

To conclude, the fairy-tale genre, from sixteenth-century social critique to golden age animated feature and short, was an elaborate construction that became the well for various excursions into critique, pedagogy, parody, and sentimentalism. Before we analyze the uniqueness of these claims to *Shrek,* let's look more closely at the three feature films as they purport to transgress the genre boundaries of the fairy-tale cartoon.

Shrek

The original children's book (Steig, 1990) on which *Shrek* (2001) was based deals out a topsy-turvy take on "Happily Ever After." In the first film, Shrek is introduced as a loner who is quite happy with life in his swamp until his space is invaded by displaced fairy-tale creatures. The ogre emerges as a reluctant and unusual hero squaring off against the antagonist, who is the ruler of a nearby town. Farquaad is not a prince, but he desperately wants to be one in order to solidify his authority over the town of Duloc. One of many reversals of fairy-tale structure has the ogre as the hero and the "prince" as the bad guy. Princess Fiona consistently reminds viewers of the topsy-turvy nature of the film: her rescue by Shrek just "isn't right,"—her expectation of a romantic moment is sorely disappointed. This disappointment only highlights the film's spoofing of the fairy tale and its many reversals of the traditional expectations of the fairy-tale narrative.

Despite her traditional expectations, Fiona herself does not exemplify the ideal feminine, even in her pretty princess form: she fights, she accidentally kills birds with her singing, and (due to a curse) she turns into an ogre after sunset. Shrek is willing to accept Fiona, "you're pretty, but I still like you anyway," but it turns out that their kiss brings on a surprising "love's true form," and she remains an ogre after sunrise as well. Her "true" ogre form fits better with her true love, an ogre, and the story must resolve with the couple becoming the same. While in most fairy tales the girl becomes a princess (joins her true love's class), in this case she becomes an ogre (joins her true love's race). To this extent *Shrek* follows its source material where Steig's characters "lived horribly ever after, scaring the socks off all who fell afoul of them." However, the movie's sequels curtail their Happily Ever After.

Shrek 2 (2004) and *Shrek the Third* (2007) ultimately serve to contain the subversive promise of the first movie. What was seemingly transgressive becomes revealed as merely novel, and there's a containment or retrenchment as the franchise enjoys ever more financial success. *Shrek 2* was the number one box office draw of 2004 among all films released in that year (The Numbers). It also, despite some widely reported oversupply, was the best-selling DVD of 2004 (Reuters, 2005: p. C5).

The challenges to narrative expectations take a different form in *Shrek 2*. No longer is DreamWorks trying to produce something that has never been seen before; now they are, rationally, cashing in on their box office success. Many of the reversals found in the sequel in fact operate by containing or foreclosing on many of the celebrated challenges to gender norms in *Shrek*. Most of the challenges are challenges in style, not substance, and the entire film serves to reinstate gender norms that appeared to be challenged in the first film. In their gender analysis of *Shrek 2* Marshall and Sensoy (2009: p. 151) argue that "while *Shrek 2* purports to offer viewers a more progressive curriculum about girlhood in relationship to other media texts such as Disney, it ultimately reifies heterosexual white femininity as the norm." In married life Shrek and Fiona play out the same old conflicts that were such a staple of 1960s sitcom television. Indeed, in the sequels there are a number of intertextual references to 1960s television that serve to reinforce symbolically the narrative project of creating a world that echoes the values represented by media in the 1960s.

The second film does continue to spoof the traditions of fairy tales by once again casting the ogre as the hero, and this time casting not just a true prince, but also his mom, the fairy godmother, as the bad guys. The fairy godmother reads as both a meddlesome mother-in-law (à la 1960s television)—with highly traditional expectations for her son's (Charming's) marriage to Fiona—and a representative of modernism— via her super-exploitative potion factory. The fairy godmother at one level seems to be just trying to set the story right: "There are no ogres in Happily Ever After stories!" She also polices the expected class system of the fairy-tale kingdom. Charming is a real prince, the king has jumped class (and species) to become ruler, and Shrek himself is persistently uncomfortable in the role of prince-in-waiting.

Once again, in this sequel, there is an ogre at the Happily Ever After. Although they could kiss before midnight and keep their handsome, human forms, Fiona does not want Shrek to change for her. In the end, we arrive at what appears to be the same Happily Ever After that concluded *Shrek,* but this time Fiona has fully embodied the traditional wife role and elided all semblance of gender transgression that was hailed in the first film. The fairy tale has been played with and played up for laughs, but the gender norms have regressed in this offering of the franchise.

Shrek the Third (2007) furthers the containment of some of the most promising challenges that were hinted at in the first film. At the beginning of the film, Shrek is filling in for the king with Fiona at his side. At no point is it suggested that the Queen could rule or that Fiona is the rightful heir. Somehow the male ogre is the more acceptable choice than any of the female options. When he realizes that an ogre just is not king material, Shrek looks for a long lost heir to take his place, Arthur. In one of the trademark reversals of the franchise, Arthur is depicted as a loser who is bullied at school, even by the role-playing game geeks; he is still apparently better qualified than the Queen or Fiona. This smacks of precisely the conventions that were thumbed at in the first film, but in *Shrek the Third* they seem to be at best taken for granted or at worst embraced. Fiona and the Queen each take some steps outside of traditional gender roles, but these forays are short lived and only partially successful. The other princesses are talked out of their complacency, assuming the "waiting to be rescued" position, only to fail in their efforts to rescue themselves, the kingdom of Far Far Away, and Shrek. This suggests only a limited expansion of their roles and largely for the laughs that are achieved at the expense of any substantive transgression. A potent example is the vision of Snow White calling birds and woodland animals using her singing voice and then flinging them on the unsuspecting guards.

As with the previous films a major theme is that ogres do not belong in the role that Shrek has found himself fulfilling. In this film he is not only not cut out to be king, but also because ogres are not nurturing, he is not cut out for parenting either. In the end he embraces fatherhood, but abdicates the throne despite evidence through the narrative that he is up to that role as well. Shrek, as he is developed through three films, is more the fool in a European carnival, than an embodiment of the carnivalesque. The main difference is that the ogre who would be king chooses to take the crown off himself before the end of the party. Shrek's abdication of the throne suggests that social and political structures need not stand in the way; instead, his return to the swamp is represented as individual choice and not at all a consequence of social discrimination. The transformation of the villains, all but Prince Charming, following Arthur's speech ("The only person standing in your way is you!") reinforces this notion that it can be difficult when everyone hates you, but you can choose how to respond; villains can become gardeners instead of villains if they choose to do so. Ogres can be nurturing and they can be king, but Shrek just prefers to relinquish the latter responsibility for the more enticing responsibility of fatherhood back in the swamp. In the end Shrek and Fiona refuse the gift of a live-in nanny (one of the seven dwarfs), and each participates in the full gamut of parenting tasks—Happily Ever After, until the next sequel in 2011. This forestalling of the Happily Ever After may well be the most significant transgression of fairy-tale narrative that the franchise ultimately makes.

Consistent with Martin's (2006) discussion of the pantomime, in later *Shrek* films there are a few isolated nods to gender bending (the ugly stepsister and Pinocchio). However, for the most part sexual transgressions are set aside for class reversals and even these are contained by the narrative in the same way that the carnival, the harliquinade, and the sitcom restore the "natural" order by the end of the episode.

Novelty, Competition, and Mainstreaming

The success of *Shrek* established Jeffrey Katzenberg's DreamWorks Animation Studio as a viable challenger to Disney (the studio Katzenberg helped revive in the early 1990s). As a blockbuster, *Shrek* is accompanied by cross-marketing, happy meal toys, DVDs, et cetera. Its success, not surprisingly, creates a franchise that inevitably explains the shift in narrative and thematic tone in the sequels. In the end the novelty of *Shrek* as an alternative to Disney (and Pixar) is more significant in its success than in its playing with genre expectations.

According to Marshall and Sensoy (2009: p. 152), *Shrek* uses humor as social critique while reinforcing social structures. They write:

> *Shrek 2*, for instance, plays on rather than subverts fairy-tale conventions and plots. The film offers allusions to popular tales such as "The Three Little Pigs," and "Little Red Riding Hood," and makes digs at Disney's fairy—tale variants such as "Cinderella" and "Pinocchio." These references offer the audience laughs and a context for Shrek's exploits rather than overturn any familiar fairy-tale narratives, such as the romance script.

We have already suggested that *Shrek* follows a formula of commentary and parody established by the animation studios of the 1930s and 1940s. For example, Warner Brothers Animation, under the direction of Frank Tashlin, made reference to Hollywood actors, famous musicians, and the animated stars of other studios in a kind of "kidding self-reference" (Maltin, 1987: p. 234).

Plagiarism was part of the competitive atmosphere of the 1930s as artists routinely took characters, gags, and stories from one studio to another. DreamWorks' digs at Disney are supported by critics who observe the parodic elements in Shrek. Coincidently, this creates a plausible defense against copyright infringements (whereas Pixar was sued twice for perceived plot and character similarities in *Monsters, Inc.*, 2001).

When Jeffrey Katzenberg was fired from Disney in 1994, he ended up attacking Pixar as a proxy for Disney. This is ironic since it was Katzenberg who had championed the company's initial foray into feature films by supporting *Toy Story* (1995). After a conversation with John Lassiter about his new film *A Bug's Life* (1998), Katzenberg announced that DreamWorks' first animated film would be *Antz* (1998), produced by Pacific Data Images (PDI) (Prince, 2008: pp. 165–71, 201–2).

Animated cinema since the renaissance of Disney in the 1990s (including the subsequent success of Pixar) is consistently ranking in the top ten box office earners. *Shrek* is successful as part of a "mainstreaming" of animation after Pixar. It is successful in part as a differentiated movie (not Pixar, which stands as a proxy for Disney).

Further, Katzenberg takes Pixar on as a proxy for Disney. This accomplished, the two *Shrek* sequels fall back into a more traditional play at the fairy tale. This is perhaps most explicit in the musical stage show of *Shrek*, which premiered on Broadway in 2008.

Disney's Mickey Mouse was attacked soon after his rise to popularity for being too mischievous (as was Walter Lantz's Woody Woodpecker a decade later). The success of the character demanded its mainstreaming. One can argue that the same holds true for the *Shrek* sequels. Happily Ever After is a coded version of the American Dream—and it is incumbent upon the characters in the narratives to uphold the values of the implied social order.

So, in the end, claims about transgression are less interesting than the ways the *Shrek* films draw on the fairy tale and on the classic period of animation in spirit, and in execution, which makes them relevant to our time.

Conclusion

Shrek does not teach us how to be women and men. It pushes the boundaries of acceptable behavior, recognizing that comic characters cannot be too anarchic (a lesson learned by Bugs, Daffy, and Woody) and that they are mired by the American ideal of consumer individualism. More interesting is the return of classic animation strategies and techniques digitized. As teaching machines the films might make us desire to learn more about our popular culture.

In the end *Shrek*'s only transgression is the stylistic elements that enable it to stand out in comparison with Disney animated features. The goal of the *Shrek* franchise was to achieve box office gross profit and to create a viable industrial alternative to Disney in the marketplace. To return to our starting point, real satire is rebellious, requiring a rigorous commitment to the transgressions implied in the narrative. As a character, Shrek abdicates every opportunity to assume social responsibility in favor of individual choice. As a franchise, the films ultimately sacrifice narrative subversion as an unnecessary financial risk. Ultimately, DreamWorks usurps Disney as the custodian of an Americanized fairy tale. The filmmakers abdicate responsibility of social commentary in favor of a message that valorizes a classless individual coming to terms with *his* place in the social order. Ultimately, the *Shrek* films teach us that we can be "Happy ever after in the far far away of the American dream."

CHAPTER 7

Kantian Cosmopolitanism and the Dreamworkification of the Next Generation

Marianne Vardalos

> We needed to find our own path, a sensibility that's a little subversive. Shrek defined us.
>
> Jeffrey Katzenberg, cofounder of DreamWorks

With a caliber of marketing savvy that can only be developed after years of experience in the culture industry, owners Jeffrey Katzenberg, Steven Spielberg, and David Geffen used the word "subversive" to describe their new enterprise DreamWorks Animation. Movie critics followed suit, calling Shrek an *anti – fairy tale* and attributing the appeal of the franchise to its subversive tone in contrast with the decency characteristic of Disney Animation. One typical reviewer writes, "Sporting an exuberant irreverence toward fairy tales, wickedly subversive humor that up-ends the conventions of the Disney animated musical (...) 'Shrek' is probably the most fun you'll have in a theater this summer" (Leong, 2001), while another writes, "Subversive humor, [has] long [been] the calling card of the Shrek films" (O'Connell, 2007). Reviewers may be connoisseurs of the industry, but such proclamations reveal a gap in their historical knowledge of Hollywood. Since its genesis almost a century ago, Hollywood's methods of satire and superficial criticism have seldom been used as catalysts for social change, only diversions intended to serve and reinforce the status quo. DreamWorks Animation is not the exception to the historical trajectory of Hollywood; it is the rule.

In *Negative Dialectics,* Adorno (1973) argues that capitalism as a repressive order has effectively rendered benign any antithetical forces that could bring about its demise. As such, the revolutionary moment of transformation to any alternative, such as socialism, has passed. To label a cultural product as subversive is to imply that it is intended (or likely) to overthrow the dominant order of techno-capitalism and to undermine the market economy. Though a variety of animation studios have been labeled subversive since the golden age of animation in the 1930s, the term has generally been used to describe artists who were deliberately intending to challenge not the institution of capitalism but the conservatism of the industry or the animation style of one of the other studios. Warner Brothers studio was considered to be subversive in the 1940s, because cartoonists like Tex Avery were unwilling to continue working within the safe, formulaic parameters of animation that had been established by the major studios like Universal and Disney (for a discussion on ideological and commercial tensions between Disney Corporation and Warner Brothers cartoons, see Sandler, 1998). Historical evidence suggests that Jack Warner, himself, and the other major studio heads were committed to producing cultural products with pro-American and pro-capitalism themes so any subversive tones did not originate from them.

Sustained analyses of Disney, such as Henry Giroux's *The Mouse That Roared,* have not outlived their salience; Giroux's purpose was far higher than one of a whistle-blower. Were he dedicated only to dismantling the Disney empire, his work would be senseless, but, on the contrary, his objective was to demonstrate how media culture is highly invested in perpetuating a certain worldview. Just as Disney legitimates particular subject positions and defines history, childhood, beauty, truth, and political agency, so too does DreamWorks. For this reason, cultural critique must not rest, as scholars remain obligated to recognize the ways in which the culture industry continues to alter the popular imaginary.

Disneyfication, Disneyization, and DreamWorkification

After decades of conventional thought that praised Walt Disney for defining the literary and cultural sensibilities of generations by introducing wholesome expressions of American childhood, Disney animation was officially out of fashion until it partnered with Pixar Animation. Supporters of the corporation's vision, products, and sites will argue that Disney is of ideological importance because it reflects American life and values; it is not so complex and sinister as the criticisms suggest, just the expectation of society as a perfect expression of entertainment, a little education, and fun. There is also the argument that Disney's endless production of goods and services fulfills modern society's needs. For our purposes, however, we focus on all those critiques that refer to a transformative process of Disneyfication, whether it be the "infantilization" of adults encouraged to retreat into images and fantasy or the "techno-centricism" of society's growing dependence on automation. In some analyses, Disney World is a cautionary tale about the dangers of intellectual illusions, spaces where experiences are manufactured by machines. In his essay "The Precession of Simulacra" in *Simulations,* Jean Baudrillard (1983) presents the concept of Disneyfication as the process whereby the authentic is made to appear inauthentic to reified populations. He writes:

> Disneyland is presented as imaginary in order to make us believe that the rest is real, when in fact all of Los Angeles and the America surrounding it are no longer real, but of the order of the hyper-real and of simulation. It is no longer a question of a false representation of reality (ideology), but of concealing the fact that the real is no longer real, and thus of saving the reality principle. The Disneyland imaginary is neither true nor false; it is a deterrence machine set up in order to rejuvenate in reverse the fiction of the real. (Baudrillard, 1983: p. 25)

Baudrillard's description of the process as a "deterrence machine" is salient precisely because it implies a strategic motivation on the part of Disney. In military strategies, deterrence measures are taken to prevent hostile actions, and as Allan Bryman (1999) points out, Disneyfication is precisely about combating aggression from opposing ideologies. According to Bryman the theory of Disneyfication has been developed by several different authors, all of whom highlight and usually critique a variety of processes by which Walt Disney as a corporation has whitewashed, sanitized, and trivialized the unsavory aspects of American culture and its underlying values: unbridled capitalism, racism, patriarchy, and anti-miscegenation. Using techniques like idealization, censorship, distortion of facts, and the cleansing of otherness, the Disneyfication process has succeeded in controlling not only its version of reality but also real-world development. Once restricted to the realms of cultural theory and social sciences, the term has now entered the vernacular and is commonly invoked to describe processes whereby something real is made inauthentic with the purpose of deceiving an audience. Perhaps due to media literacy projects inspired by critical cultural studies, audiences are beginning to recognize culture as a primary socializing agent in North America, one that regulates meanings, manufactures desires, and determines values and norms. For this reason, Disneyfication is generally understood to be a process of manipulation that transforms something authentic into an engineered and highly controlled facsimile.

Disneyization, which is often assumed to be an alternative name for Disneyfication, differs in that it is concerned with the intention of expanding the homogenized, common culture of consumption, by making all people believers of capitalism. Disneyization is more concerned with the intention of spreading the worldview around the globe in an imperial act of frontierism. In this regard, Disneyization resembles more George Ritzer's thesis of McDonaldization.[1] According to Bryman, "Disneyization is the process by which the principles of the Disney theme parks are coming to dominate more and more sectors of American society as well as the rest of the world." In his development of the concept, Bryman presents what he sees as four dimensions of the process: theming, hybrid consumption, merchandising, and performative labor (1999: pp. 30–6). Disney's theming has always aimed to represent the American Way of Life, so in its decision to rebrand itself by joining Pixar, the company remained true to its theme even when producing characters—from a feminist princess in Princess Diaries, to an anti-consumerism robot, Wall-E—markedly different from and almost hostile to traditional icons. Bryman defines merchandising as "the promotion of goods in the form of or bearing copyright images and logos" (Bryman, 1999: p. 36), so Disney's new characters, updated icons, allowed for dedifferentiation of consumption by attracting the next generation with a message of, "this is not your parents' Disney." Characters with values seemingly more progressive than those of the 1940s and 1950s permitted the next generation of fans to consume differently, yet to consume all the same. The brands are synergistically cross-promoted in the same manner as the past, licensed, and sold to consumer giants like Walmart and McDonald's as well as smaller chains like Dollorama. Disney also operates its own stores in virtually every mall in the world's largest cities. Beyond merchandising, these operations illustrate the fourth of Bryman's characteristics of Disneyization: performative labor. The use of coercion to force employees to behave in a given way is par for the course in Disney owned institutions even if they are in Tokyo or Cairo.

Both Disneyization, which is about cultural consumption promoted through expansion, and Disneyfication, which entails the cultural production of a worldview, are integral to a new process that we are delineating in this chapter, that of DreamWorkification. It is at once a process of producing the worldview supportive of neoliberalism and a process of ensuring that the neoliberal doxa and no other penetrates every corner of the earth. DreamWorkification should be seen as calculated and as more intensely damaging than Disneyfication and Disneyization have been in the past because it involves greenwashing, the technique of appropriating radical and subversive criticism and rending it benign. What can be detected in DreamWorks' productions, such as *Shrek*, is a Kantian version of cosmopolitanism—one that thinly veils the universalizing mission of the Enlightenment project. The appearance of subversion in *Shrek* films, or any products from DreamWorks Animation, is better understood as the result of marketing savvy and the industry's the ability to adapt not to the changing needs of consumers but to the changing needs of the market. While there is an illusion that DreamWorks is responding to a hip, new anti-Disney generation, it is in fact retaining much of the essentials of the original Disney format, including deception, to legitimate a particular worldview in manufacturing its audiences' tastes. Disney's presentation of "entertainment" has, in many ways, become the cartoon formula now being copied by DreamWorks Animation. As a former Disney employee, Katzenberg is aware of the commercial possibilities and popularity of animation done the Disney way.

Irreverence is Not Subversion

A central tenet of the Frankfurt School's understanding of the culture industry is that it is an essential element of the productive apparatus, which promotes the processes of domination. Since the process of domination entails the reification and totalization of the Enlightenment project through the ideals of individualism, democratic participation, and scientific/technological progress, these values will always be supported in cultural texts produced by the industry. Satirical animation is worthy of analysis not only because it is an object of culture but because its promotion and perpetuation all take place in the realm of cultural production. The Frankfurt School's assessment of the social and political consequences of the advent of mass media informs this analysis because animated films and cross-promotion of them through large and complicated marketing systems serve the interests of the ruling classes and amount to nothing less than propaganda for neoliberal ideologies. The cultural leadership exercised by the ruling classes (rather than the coercive effect of state policing) always ensures that the mandates of production are achieved (Althusser, 1972); therefore, the production of mass culture cannot be independent of the economy and cannot be subversive.

The description "subversive" is used for the capacity of something to overturn or bring down an institution, while the term "radical" describes a foundational change or return to the genesis or root. To refer to the subversive power of humor or satire is to be arguing that it can expose the rationality and ideology of political and moral power held by the dominant order. In the case of *Shrek,* then, the description subversive would mean that the cultural text is aimed at or capable of overturning or bringing down not only techno-capitalism but liberal humanism and all its forms of political, economic, and social oppression, subjugation, and exploitation. Contemporary liberal humanism, which is based on producing and consuming at a frenetic pace, has yet to become aware of its own historically conditioned past. It remains incapable of cognitively mapping the ideological forces of imperial neoliberalism that function within and condition a predominantly Eurocentric, capitalist, patriarchal, global economy.

With the *Shrek* franchise, DreamWorks is preying upon the human impulse for dissonance and anarchy when things are not right in the real world. Since audiences hold the belief that artistic expression possesses the possibility of dissent, in other words, that art can change the world, they see the text, a movie in this case, as something that can make things better. But, insofar as media culture is used by techno-capitalism to control individual consciousness, the *Shrek* series poses no threat to the institutions of global capitalism and liberal humanism and possesses social and political implications no differently than traditional animated films like Snow White or Cinderella. As long as the project of domination associated with the Enlightenment continues, the popularity of any cultural product based on its violation of social norms should be understood as the industry's successful attempt to manipulate desires so that they are hospitable to the shifting needs of global capitalism. For efficient expansion of the project, modernist values of national citizenship, homogeneous culture, and U.S.-centricity must be replaced with postmodern values of hybridity, marginalization, and delocalization. The notion of cosmopolitanism as presented in the *Shrek* series expounds these very values, making them not only palatable but inevitable in the minds of the audience. Applying this illusion of difference as developed by Adorno and Horkheimer (1990), specifically to recent animation films, Hinkins writes:

> All recent animated children's films produced by such corporate giants as Disney/Pixar and DreamWorks, despite advocating consumer awareness and criticism of the consumer system have also attempted to take advantage of a positive audience response to the inclusion of such values in its narrative by allowing for the promotion of the sale of innumerable short-lived consumer products which are a by-product of the film, and vigorously cross-promoting their films through the internet and other media outlets in the hopes of increasing profits. (Hinkins, 2007)

What is mistakenly referred to as subversion in the *Shrek* enterprise is best described as irreverence. There are occasional moments of race/class/gender iconoclasm, although some researchers have already disputed that the *Shrek* films break down stereotypes in any meaningful way. Maria Takolander and David McCooey (2005), for example, conclude that the three films ultimately support patriarchal ideology rather than offering any real alternative. Daren Brabham (2006) examines the character of Donkey with the use of Stuart Hall's three tropes of blackness—the native, the slave, and the court jester. Brabham concludes that the depictions of Donkey, in both representation and dialogue with other characters, serve the present order by helping to disguise grossly retrogressive views of racial equality. Unger and Sunderland's account of gender depiction (2007) in the *Shrek* films is another study that highlights how the intertextual structure of the film and other features encode both the challenges to and the confirmation of gender stereotypes.

The DreamWorkification of William Steig's *Shrek!*

Critical theory suggests that the productive apparatus, in its function of domination and control, always "fuses the old and familiar into a new quality" (Adorno, 1991: p. 85). Hence, the presence of unfamiliar themes, like those of exotopy, or otherness, in *Shrek*, serves to disguise the constant sameness that governs capitalism's exploitative relationship to the past. Of this irony, Adorno and Horkheimer (1990: p. 134) write:

> What is new about this phase of mass culture compared with the late liberal stage is the exclusion of the new. The machine rotates on the same spot. While determining consumption it excludes the untried as a risk. The moviemakers distrust any manuscript which is not reassuringly backed by a bestseller.

Indeed, *Shrek* was based on the children's book *Shrek!* by William Steig, an award-winning cartoonist, known for writing on themes of marginalization and the experiences of Jewish immigrants in twentieth-century America.

According to the biographer Iain Topliss, as the child of Jewish immigrant parents firmly dedicated to socialism, Steig knew outsiderness well. From a young age, Steig was encouraged to integrate into American society by becoming proficient in the fine arts, such as writing, drawing, and painting. Topliss (2005) writes:

> Steig proudly insisted he grew up to be an all-American boy, the parents were not religious, and Steig himself, while remaining culturally Jewish, also rejected Judaism... His humour springs naturally from a lower-class viewpoint and when it criticizes it does so with understanding, validating what it finds amusing... At their best, Steig's lower class cartoons express an unsentimental sympathy for the view from the bottom of the social hierarchy.

Topliss quotes Steig's description of himself from an interview:

> My father was a socialist—an advanced thinker—and he felt that business was degrading, but he didn't want his children to be laborers. We were all encouraged to go into music or art... If I'd had it my way, I'd have been a professional athlete, a sailor, a beachcomber, or some other form of hobo... anything but a rich man... I feel this way: I have a position—a point of view. But I don't have to think about it to express it. I can write about anything and my point of view will come out. So when I am at work my conscious intention is to tell a story to the reader. All this other stuff takes place automatically.

It is plausible if not likely that Steig's "point of view," as he calls it, was deeply impacted by what Jewish immigrants from Europe found when they arrived in America. The historian Neal Gabler (1987) writes:

When they landed in America, they expected to find a place where the little guy could make it to the top. Jews instead found a Protestant Élite whose mission was to educate the immigrants and keep them in their place.

In the documentary *Hollywoodism: Jews, Movies and the American Dream* (Jacobovici, 1998), it is argued that the Protestant establishment championed the social hierarchy of the United Kingdom on American soil, painstakingly recreating the stratification that it had left behind. Jews and other immigrants from Europe were denied access to the good neighborhoods, to professions, or to any opportunities to better themselves. Their opportunities were limited to working in dry goods, and the manufacture of cloths, gloves and furs.

When the film industry began to grow in the early 1900s as the result of Thomas Edison's new technologies, Jews approached the industry as distributors, not artists. They offered movies to the masses in small mom and pop outfits. While most moviegoers at the time were the immigrant classes, Jews saw the industry as having the potential to attract the middle classes, those with money but without the ancestry to gain entry into the upper-class circles. The problem was that productions were limited to the Protestants, who created movies with heavily racist plots, such as *The Birth of a Nation* (1915), in which characters without British ancestry were portrayed as barbaric and dangerous. For the upper-class Anglo-Saxons, knowledge of and exposure to high culture were the primary methods of gaining and signaling status, while low culture, including the entertainment industry, was relegated to the working classes and therefore offered crude, simplistic, nationalistic narratives.

Unlike the Protestants, the Jewish immigrants saw high culture as not separate from but integral to popular culture, and with a commitment to accessibility, validated the relationship between the two. To diversify the offerings, Jews soon began to incorporate high culture into the film industry by producing their own films for distribution. This gesture was intimidating to the establishment, which felt that the "Jews had overstepped their boundaries" (Jacobovici, 1998). Threatened by the growing popularity of the Jewish run cinemas, in 1908, Thomas Edison tried to shut them out with a ban on Jewish production, and when he lost, he and other Anglo-Saxon members of the establishment bullied the Jewish filmmakers out of New York.

California, according to Jacobovici, was still a relatively new territory where the Protestant social hierarchy was less entrenched than it was on the east coast. There Jews tried to establish "an empire of their own," a social order that did not deny them opportunities. As Jacobovici points out in the movie's narration, "Hollywood was a dream dreamt by Jews who were fleeing a nightmare." In establishing the five major studios of Hollywood, these Jewish immigrants were making the point that a parochial Jewish peasant, by having a gentile demeanor, can pass and live without prejudice. The film industry reflects its origin in its themes of passing. Cultural texts depicting the American Way were, in fact, constructions of precisely this ideal.

Thorstein Veblen's (1925) theorization acknowledges the act of consuming culture in liberal societies as not only an attempt at class distinction, but also an act of class emulation. Though many attribute Veblen with describing conspicuous consumption among the upper classes, he was in actuality referring to the nouveau riche. Unlike the long-established families, who were discrete with their expenditures, those with new money purposely drew attention to their spending in order to buy status and gain entry into the elite social circles. Veblen detected in conspicuous consumption an element of performance that propagated the intensification of domination among and within the classes and ensured the longevity of capitalism.

Cosmopolitanism: From Disney's Mythical America to DreamWorks' Mythical World

In what Adorno and Horkheimer called the "continuing mythology of the Enlightenment," the call for cosmopolitanism is next in a series of transformations in the legitimacy of domination. We have argued that the central value being presented in the *Shrek* series is the possibility of, indeed the *necessity* of, cosmopolitanism. We have also argued that this value should not be viewed as a potential counterforce against the project of domination, because the strategies of domination are also always in transformation. In its promotion of the value of cosmopolitanism, DreamWorks Animation further legitimates, reproduces, and intensifies struggles among classes, and normalizes domination— of nature, among class factions, between nations, and over people. Although Frankfurt School members construct their argument in several books, Jere Surber (1998: p. 135) briefly summarizes their critical position on the pervasive idea that the Enlightenment can usher in emancipation from domination:

> In place of the former structure of domination emerged an even more insidious complex of structures: the alimentation of human beings from

nature, which now appeared merely as a field for technological manipulation and control; the blind mechanism of the capitalist market, which while potentially satisfying human desires, resulted in the division of society into competing and mutually hostile classes based on human exploitation; and the bureaucratic administration of the social system, replacing any sense of human community or solidarity with its own impersonal and purely formal procedures.

In addition to the importance of the productive apparatus, the Frankfurt School offers an understanding of subjectivity in the advanced industrial society, which is central in this analysis of the idea of cosmopolitanism in the *Shrek* series. The traditionalist Marxist proletariat, expected to be the historical engine of radical social change, is actually absorbed into the system of production and reproduction. It is not that the subject is completely stripped of agency, but that he or she exercises agency within a restricted realm of choice, determined by the needs of advanced industrial capitalism. Unaware of the dominant ideology, what we have been referring to as the neoliberal doxa that permeates the movie industry and all culture products, the subject remains convinced that he or she is free, rather than a central figure in the promotion of neoliberalism. In the words of Adorno and Horkheimer (1990: p. 134): "as naturally as the ruled always took the morality imposed upon them more seriously than did the rulers themselves, the deceived masses are today captivated by the myth of success even more than the successful are. Immovably, they insist on the very ideology which enslaves them."

Like the Frankfurt School scholars, the contemporary theorist Ziuaddin Sardar sees the discourse of cosmopolitanism in postmodernism not as transformation away from domination but as continuation of domination in the form of new imperialism. He writes:

> Colonialism was about the physical occupation of non-western cultures. Modernity was about displacing the present and occupying the minds of non-western cultures. Postmodernism is about appropriating the history and identity of non-western cultures as an integral facet of itself, colonizing their future and occupying their being. While postmodernism is a legitimate protest against the excesses of suffocating modernity, instrumental rationality and authoritarian traditionalism, it has itself become a universal ideology that kills everything that gives meaning and depth to the life of non-western individuals and societies. (Sardar, 1998: p. 13)

Sardar's new imperialism, in its recognition that postmodernism preserves and enhances all the classical and modern structures of oppression and domination, is equipped to explain allegedly subversive texts supporting cosmopolitanism as both enactment and representation.

Embedding Kant's Cosmopolitanism in *Shrek*

Although themes of cosmopolitanism pervade much of Immanuel Kant's work, it is in the essay "Idea for a Universal History with a Cosmopolitan Intent" (1784/1991) that readers find a prophetic prediction that one day the whole world will be governed by a global government of republican representatives. Several imminent scholars, like Hegel, have since revealed the Kantian illusion of cosmopolitanism to be a thinly veiled reformulation of the universalizing project of the Enlightenment, and contemporary critics stay vigilant in demonstrating how the movement has been appropriated to revitalize a neoliberal capitalist imperialism that imposes upon different societies a singular form of life. In the *Shrek* films, the Kantian prediction of cosmopolitanism is embedded so that its discourses serve to consolidate the liberal humanist values of the power elites by promoting the global expansion of techno-capitalism, social hierarchies, and state-centered power.

In conventional thought, cosmopolitanism invokes an image of one world—connected by one market, ruled by one governing body, and condemned to one destiny. Contemporary variants of cosmopolitanism, like its predecessor, universalism, are premised upon a neoliberal understanding of globalization as an integrative, universalizing process, a great equalizer, and the irreversible fate of the world. The prevailing understanding is embodied in Anthony Giddens' work on the consequences of modernity. He writes:

> One of the fundamental consequences of modernity... is globalization. This is more than a diffusion of Western institutions across the world, in which other cultures are crushed. Globalization—which is a process of uneven development that fragments as it coordinates—introduces new forms of world interdependence, in which, once again, there are no "others." (Giddens, 1990: p. 175)

This brand of cosmopolitanism posits that the unity of mankind is not an ideological imperative, as it was in the projects of the Enlightenment and modernization, but a biophysical fact evident in intensified mobility—of people, capital, and information—as a central feature in the reconfiguration of geopolitical processes. The idea of increased mobility attributed to globalization assumes a freedom of movement, real and virtual, and an increase in the pursuit of happiness for those who participate in the reproduction of these processes while ignoring the asymmetrical relations required *by* the process. A more critical view recognizes that cosmopolitanism lacks the commonly assumed unity of effects, and actually divides human beings into grossly disparate power relations. In place of the former structures of domination, inherent in colonialism and modernity, the era of globalization represents an even more insidious structure, one that intensifies the alienation of humans from nature, further divides them into mutually hostile classes, and replaces any sense of community with impersonal and dehumanizing procedures. The idea that globalization requires integration conceals its true requirement—of polarization, through the simultaneous processes of globalization and localization. These parallel processes are not, according to Zygmunt Bauman (1998: pp. 2, 105), a spontaneous historical movement, but rather a deliberate strategic act that supports and reinforces the cultural and economic forces conducive to the perpetuation of domination. He explains the processes this way:

> What appears as globalization for some means localization for others; signaling a new freedom for some, upon many others it descends as an uninvited and cruel fate. Mobility climbs to the rank of the uppermost among the coveted values—and the freedom to move, perpetually a scarce and unequally distributed commodity, fast becomes the main stratifying factor of our late-modern or postmodern times.... Mobility and its absence designate the new, late-modern or postmodern polarization of social conditions. The top of the hierarchy is exterritorial; its lower ranges are marked by varying degrees of space constraints, while the bottom ones are, for all practical purposes, glebae adscripti.

The predication that cosmopolitanism, or the cultural process of globalization, is spontaneous, necessary, and beneficial for all, rather than an orchestrated and thought-out project of cultural domination, has been in vogue for some time. It is an idea that effectively legitimizes and normalizes the destructive forces of this process, rather than exploring the notion of globalization through a sustained critical eye, without veiling its contradictory logic as it pertains to the numerous realms of social life, including the psychic and ontological well-being of those who reside under its banner.

Kantian cosmopolitanism, as it is portrayed in *Shrek,* proves that the only entity that flows freely across borders with the power to impose its own logic is capital. Evidence of the presence of cosmopolitanism is always substantiated with a litany of superficial illustrations such as being able to purchase spring rolls and samosas while walking through the streets of London or watching an Indian film en route to Africa for a conference. Such examples inevitably reveal that the direction of this movement of ideas, people, and objects seems to be biased in favor of the wealthier nations or the bourgeoisie of the poorer ones. The *Shrek* movies remain painfully silent on issues of cultural power—or any power for that matter.

The pro-cosmopolitan message in *Shrek* (2001) is that Global citizenship means diversity not conformity; whereas universalism views diversity as an obstacle to order, cosmopolitanism embraces otherness. The villain, Farquaad, exclaims that he is "entitled" to rule the kingdom despite his lack of royal blood. Farquaad's claim to be the "rightful King" is based on his success in ruling the fiefdom of Duloc, a perfectly controlled town, which he has cleansed of nonhuman fairy-tale entities, or the "trash poisoning [his] perfect world." The presence of the "others," the monstrous and the carnivalesque, results in destabilization of the simulacrum of a "perfect world." A Bakhtinian reading suggests that the fiefdom of Duloc and Farquaad are meant to represent the established Jews who had gained wealth but were still denied acceptance into the Protestant elite. Farquaad's desire to control the less desirable elements of fairy tales, the grotesque, is similar to the established Jews, who were passing as Americans, and were reluctant to join the war and integrate European Jewish refugees. Though the humor in the film is based on the removal of unseemly details from the Brothers Grimm fairy tales, by Disney, the desire to control in order to portray a perfect world is parallel. In Duloc, even the audience's responses are fed to them on cue cards, again suggesting manipulation of viewers who were spoon-fed.

In *Shrek 2* (2004), the pro-cosmopolitan message is: race and class stratification will make way for the era of hybridity. Hybrids pepper the cast of characters in the film. Fiona is a hybrid herself, with a human mother and a frog father. Donkey mates with a dragon to create flying donkeys. In the *Shrek* films, the tale of cosmopolitanism is embedded in a plot that shows a kingdom in transition from a style of governing that cleanses the "other" to one that appropriates the "other." The core of power is Far Far Away, while the marginalized categories of cosmopolitanism are represented in anthropomorphized characterizations of many groups who have been outsiders throughout history: the grotesque (ogres), the women (princesses), the disabled (the three blind mice), the LGBQ (transgendered stepsisters), the continental Europeans (three little pigs), the Scots (Shrek), the Latinos (Puss in Boots), the hippies and mystics (the wizard), the ebonic-speaking ghetto dwellers (Donkey), and the criminals (the villains).

When the King announces that he needs to prepare for death, neither Fiona nor Shrek are considered appropriate replacements, despite being next in line to the throne. "An ogre as King?" Shrek asks. The King doesn't encourage him to reconsider, nor does Fiona. No one considers Fiona, the daughter of the King and the Queen, as the natural heir; instead, the King informs them of a nephew, "Arthur," who is fully human and therefore fit to be the next King. Shrek reluctantly leads the resistance against Charming, but only for his own comfort and stability. The war over the center of power is between two humans, both with royal ancestry, only their accents revealing to the audience that Charming is purebred British, while Arthur is hybrid American. The accents are meant to contrast the old *Pax* Britannia, which displaced the other, with the new *Pax* Americana, which includes the other.

The final pro-cosmopolitan discourse detectable in the *Shrek* series is that governing will be an act of inclusion not exclusion. Faced with the prospect of losing the throne to "Arthur," the nephew of the King, Prince Charming needs to assemble a military of mercenary fighters from the villains ousted from Far Far Away. He refers to them as "freaks" to show his reluctance in working with them, but in his bid to mobilize the crowd of underprivileged outcasts who see him as the enemy, Charming tells them, "we're more alike than you think." He finally persuades them to fight with him by promising them redemption for their past lives: "Someone decided we were the losers—so who will join me? Who wants their happily ever after?" Convinced of the moral necessity of their war, the villains raise their arms (and hooks) in solidarity. Arthur has also appealed to the margins to create an army, but in contrast to Charming's army of villains, Arthur's is composed of women, animals, hybrids, and the gender ambiguous.

Arthur's potentially benevolent manner of ruling is contrasted with Charming's in several ways. Where Charming kills nature for his future by decapitating five animals in a theater performance, Arthur's kingdom will "harness" nature with the formation of an alliance of princesses and animals (it is noteworthy that women are relegated to the place of nature in the man/nature dualism). Rather than lead his army into a bloody battle, he begins with dialogue, encouraging Charming's army not to surrender but to be included in the folds of the new empire. "Don't be outcasts," he says, encouraging the villains to take this opportunity to cultivate the more humane side of their character. "I grow daffodils," says a decidedly less villainous Hook. The warriors on both sides embrace not just one another, but the new idea of being ruled by a leader who offers justice for all.

A Non-Kantian Cosmopolitanism

A non-Kantian cosmopolitanism is forged upon the value of difference that takes seriously the inequalities of globalization processes, but Kantian cosmopolitanism depends on them. In the *Shrek* films, the stories emphasize the requirement of solidarity and resistance while at the same time undermining their value in rethinking the neoliberal doxa. Cosmopolitanism in these films is still a neoliberal project rather than a resistant practice. The messianic meta-narrative of Far Far Away suggests that the perfection of man will come as we progress and leave tradition and nontechnical, noncapitalist ways behind. The marginal characters representing anything other than new world consumerism, Gingy, the three pigs, the stepsisters, do not present the multiple possibilities and the other ways of being; they preclude them. The ways of the gingerbread people, or those of the pigs, stepsisters, or ogres, will not be incorporated into the governing of Far Far Away. As such, Arthur's promises of pluralism veil an imperial project that requires those subjects who have hitherto been marginalized, Hindus, Muslims, the queer community, and women. Ironically, however, as is illustrated when Cinderella and Snow White and nature's creatures are all reduced to soldiers to deter the threat to the liberal doxa, the dominant values remain unshaken. Kantian cosmopolitanism resorts to the same violence and exclusion of imperialism, the very process from which it claims to differ.

Note

1. Ritzer defines his theory of McDonaldization as "the process by which the principles of the fast-food restaurant are coming to dominate more and more sectors of American society as well as the rest of the world" (Ritzer, 2000: p. 1).

CHAPTER 8

Shrek: Simple Story or Nonhuman Transactor?

François Dépelteau

Basic Epistemological Principles of Transactional Sociology

Some positivist practitioners of social sciences think that objective knowledge is accessible to human beings. By this they mean a direct and "pure" knowledge of the object as it is in reality, without any interference from the methods, theories, technologies, tools, observers, and other factors involved in the production of knowledge. In this respect, they believe we have to and can neutralize the effects of our subjectivity—of our mind, values, and body—on the process of observation by using one Scientific method. Then, like an angel or the Cartesian mind, we could see the world from an external, detached and disembodied position. In sum, Science would require a neutral and cold observing machine looking at external objects as they are in reality.

Others claim that this cold observer and his detached observing position do not exist. These are positivistic myths or dreams, they say. Many of these non-positivists pretend that "objects" are only social constructions made by subjective observers and their concepts, methods, texts, discourses, and so on.

Many social scientists think we have to choose between being cold observing machines or subjective observers. Yet, there are other options beyond the positivist dream of pure facts and radical social constructionism. We can develop a third option by starting from thinkers such as N. Elias, M. Mann, J. Dewey, and B. Latour. They can help us to develop different epistemological principles and ontological views. I call this other option: transactional sociology. Why do we need another option beyond objectivism and subjectivism? It can help us to have a better understanding of a complex social phenomenon like *Shrek* and any other social phenomenon. I explain later that transactional sociology is a good alternative in comparison to social theories which look like simple stories. But for now, I would like to focus on some basic epistemological principles in order to briefly illustrate how transactional sociology produces knowledge about Shrek and any other social phenomenon.

B. Latour (1988, 2004) has constantly challenged the myth of Science by observing "science-in-action" in laboratories like an ethnographer. In brief, he found that fluid scientific knowledge emerged from complex networks involving human and non human actors, and not from detached experts who only see pure facts. In other words, scientific knowledge emerges from the assemblage of experts, technicians, computers, graphics, notes, tubes, rats, gases, and so on. Therefore, producers of scientific knowledge are always embodied in the world. By making their observations, using one tool or another, by relying on specific concepts, discussing with other experts, looking for money, publishing articles, quoting other articles, competing with other laboratories, making tables and graphs, they are transacting in complex fields of interdependent actions where fluid knowledge is produced through specific assemblages of all these interdependent actors.

What about our green ogre? Well, in order to understand *Shrek* and any other social phenomenon, we need to realize the ogre is neither an object of knowledge nor a construction or tool made by other actors. We really have to move beyond classical dualisms opposing realism and constructivism, or objectivism and subjectivism. It can be done by developing a transactional toolbox of principles and concepts used to study the social universe as a moving assemblage of dynamic social processes.

Overall, the main guiding idea of this transactional analysis is quite simple: Shrek is a transactor.[1] He is vibrant and active in complex fields of transactions, including when we think and talk about him. Far from being a simple object or tool used by other actors, Shrek contributes to the constant production of the world by being engaged in various types of transactions. The following list is not exhaustive but we can identify economic transactions where Shrek is part of business games based on profit. There are also ideological transactions where Shrek's transactions are related to the production and diffusion of values, worldviews, norms, et cetera, coming for instance, from contemporary social movements and neoconservative countermovements. We will come back to this dimension of Shrek. There are also scientific transactions where Shrek transacts with social scientists like the authors of this book, their theories and methods, and readers like you. All of these fields of transactions are more or less interpenetrated. What is happening in one field can influence the transactions of some other fields. The connections between interdependent fields are empirical relations between specific human or nonhuman transactors who are active in different fields. As shown in schema 8.1, one of these connections could be made for instance, if the actions of activists of a neoconservative countermovement are influenced by the reading of this book, or if some political actions made by these activists influenced the content of this book (scientific field ↔ political field).

What matters for now is that when Shrek is active in a scientific field, when he becomes an observed phenomenon like in this book, he is not powerful enough to simply impose himself as a solid "thing." He cannot simply neutralize observers and their theories and methods. Like any other transactor in any scientific field of transactions, Shrek is engaged in relations with observers and their theories and methods, but also with publishers, readers, and so on. Each interdependent human and nonhuman actor plays a role, or has some "agency," in social

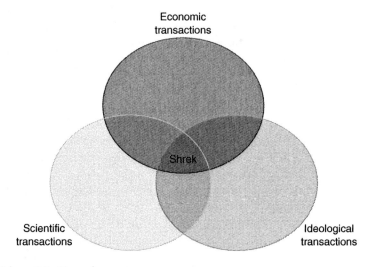

Schema 8.1 Types of transactions

relations and, therefore, affects the liquid (rather than solid) result of these relations—the result being some fluid, changing knowledge in the case of a scientific field of transactions. This is why we always end up with diverse interpretations, explanations or perceptions of Shrek and any other observed phenomenon in social sciences.

In other words, this diversified book on *Shrek* is a good illustration of one important transactional phenomenon of what B. Latour (2004) called the "science-in-the-making." The "known," and by this I mean any observed phenomenon as it is known by us, can take many forms depending partly on the type of social theory and research method used by the observer. Indeed, Shrek can be seen as a living entity acting according to predefined evolutionary laws; an entertaining strategy used to divert the attention of people from more important political issues; or an illustration of various forms of discourses and representations of political regimes. In this sense, social theories and methods are not simply detached from the "objective reality" they try to represent. Without denying the existence of Shrek as a real nonhuman transactor, we can say that social theories and their related research methods contribute to shape the reality we observe as far as the "known" is concerned. With different concepts, tools (interviews, surveys, content analysis, statistics, tables, software, etc.) and ontological views, theories and methods transact with the observers by orienting the observations on some real or imagined dimensions of the reality (gender issues, evolutionary effects, attempts to dominate people, representations of political regimes, etc.).

We should not conclude that knowledge is simply determined by theories and methods. Even if some theories and methods are more powerful than others, they do not simply self-act on (or determine) the observer and the observed phenomenon—as many positivists believe. Theories and methods *in action* transact with observers and observed phenomena. Indeed, the best observer of the world always uses one theory and method in her own way, with more or less "agency" and flexibility. The observer cannot or should not try to force theories, methods and observed phenomena according to her own goals, interests, values and desires. But she is not an angel. She has a personality, a history, subjectivity; she is also transacting with the theory, the methodological tools and the observed phenomenon. The actors are always interdependent. Furthermore, the development of one research is never the kind of mechanical process as described in many textbooks. Research is always full of hesitations, contingent and unexpected problems, and more or less accurate choices. As shown in schema 8.2, observers, theories, and

Shrek: Simple Story or Nonhuman Transactor? • 107

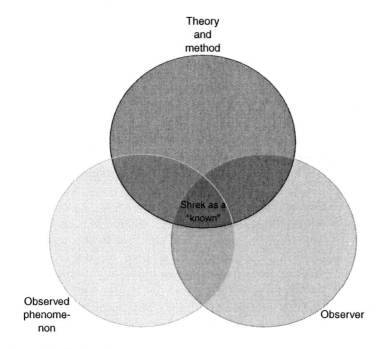

Schema 8.2 Shrek as a known

methods transact with many other transactors in one research project, and they are affected by them in one way or another (like they affect them). Theories and methods exist through transactions where all the transactors make each other without simply determining each other. In this sense, the observed phenomenon also transacts in a scientific field. The fact that Shrek is observed, discussed and interpreted does not cancel the other fact of his existence as a transactor. This preservation of a transactional realism helps to understand why it can be more difficult to argue that Shrek is a red submarine than a green ogre, even if the form taken by the "known" is quite flexible due to the interdependent actions of the observer, the theory and method.

In sum, there is no such a thing as a separated, detached "scientific" fact in this complex universe made by multiple transactions. More generally speaking, there is no such a thing as independent, all powerful or passive, actors. There are just relations between transactors and their fluid transactions produce liquid and complex phenomena. This is what this chapter is all about. Indeed, despite its simplicity due to the lack of space and the limited knowledge of its author, this text insists on the complexity of the green ogre by relying on transactional sociology. In this logic, I want to show that *Shrek* cannot be reduced to any simple story. For instance, *Shrek* cannot be reduced to pure entertainment, a simple commercial product made to make profit, or an attempt made by one dominant group to maintain the capitalist or patriarchal social order. And he is not only driven by a natural law of evolution when he falls in love with Fiona.

I am not rejecting these explanations or any other theory. Each of them might—or might not—help us to see some transactions related to Shrek. However, I am saying that in order to understand the complexity of Shrek, the ogre should be seen as a nonhuman transactor involved in many transactions with many other transactors—including contemporary social movements and other vibrant observers like social scientists, journalists, lay persons and children. In this sense, Shrek is an amazing money machine; he is entertaining; and he might be driven by basic sexual and reproductive impulses. Nevertheless, he is also part of much more complex transactions between multiple human and nonhuman transactors. In this text, I quickly underline the importance of his creators, contemporary social movements such as the gay and lesbian movement, and a wide audience made partly by children.

In the second part of the chapter, I will present some basic ontological views of transactional sociology. This is the approach I am proposing to deal with the high complexity of social phenomena.

In the third and fourth parts, I will try to add to the complexity of the fat and stinky ogre by showing what transactional sociology can add to our knowledge about Shrek. This job will be done in comparison to one virtual but potential simple story about Shrek. This imagined story is inspired by quite famous N. Chomsky's critical theory of "manufacturing consent." In brief, the "rebel without a pause" explained how and why the "owners of the society" manipulate the mind of passive people with entertaining products like Shrek. Why choosing this critical theory rather than any other one? Firstly, the theory of manufacturing consent is representative of many explanations of mass consumption influenced by the texts of L. Althussser, the Frankfurt School and even S. Hall. N. Chomsky presented entertaining and mass consumption products like *Shrek* as contributing to the status quo. Consumers are seen as being passive and simply manipulated by the dominant class and their ideology. In this type of theory, only self-declared and noisy protesters to the social order are seen as being active and creative (see Walkerdine, 2009: pp. 5–8). In this sense, criticizing Chomsky's theory is criticizing all these theories which are, I think, nothing more and nothing less than simple stories. Another reason for choosing N. Chomsky's stories is because I like them. I think that this is exactly the kind of social approach we need to evaluate and criticize if we want to improve this sad and cruel world based on oppression and exploitation. Many other theories do not deserve to be criticized. Even if we would improve them, as transactors, these theories would have very little positive impact on the production of this world as we know it. So why should we care about them? I hope that transactional sociology also deserves to be harshly criticized.

Basic Ontological Views about Our Social Universe

A world of social configurations full of power relations (and also other relations)

Human beings live in a world characterized by huge social inequalities. As a matter of consequence, centuries after T. Hobbes published the *Leviathan,* life of too many is still "solitary, poor, nasty, brutish and short." We know how to develop amazing technological tools such as spaceships, complex computers and nuclear plants. We can even transform living organisms thanks to our science. But socially speaking, we are still surprisingly involved in destructive power relations through multiple fields of transactions.

Generally speaking, power relations can be found in four main sources of transaction in this world (inspired by Mann, 1986: p. 2):

(i) political transactions, where people are conflicting, making alliances, demonstrating, for the control of laws, population, taxation, and territory;
(ii) economic transactions, where individuals compete for the accumulation of wealth;
(iii) ideological transactions, where people contend over school curriculums, give speeches, write texts, make movies, interpret and preach the words of God, and so on for the control of worldviews, values, norms, et cetera;
(iv) military transactions, where generals, soldiers, child-soldiers, et cetera, fight for the control of space and resources on land, sea, and air through the use of weapons and various forms of violence such as torture, terror, and massacres.

All of these types of transactions are more or less interconnected or interdependent. Social transactions are not limited to spectacular power relations. They happen through various fields of transactions like couples, families, schools, towns, corporations, social movements, bookstores, armies, shopping malls, et cetera. Our liquid world is comprised of billions of fields of transactions emerging, changing or disintegrating through power relations but also on the basis of emotions such as love, hate, friendship, disgust, fear, and so on. Billions of individuals constantly mobilize various resources to achieve different goals in one field of transactions or another: getting an education, finding a job, trying to get elected, seducing another person, destroying an enemy, invading a territory, making more money, having more prestige, having a child, changing the mind of other people about their needs and dreams or their worldviews, et cetera. Of course, these billions of people are also driven by unconscious motives or desires.

Most of the time people act on an individual basis, but again, they are also part of various fields such as couples, families, elites, social classes, clans, tribes, pressure groups, corporations, governments, social movements, countermovements, neighborhoods, and political parties. Some of these fields look quite stable most of the time in the eyes of someone who does not see that they are made by complex and fluid transactions. In reality, and like anything else in this universe (living organisms, rivers, clouds, planets, etc.), these fields of transactions are in constant movement. They change all the time even if our human eyes cannot see most of the ongoing transformations. These constant changes are also difficult to see because most people refuse to face the messiness of our social universe. They are afraid by the liquidity of social phenomena like they are scared by death. They prefer to see their "society" as a functional and stable entity, believing that some strange forces like "social structures," the "Market" or the "System" assure the continuity of the order of things. Fears and frustrations play a significant role in the success of simple stories about ourselves and our universe (Freud, 1969; Elias, 1987). Rulers are much more efficient when they base their ideological work on fears and frustrations.

A World of Inequalities

In an unstable magma of multiple and complex transactions, some actors mobilize much more resources than others and, in this respect, are more successful in their ability to pursue and attain goals through mastery of human and nonhuman actors in specific fields of transactions.[2] For instance, some had more "extensive power" than others, that is, "the ability to organize large numbers of people over far-flung territories in order to engage in minimally stable cooperation" (Mann, 1986: p. 7). These people usually become presidents, dictators, charismatic leaders, prime ministers, and so on. In fields of transactions such as States, private businesses, social movements, armies or even classrooms, power is also more or less "intensive," meaning that some people are more efficient than others "to organize tightly and command a high level of mobilization or commitment from the participants, whether the area and numbers covered [are] great or small" (Mann, 1986: p. 7).

A World of Egocentric People

I believe one of the main problems we are facing, is the lack of understanding about the transactional nature of our universe. In fact, most of us cannot or do not want to see that we are all in a constant state of interdependency with other human and nonhuman transactors. Most people adopt an egocentric mode of perception of the universe (Elias, 1978). They see their environment only from their own perspective, as if they were at the center of the universe. Instead of seeing themselves as interdependent coproducers of their families, schools, villages, States, or global economy, they think they are determined by them or that they can interact "with the System," as they say. Many specialists of the social see these social phenomena as "social things," that is, external and constraining/enabling substances. They cannot think in a transactional way. The same is true about our interdependency with nonhuman transactors. Many of us are so egocentric that we cannot even see—or do not want to see—our interdependency with nonhuman transactors such as water, air, soil, trees, animals and plants.

A Complex World Where People Prefer Simple Stories

In this world of limited social intelligence, many people favor simple stories showing how everything that happens results directly from a few independent, conscious, and self-motivated characters (Tilly, 2002: p. 26). These stories are usually easier to grasp than detailed analyses of opaque and diversified transactions and their unintended effects.

Rigorous social scientists have a hard time competing with good story tellers who can find more or less large audiences by telling spectacular and Manichean stories. Preachers, for instance, claim that some individuals are "sick" because one powerful God is punishing them for their sexual "sins."

Surprisingly, many intelligent social scientists write similarly simplistic fairy tales, telling how the world is produced or manipulated by a few powerful entities such as social classes, elites, heroic social movements or social systems. Many of them invoke deep "structural" forces in their social stories. Their "structures" almost looked like the scientific translations for gods and demons. Such stories are usually associated with the use of "scientific" methodology, reductionist theory and reifying concepts such as "system," "function," or "superstructure."[3] In sociology, structuro-functionalists, for instance, told a reassuring story. It was the story of some consensual norms and values which stabilize the social order by imposing themselves on "normal" individuals. In this story, "development" was a universal process of differentiation leading to (American) democracy. It was a very comforting story, especially to those who were American and under the impression of being "normal."

Most of the critical thinkers prefer social stories with major conflict between the bad guys (the oppressors) and the good guys (the oppressed). Some of the books which they favor were written by one of their best social storytellers, K. Marx. I say "some" books (like *The Communist Manifesto*) because Marx could also be an amazing and complex social analyst (for instance, in *The Capital*, volume 1). However, in some of his texts—usually the ones he refused to publish or the ones he published because he was looking for a wide audience to mobilize—Marx wrote exciting social stories. They were about two social classes which were involved in a struggle because they lived in a society founded on a deep contradiction. The capitalists (the bad guys) could make profit only by exploiting the workers (the good guys who most can identify with). The bad guys were protected by cynical and vicious subordinates (politicians, priests, foremen, policemen, judges, etc.) who helped them make a profit by keeping the poor workers ignorant and quiet through repression and ideological manipulation. But in the end, Marx said, the good guys will win the battle and they will be happy forever when they live in a classless, communist society. Marx wrote a simple story with a nice ending, especially if you aspired to be a communist ruler.

In sum, various people like popes, politicians and intellectuals produce different social stories in this world of transactions including power relations. Why? Because many people enjoyed the simplicity of these stories, but also because the stories are very efficient resources for controlling different political, ideological, economic and military fields of transactions. Needless to say this world is a vast battlefield of simple stories.

Now, let's see how Shrek can be viewed through one typical, radical and simple story. We will compare this story with a brief transactional analysis of Shrek later.

The (simple) Story of the Modern Roman "games of the circus"

N. Chomsky and E. Herman wrote one of the most entertaining contemporary social stories: *Manufacturing Consent* (2002). Today, N. Chomsky is certainly one of the best leftist social storytellers. In 2005, he was nominated as the leading living public intellectual in *The 2005 Global Intellectual Polls*. One year later, the magazine *New Statesman* voted him as the seventh "Hero of our time."

In brief, *Manufacturing Consent* is a story about the failure of American democracy. N. Chomsky told us that a few transnational conglomerates (Disney, AOL Time Warner, Viacom, etc.) control the media. These media outlets "serve, and propagandize on behalf of, the powerful societal interests that control and finance them" (Herman and Chomsky, 2002: p. xiii). The bad guys—"a pretty narrow group" of "people with real power" "who own the society" (Chomsky, 2002: p. 18)—are worried that the "bewildered herd" (the victims we can identify with) could eventually use their vote to defend their interests. Therefore, after learning how to use state propaganda during the two world wars, the bad guys started to use newspapers, movies, professional sports, et cetera to entertain "the people," to divert their attention from real problems and solutions. By doing so, the elites and their subordinates (the "specialized class") managed to "seriously weaken the 'public sphere,' which refers to the array of places and forums in which important matters to a democratic community are debated and information relevant to intelligent citizen participation is provided" (Herman and Chomsky, 2002: p. xviii). They created a "depoliticized consumer culture" which is related to "a world of virtual communities built by advertisers and based on demographics and taste differences of consumers. (...) These virtual communities are organized to buy and sell goods, not to create or service a public sphere" (Herman and Chomsky, 2002: p. xviii). In this sense, major newspapers such as *The New York Times,* professional baseball games or blockbuster movies (like *Shrek*) are seen as "the contemporary equivalent of the Roman 'games of the circus' that divert the public from politics and generates a political apathy that is helpful to preservation of the status quo" (Herman and Chomsky, 2002: p. xviii).

The main point here is the following: N. Chomsky's radical theory corresponds to what C. Tilly calls "dominant modes of story-telling":

> They typically call up a limited number of actors whose dispositions and actions cause everything that happens within a delimited time and space. (...) As a consequence, stories inevitably minimize or ignore the causal roles of errors, unanticipated consequences, indirect effects, incremental effects, simultaneous effects, feedback effects, and environmental effects. (Tilly, 2006: p. 17)

In this logic, simple stories "rework and simplify social processes," and "they include strong imputations of responsibility" (Tilly, 2006: p. 16). N. Chomsky's story is full of clear and simple characters, morally repulsing examples, fascinating conspiracies, and a potentially good ending—should the masses be finally awakened by kissing critical intellectuals such as N. Chomsky. It does not mean that Chomsky's theory is a fairy tale. I think Chomsky's story could become an interesting analysis of some important (and unpleasant) aspects of our world. However, the narrative would need substantial improvements to become a rigorous mode of perception of a *complex* social universe rather than just a good simple story. Let's see how Shrek becomes more complex through transactional sociology.

Shrek and Transactional Analysis

Keeping the complexity in mind without seeing the total field of transactions

The transactional analyst faces a constant paradox. On one hand, he wants to avoid any reductive analysis of the social phenomenon he is studying. On the other hand, he is obliged to be more humble than many story tellers who can see "societies," "infrastructures," interactions between "social systems," "micro and macro levels" or hidden and invisible fundamental dynamics. The transactional analyst is an ascetic, an obsessive empiricist always looking for traces, and some kind of a masochist: (i) relatively speaking, he is obliged to see small phenomena—basically, traces of contextualized transactions between specific human and nonhuman transactors; (ii) he is constantly conscious about his partial blindness and ignorance even if he is desperate to discover something else other than his own limitations as an observer. Indeed, in relation to his research question, the transactional analyst is restricted to the observation of what seems to be the most important transactions identified with his limited mode of observation and knowledge. In this respect, the "known" never corresponds to the observed phenomenon. It is always more simple even if we are looking for the complexity of phenomena.

Let's be honest here. The selection of transactions I propose in this chapter is a ridiculous simplification of the reality. Beyond the typical lack of resources I would need to go deeper in the history of traces left by transactions related to Shrek, my only excuse is that any research is always the result of transactions between the "knowing" and the "known" (Dewey and Bentley, 1947). Alas, nobody can see the total field of transactions which make any social phenomenon. There are not enough resources, too many transactions and not enough traces. However, I wish that my limited choice of foci can provide a better understanding of Shrek and show the possibilities of transactional sociology.

Seeing Traces of Significant Transactions

The observer is condemned to look at the most important transactions which have made a phenomenon like Shrek. But what are the most important transactions? How do we choose them? As I mentioned on several occasions by being inspired by B. Latour, human and nonhuman transactors exist and are noticeable when they make differences and leave traces: "If I want to have actors in my account, they have to do things, not to be placeholders; if they do something, they have to make a difference" (Latour, 2005: p. 154). In this sense, transactors do not have to be reflexive to make a difference and leave a trace. A knife cuts some meat. It (trans)acts (without thinking) because it left a trace; it made a difference:

> *any thing* that does modify a state of affairs by making a difference is an actor (...) Thus, the question to ask about any agent are simply the following: Does it make a difference in the course of some other agent's action or not? Is there some trial that allows someone to detect this difference? (Latour, 2005: p. 71)

Some Important Transactions behind Shrek

As entertaining as they may be, *Shrek* movies are not simply the equivalent of the "Roman circus games." Of course, these blockbuster movies are commercial products. I have no doubt that some very wealthy people are enjoying the amazing profits they are making with the movies, the popcorn, and all the other related products they sell. As a parent, I also witness my kids' fascination toward anything related to Shrek, particularly during times when neoimperial invasions, corruption, scandals, lies, et cetera consume the "free and democratic world" outside of the movie theater. It is no wonder I have been tempted so many times by N. Chomsky's theory about entertaining the masses in order to divert our attention from political problems. However, Shrek is much more than a clown used by the King to divert his passive and ignorant subjects. He is a transactor involved in multiple fields of transactions. Let's see what the main traces are that I found in this brief observation to support my thesis.

Economic Transactions with Capitalists and Famous People

In February 2008, *TF1* presented *Shrek 2* in France. More than 7.5 million French people watched it (Médiametrie—TF1, 2008). *Shrek the Third* had generated more than 800 million US dollars in worldwide revenue by the end of October 2007. Some people are richer than they were before. And by investing this amazing profit, they are still making many more differences.

By transacting with them, Shrek also makes some people famous. Thanks to Shrek's successful transactions with so many viewers and critiques of cinema, the *DreamWorks* executive Jeffrey Katzenberg has been described as a "genius" able to bring children, teenagers and adults in the same theater (Weinman, 2007).

Shrek (the people behind its production and marketing, of course) also transacted with other big moneymakers such as McDonalds. Some people behind the big, rich, red and yellow clown have used Shrek to hide their greasy hamburgers behind some fresh fruits and vegetables when they transact with kids:

> Bill Lamar, chief marketing officer, McDonald's USA, from left, Roger A. Enrico, chairman, DreamWorks Animation SKG, and Mary Dillon, McDonald's global chief marketing officer, introduce McDonald's "Shrek the Third" global promotion Tuesday, May 8, 2007 at a McDonald's

restaurant in Chicago. McDonald's "Shrek the Third" program is the company's single biggest promotion of fruit, vegetables and low-fat milk, and features Happy Meal toys created in eight languages and an innovative online kids community. (McDonald's, 2007)

Shrek *Transacting with Progressive Movements*

We could multiply the traces of economic transactions left by *Shrek* movies. But let's come back to the main thesis: the complexity of Shrek (see schema 8.3). On one hand, Shrek has transacted with millions of happy (or "alienated") consumers in capitalist fields of transactions by showing his lack of good manners, making people laugh, promoting hamburgers, reshaping toothbrushes, publishing books for kids, showing his fat ugly face on posters in kids' bedrooms, participating in the consumption of coke and popcorn in movie theaters, and so on. But on the other hand, Shrek also integrates and diffuses worldviews, ideas, values, emotions, et cetera of progressive social movements. In this sense, I think that what R. Eyerman and A. Jamieson (1998) wrote about

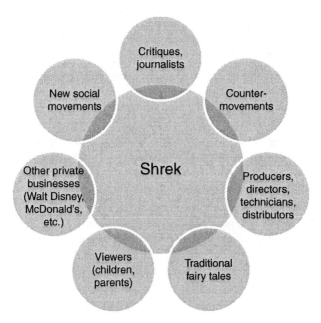

Schema 8.3 Shrek and its various transactors

famous artists such as Picasso, Dylan, Copland and others is also true about Shrek.

The "form" of Shrek cannot be understood if we disconnect him from social movements. And these movements cannot be fully understood if we forget about Shrek's recent contribution (and other books, movies, etc.) to the reformulation and diffusion of values, worldviews, et cetera:

> So many of the leading artists, writers, and composer/musicians of the twentieth century have been involved, at formative periods of their lives, in political movements. This does not mean that the monumental artistic achievements of Picasso, Kollwitz, Rivera, Gorky, Brecht, Sartre, Weill, Copland, Bernstein, Baez, Dylan, and all the others can be reduced to their political involvements. But it does suggest that, without having taken active part in social movements, these individuals would have produced very different works. And, in most cases, movement involvement remained central to their artistic production. Their engagement was objectified in their art, and the movement thus came to be embodied in them. When the movements in which they had been involved were no longer active, the ideas and ideals of the movements lived on in their art. And, in many cases, they served to inspire new movements by helping to keep the older movements alive in the collective memory. (Eyerman and Jamieson, 1998: p. 12)

Many aspects of Shrek's movies are linked to changes desired by some activists in contemporary social movements, such as the gay, bisexual, lesbian and transgender movement. In this respect, I think one of Shrek trilogy's goals—not the only one, of course!—has been the recognition of so-called deviant people and other "losers" as legitimate and respectable members of the society. With other large audience movies such as *Philadelphia* (1993), *Brokeback Mountain* (2005) and *Milk* (2008), Shrek has supported this claim by presenting various "weird" characters as being recommendable and good people. Some friends or allies of Shrek—such as the wolf and Pinocchio—can be seen as transgendered in one way or another. Nevertheless, they are good guys. Like in *Philadelphia, Brokeback Mountain* and *Milk,* the bad people are those who neglect gay and lesbian rights. Let's see some examples. In the movies, Prince Charming—who should be the hero if *Shrek* were a "classical" fairy tale—is presented as a blond, superficial, frustrated and clear heterosexual macho-male. In *Shrek 2,* he is such a looser that he is unable to seduce princess Fiona without relying on a magic potion made by his . . . mother!

Another example: in *Shrek* (2001), Lord Farquaad (bad guy) has no room in his kingdom (a totalitarian regime) for "deviant" people. Furthermore, the same dictator tries to force Fiona to marry him in order to become a real king. Fiona is courageous and she has a lot of "agency." She stays as a "deviant" by accepting to be a full-time, green, fat female ogre, basically because she loves Shrek and refuses the high status offered by Lord Farquaad. Farquaad rejects Fiona the moment he realizes she is not the beautiful and docile princess he expects. And he is finally eaten alive by a weird female dragon that has an unconventional affair with one talking but nice donkey—who speaks like an American black person.

Once again, who are the good guys in the film? Two ogres, one talking donkey, a dragon who falls in love with the (black) talking donkey, and so on, in brief, the marginal people. Who are the bad guys? They are the ruler of the clean and orderly society, the awesome and ambitious prince charming, and his mother who seeks power in and of itself. The dominant class does not win the image contest in these movies. Even the King Harold—Fiona's father—is weak, cowardly and a little bit "slow," as the Queen says in *Shrek 2*.

Let me give more examples of traces of connections between these social movements and *Shrek*. Most of the "new" social movements' activists are very different from their left-wing ancestors of the early twentieth century at least on one point: they are not looking for power. This is, I guess, one positive legacy of the totalitarian nightmares of the twentieth century, including the communist ones. The quest for changing society does not imply a total revolution, a coup d'état and the destruction of the "objective enemy" with new social movements such as feminism and pacifism. As Touraine (1977) explains, many contemporary social movements have been democratic (but not all of them!) because they have not tried to change the totality of the society. In this sense, Shrek can be contrasted with classical political leaders such as Lenin. In the first movie, he is presented as an antisocial ogre who just wants to live a quiet life in his swamp. He wants to be alone. But even a powerful and terrifying ogre cannot control the evolution of his life and the rest of the world. Whether he likes it or not, Shrek is condemned to be social, that is to be involved in fields of transactions he cannot control by himself. So, one day Lord Farquaad decides to clean his kingdom from any magical creatures. This is clearly presented as an organized and centralized purge which follows one disorganized pogrom made by peasants against the ogre. The metaphor with the Holocaust is quite clear.

When some refugees try to hide themselves in Shrek's swamp and ask for his help, Shrek refuses at first. He rejects the role of the hero, of the revolutionary leader who can mobilize the oppressed and challenge the "system" or the dominant class. He finally and reluctantly accepts to meet Lord Farquad only because it seems to be the best solution to get rid of these annoying refugees from his swamp.

SHREK
I live in a swamp. I put up signs. I'm a terrifying ogre! What do I have to do to get a little privacy? [HE OPENS THE FRONT DOOR TO THROW THE WOLF OUT AND HE SEES THAT ALL THE COLLECTED FAIRY TALE CREATURES ARE ON HIS LAND.] Oh, no. No! No!

(...)

SHREK
[SIGH] Okay, fine. Attention, all fairy tale things. Do not get comfortable. Your welcome is officially worn out. In fact, I'm gonna see this guy Farquaad right now and get you all off my land and back where you came from! [PAUSE. THEN THE CROWD GOES WILD.] Oh! [TO DONKEY] You! You're comin' with me.
(Elliott et al., 2001; caps and boldface added)

Another similar example: when Fiona asks him to be her loving prince charming, Shrek declines the offer and brings her by force to the evil Lord Farquaad. Once again, the ogre is not interested in power and wealth. Like many supporters of contemporary social movements, he is looking for a peaceful and decent life which is not corrupted by politics. I think the swamp is not only reflecting the wild and pure Nature that many ecologists have in mind these days when they think about our polluted and industrialized world. This swamp is also the opposite of the highly "civilized" court society presented at the beginning of *Shrek the Third*.[4] The swamp is a place where one can fart without violating any social norm or etiquette; a place where there is no prestige and no social competition based on highly normalized presentation of the Self; a place where Shrek feels at home, where he can relax and be himself for himself. This representation of freedom and happiness is far, far away from the revolutionary dreams of classical left-wing activists. It is clearly influenced by the individualistic quest of the real Self and pleasure one can find in many contemporary movements.

In the second movie, Fiona and he have to go to the kingdom of Far Far Away (Hollywood) to meet Fiona's parents, the King and the

Queen of this capitalistic, organized and superficial society. Though Shrek is offered the chance to become famous and enjoy the easy life of the court, he made it very clear to Fiona that their future was in the swamp. In the third movie, the somehow pathetic king of Far Far Away dies. Shrek is told that he is the potential new king. He will do everything he can—including leaving his pregnant wife—to find the king's nephew and bring him to Far Far Away as the new king. In all these stories, Shrek will finally become the hero and contribute to saving the victims from the bad guys. But he does it reluctantly and mostly for altruistic motives. The main point is that he is never looking for wealth, prestige and power. In fact, he seems to be afraid of power which is associated with superficial life or totalitarian plans. Real life is elsewhere—in the stinky swamp with no State. However, like many contemporary social movements, in order to realize himself, Shrek has to constantly fight against political transactors who are trying to control the main political institutions (Lord Farquaad, Prince Charming, the stepmother, his own stepfather in *Shrek 2*...). Once again, Shrek does not correspond to the Leninist conception of rebels and social movements. If he could just control his life, he would prefer to be "depoliticized" by living as an ogre in his swamp. Unlike N. Chosmky, he is not the representation of the typical heroic rebels who is denouncing the social order and looking for a revolution to save oppressed people. Shrek looks more like the contemporary social movements described by A. Melucci in *Challenging Codes: Collective Action in the Information Age* (1996). He is trying to control his own identity, body and social relations by working hard to choose his way of life in his idealized swamp, with his love Fiona, who happens to be a princess—nobody is perfect!

In this sense, Shrek is the legacy and a part of contemporary social movements such as the peace movements, the environmental movements, the student movements of the 1960s and early 1970s, feminism, and the gay and lesbian movements of so-called post-industrial or post-materialist societies (Habermas, 1984, 1987; Inglehart, 1990; Touraine, 1995). At the same time, and in spite of his individualistic and apolitical conception of self-fulfillment and happiness, Shrek is like any other individual living with other human beings: consciously or not, he is social. Like it or not, his adventures are teaching him that he is moving from one field of transactions to another by being constantly in a state of interdependency with other transactors (annoying talking animals, family members, enemies, etc.). Therefore, his life is full of positive and negative emotions, desires, duties, moral dilemmas, temptations, achieved and underachieved goals, and power relations. He does not control the dynamic of his life even if he contributes to the structuration of fields of transactions such as his family and the kingdom of *Far Far Away*. Therefore, by watching these stories, children and adults are learning that everything is social (relational). And they are also exposed to the negative legacy of so many attempts made by so many leaders who wanted to create a perfect society. Like so many contemporary activists, Shrek would prefer to stay far, far away from wealth, power and prestige. However, he is reluctantly condemned to be part of a political world because he is a social actor (or a "transactor").

Like Radical Intellectuals, Neoconservatives Attack Shrek

The American countermovement organization *The Traditional Values Coalition* (2005a and 2005b) recognizes that the entertainment provided by *Shrek* is part of a political battle related to serious issues. I agree with them, but not for the same reasons! This coalition urges their members to resist what they see as the challenges raised by the gays and lesbians against the traditional and patriarchal family and sexual genres. For instance, under the subtitle *What can be done?*, they explain:

> If the transgender movement is not already active in your community, it will be. Wherever there are homosexual activist groups, you will find transgendered individuals working alongside them to establish policies and recruitment programs in public schools and to change laws to redefine what it means to be male or female. Here are some suggestions for action:
>
> • Monitor city and state legislative proposals that contain the word "gender" in them. Gender is code for cross-dressers, transvestites, and transsexuals. Inform your local politicians of this cultural agenda so they will recognize it when activists attempt to push through legislation.
>
> • Oppose Gay Straight Alliance clubs on school campuses. These are recruitment programs to lure children into sexually destructive lifestyles. These GLSEN-sponsored groups are now promoting cross-dressing for children.
>
> (Traditional Coalition Values, 2005a)

For this organization, Shrek is active in their community and deserves to be counterattacked. By reacting to it, they show that Shrek is not only about entertainment. For neoconservative people, there is an ongoing political battle out there. Parents should do the "right thing" by protecting their children against "deviants" like the green ogre and his perverse friends.

Like N. Chomsky's theory to some extent, these neoconservatives tell another simple social story where DreamWorks is presented once again as a monolithic block. But this time, entertaining commercial products like *Shrek* are part of a dangerous movement pushing for significant change of the social order. (Even Larry King helps Shrek in his malicious attack against heterosexuality!):

> The DreamWorks' animated film, "Shrek 2," is billed as harmless entertainment but contains subtle sexual messages. Parents who are thinking about taking their children to see "Shrek 2," may wish to consider the following: The movie features a male-to-female transgender (in transition) as an evil bartender. The character has five o'clock shadow, wears a dress and has female breasts. It is clear that he is a she-male. His voice is that of talk show host Larry King. During a dance scene at the end of the movie, this transgendered man expresses sexual desire for Prince Charming, jumps on him, and both tumble to the floor.
>
> In another scene in the movie, Shrek and Donkey need to be rescued from a dungeon where they are chained against the wall. The rescue is conducted by Pinocchio who is asked to lie so his nose will grow long enough for one of the smaller cartoon characters to use it as a bridge to reach Shrek and Donkey. Donkey encourages him to lie about something and suggests he lie about wearing women's underwear. When he denies wearing women's underwear, his nose begins to grow.
>
> An earlier scene in the movie features a wolf dressed in grandma's clothing and reading a book when Prince Charming encounters him. Later, one of the characters refers to the wolf's gender confusion.
>
> TVC's report, "A Gender Identity Disorder Goes Mainstream," explains the transgender agenda and the effort to deconstruct the biological reality of male and female. DreamWorks is helping in this effort by promoting cross dressing and transgenderism in this animated film.
>
> (Traditional Values Coalition, 2005b)

Neoconservative people present the poor green ogre as a tool used by transgender people to change the heterosexual order of things. It is funny to note that N. Chomsky' theory presents Shrek as a conservative strategy used to preserve the order of things. However, these stories are similar in many ways because they are both simple stories. Both judge *Shrek* movies on the basis of unified actors with homogeneous goals and strategies. They both tell us that these powerful groups can shape the mind of other people by self-acting on them, just like a pool ball can push another one in a pocket. In both cases, *Shrek* movies appear as being part of a propaganda campaign made up by minorities which are manipulating the mind of innocent people like our children. In both cases, the accusers present themselves as the defenders of the innocent and manipulated people.

Simple social stories usually contain three important weaknesses. First, they objectify or reify social phenomena. Structural categories based on variables (age, sex, income, etc.) or collective actions such as social movements are transformed into solid, unified actors which exist as social "things." Second, they simply self-act on docile people. Therefore, the interdependency of the transactors is lost; the complexity and the "relational texture of social phenomena" (Melucci, 1996: p. 80) disappears. Third, simple social theories are often Manichean. Even when they engage more than two actors, they usually involve "objectively" good people (women, workers, ethnic minorities, students, "ordinary" people, etc.) and bad people (capitalists, politicians, managers, men, "deviants," etc.). The moral classification (bad/good) of the individual is usually based on two main features: (i) the structural (objective) positions of the actors in the society (as defined as a patriarchal society or a capitalist society, for instance); and (ii) implicit or explicit moral values against exploitation, domination, exclusion and ignorance (in critical theory), or social disorder, deviancy, et cetera (in "conservative" theory).

My main argument is that Shrek has no chance if he is analyzed through a simple and critical theory. By definition of his "structural position" in the American/consumer/capitalist society, he is working for the "bad guys" no matter what he can say or do. He might be more clever and sympathetic than Snow White or Cinderella, but it does not really matter. He is guilty by (structural) association with the dominant class. In fact, his cleverness and sympathy make him even more of a target. N. Chomsky, for instance, associates the presence of progressive elements in commercial products as a strategy used by the dominant class and its elites to fool the people. Here the story seems to be more than plausible if Hollywood is seen as a unified actor which allows some progressive images (such as a superficial and opportunistic prince charming, or princesses who are burning their bras, or a transsexual stepsister) in some of their movies, as long as these images "are kept within bounds and at the margins, so that (...) their presence shows that the system is not monolithic" (Chomsky and Herman, 2002: p. xii).

Here, the problem is that this type of simple critical story usually collapses quickly when its black boxes are opened. These stories crumple, for instance, when the structural unity of the collective actors is fragmented by more detailed observations of who is whom, who is doing what, and who is related to whom. In other words, the homogeneity of interests, strategies and actions do not resist a historico-empirical analysis of the traces left by transactors. Transactors are interdependent individuals with their personalities, brains, minds, perceptions, strengths and weaknesses, and so on. Social phenomena are not simple relations of determination going from structural positions to fully or partially determined individuals, or from powerful actors to passive and powerless people. Social phenomena are unique and complex relations between many human and nonhuman transactors. Therefore, we have to study contextualized transactions between transactors and their more or less different or similar—but always specific—outcomes. One popular green ogre called Shrek emerges from contextualized transactions between specific persons involved in the production process (W. Steig's original book, the directors, the producers, actors, etc.), but also from transactions which connect all of these people to other fields of transactions such as social movements. Producers of blockbusters, directors, writers, et cetera are not all the same. They come from specific life trajectories where they have met various human actors (such as activists, teachers, gay friends, etc.) and nonhuman actors (such as radical books, other movies, etc.). Their goals, values, et cetera cannot be simply deduced from their class positions or any other similar structural category. Furthermore, Shrek cannot be reduced to his economic producers and transactions. The existence of one of *Shrek* movies implies billions of transactions between millions of people and nonhuman transactors. Children are part of this wide field of transactions. Far from being passive or just entertained, they also transact with Shrek.

Shrek *Talks to the Children*

Am I one of those social scientists who are overintellectualizing what is just plain entertainment? Do I read too many books in social science? I know that some of my respected colleagues think that we are dealing with pure entertainment, especially when we are talking about children. For instance, by reporting on the anti-Shrek campaign launched by the "Traditional Values Coalition" (2005), one journalist interviewed a film studies professor from the University of Toronto. The journalist wrote:

> "You have an image within a comic context that could be read either way," says Keil [the professor], who adds quickly that such humour is designed for parents anyway and goes way above the heads of the children in the audience. (...)
> There's all sorts of things going on in those cartoons that are pretty suggestive," concedes Keil. "But (the kids) are laughing at the pratfalls, the funny voices, the very basic humour."
> "Kids at that age don't even have pre-formed notions of sexuality."
> (McKay, 2005)

It might not be a major discovery for parents, but children are full transactors! They are "participant agents in social relations" with some "agency" (Mayall, 2002: pp. 2–3). We have to study their perceptions instead of assuming that they do not really understand or pay attention to the images on the screen. When we listen to the children, we quickly realize that Shrek cannot be reduced to entertainment.

Learning about the possibility of this book on Shrek, one journalist from Radio-Canada (Gerbet, 2009) decided to interview some children several months ago. Please, take note as to what these children got out of their transactions with Shrek. In reference to Lord Farquaad who decided to clean his kingdom from any magical creatures, one child explains to the journalist, Thomas Gerbet:

> – "I saw Shrek three times. The first time, the second time, and then a third time. The others are human and Shrek is an ogre. And I think this is very different because the others are white, and him, he is green."
>
> – "If they tell us: 'No, I do not want this one in the world', then they might reject everybody because nobody is perfect."

This boy is about ten years old. He understood the message quite clearly even if he did not make the connection with antiracist movements and any genocide. This message made sense to him probably because this child has been exposed to one form or another of antiracist or multicultural values, or just because he agrees with it for one reason or another. In this sense, Shrek's message is following the trail opened by some social movements. No matter what happened to this boy before, the point is that by telling his own stories, Shrek is reinforcing *this* antiracist message and its related values.

The political discourse against racism, exclusion and essentialism is pretty clear in *Shrek* (2001). In at least two scenes of this movie, for instance, Shrek is inviting Donkey to look beyond the appearance of things and prejudices:

[TIME LAPSE—DONKEY AND SHREK ARE NOW WALKING THROUGH THE FIELD HEADING AWAY FROM DULOC. SHREK IS MUNCHING ON AN ONION.]

DONKEY
Let me get this straight. You're gonna go fight a dragon and rescue a princess just so Farquaad will give you back a swamp which you only don't have because he filled it full of freaks in the first place. Is that about right?

SHREK
You know, maybe there's a good reason donkeys shouldn't talk.

DONKEY
I don't get it. Why don't you just pull some of that ogre stuff on him? Throttle him, lay siege to his fortress, grind his bones to make your bread, the whole ogre trip.

SHREK
Oh, I know what. Maybe I could have decapitated an entire village and put their heads on a pike, gotten a knife, cut open their spleen and drink their fluids. Does that sound good to you?

DONKEY
Uh, no, not really, no.

SHREK
For your information, there's a lot more to ogres than people think.

DONKEY
Example?

SHREK
Example? Okay, um, ogres are like onions. [HE HOLDS OUT HIS ONION]

DONKEY
[SNIFFS THE ONION] They stink?

SHREK
Yes—No!

DONKEY
They make you cry?

SHREK
No!

DONKEY
You leave them in the sun, they get all brown, start sproutin' little white hairs.

SHREK
No! Layers! Onions have layers. Ogres have layers! Onions have layers. You get it? We both have layers. [HE HEAVES A SIGH AND THEN WALKS OFF]

[SHREK AND DONKEY ARE SITTING AROUND A CAMPFIRE. THEY ARE STARING UP INTO THE SKY AS SHREK POINTS OUT CERTAIN STAR CONSTELLATIONS TO DONKEY.]

(...)

DONKEY
That ain't nothin' but a bunch of little dots.

SHREK
You know, Donkey, sometimes things are more than they appear. Hmm? Forget it.

(Elliott et al., 2001; caps and boldface added)

On transgender issues, Shrek clearly influences the perceptions, the judgments and eventually the transactions of children. This is how one little boy described the transgendered stepsister in Shrek. He was entertained by this character but it also influenced his perception of transgendered people. Next time he will have to deal with a transgendered person, he said, he will not be shocked because he already saw one in Shrek:

– The child (talking about the stepsister): "He is a boy with lipstick, a lot of makeup and one red dress. I laughed a lot because I did not know we could do that"

– The journalist: "And how would you react if you would see someone like that on the street?"

– The child: "I would react like...A little bit like...I don't know what is going on with this person. But I already saw this person (in Shrek's movie), so I know what it is.

(Gerbet, 2009)

In *Shrek the Third*, Fiona, her Queen mother and other princesses (Cinderella, Snow White, etc.) are hijacked by Prince Charming (the macho man) in the castle after his coup d'état. Trying to fight back, Fiona encourages the other captive princesses to fight back:

SNOW WHITE
Who cares who's running the kingdom anyway?

FIONA
I care. [FIONA STEPS FORWARD AND CHALLENGES THEM.]

QUEEN
And you should all care too.

(...)

FIONA
Alright everyone, we need to find a way out, now. [THE PRINCESSES NOD IN AGREEMENT.]

SNOW WHITE
You're right. [TO THE OTHER PRINCESSES] Ladies, assume the position! [SLEEPING BEAUTY FALLS ASLEEP STANDING UP. SNOW WHITE QUICKLY ASSUMES HER POSITION BY LYING DOWN AND PUCKERING HER LIPS. CINDERELLA DUSTS OFF A SPOT, SITS DOWN AND CROSSES HER LEGS.]

FIONA
What are you doing?

SLEEPING BEAUTY
Waiting to be rescued.

FIONA
You have got to be kidding me.

SNOW WHITE
Well, what do you expect us to do? We're just four... [NOTICES DORIS] I mean, three, super hot princesses, two circus freaks, a pregnant ogre and an old lady. [THE QUEEN SMILES AND THEN CASUALLY WALKS BY THE PRINCESSES.]

QUEEN
Hmmm. Excuse me. Old lady coming through. [SHE WALKS RIGHT UP TO THE BRICK WALL, TAKES A DEEP BREATH AND LETS OUT A YELL.]

QUEEN
Hiiiyyyiiiaaaah! [SHE HEAD-BUTTS A HOLE RIGHT THROUGH THE BRICK WALL. FIONA AND THE PRINCESSES ARE IMPRESSED.]

PRINCESSES/PUSS/DONKEY
Whoa.

FIONA
Mom!?

QUEEN
Well, you didn't actually think you got your fighting skills from your father, did you?

(...)

FIONA
Okay girls, from here on out, we're gonna take care of business ourselves. [SNOW THINKS FOR A MOMENT AND THEN GLANCES AT THE OTHER PRINCESSES. THEY NOD. SNOW LOOKS DETERMINED. SHE RIPS OFF A SLEEVE, REVEALING A DOPEY TATTOO. SLEEPING BEAUTY TEARS THE BOTTOM OF HER DRESS. THE QUEEN PUTS LIPSTICK SMUDGES UNDER HER EYES (A LA A FOOTBALL PLAYER). CINDERELLA SHARPENS THE HEAL OF HER GLASS SLIPPER. DORIS BURNS HER BRA. THE PRINCESSES PLACE THEIR HANDS OVER FIONA'S. PUSS AND DONKEY'S HANDS COME IN LAST.]
(Price et al., 2007; caps and boldface added)

The reference to feminism is crystal clear in the movie. Once again, listen to one little girl's comment (around eight to nine years old): "She [Fiona] is like a princess, but not a princess like Snow White... I don't really like princesses." (Gerbet, 2009). Fiona's stories reinforced the rejection of the old model of the young and beautiful young woman who is waiting to be discovered and kissed by prince charming to wake up... and get married. Fiona offers another model, and she can help little girls to affirm that they "don't really like (traditional) princesses." Another little girl recognized some ecological values in Shrek's strong attachment to his swamp. She said: "He [Shrek] did not cut any trees to build his house [in the swamp]. He helped me to understand how save Nature."

Brief Conclusion

We could go on and on in terms of observing Shrek's transactions. I think we have enough information to conclude that, like so many "transactors," Shrek should not be reduced to a simple story. Shrek is not about an invasion of gays and lesbians in your community. He is not one of the last ideological weapons used by the "owners of the society" to keep the citizens quiet and alienated. And he is not simply the product of social movements. Even with Shrek, we need various and multiple modes of perception in order to get closer to the complexity (and the messiness) of our social universe. Why? Because he is a "transactor" transacting with many other transactors in various and complex fields of transactions. I believe this is what studying the social universe is about: doing the best history of traces of significant transactions we can with our limited resources. At least, social scientists should start from there even when they have bigger epistemological ambitions.

Notes

1. A transactor is an interdependent actor, or a social actor, if the notion of social is defined as specific and empirical relations between human and nonhuman transactors. It means that one (trans)actor is acting as he is only because he is transacting with at least one other transactor. For instance, the actor[A] is acting as a brother only because he is transacting with his sister, and vice versa. The same is true for employers and employees, enemies and adversaries, friends and acquaintances, colleagues and peers, professors and students, and so on. Transactors are what they are only through their transactions with other transactors. As social actors and even as living organisms, they have no independency outside of their social relations with other human and nonhuman transactors (friends, enemies, employers, air, food, water, soil, etc.). Therefore, any specific dimension of action (a word, a gesture, some courage, effort, etc.) should be analyzed as happening in some specific field of transaction. By transaction, I mean social relations between interdependent people. By interdependent, I mean that by transacting with others, these people are more or less making each other. In other words, the action of A cannot be understood without taking into account that A is transacting with the actor B—and vice versa (Elias, 1978).
2. This definition of power is paraphrased from M. Mann's definition: "power is the ability to pursue and attain goals through mastery of one's environment" (1986: p. 6).
3. A reductionist theory "is one that illegitimately attempts to reduce complexities of social life to a single, unifying principle of explanation or analytical prime mover (...) such as 'the interests of capitalism', 'patriarchy', 'rational choice' (...)" (Sibeon, 2004: p. 2). Reification "is the illicit attribution of agency to entities that are not actors or agents" (Sibeon, 2004: p. 4).
4. By "civilized," I refer to Elias' explanations in *The Civilizing Process* (2000) and *The Court Society* (1983).

CHAPTER 9

An Evolutionary Psychological Perspective on Shrek and Fiona

Gayle Brewer

Evolutionary theory outlines the manner in which natural and sexual selection have shaped physical characteristics to address specific evolutionary problems. Evolutionary psychologists propose that psychological mechanisms (such as jealousy) have also evolved in their current form because they addressed specific problems of survival or reproduction across evolutionary history (Buss, 2004). These problems include the avoidance of predators, identification of appropriate food, and importantly for Shrek and Fiona, the selection and retention of a suitable mate. The chapter interprets the relationship between Shrek and Fiona from an evolutionary perspective, with particular focus on the physical and psychological differences between men and women.

Sex Differences: Why Men and Women Select Different Sexual Strategies

In most species (including humans) there is a clear sex difference with regard to the maximum number of offspring produced and the minimum level of parental resources invested (Bateman, 1948; Trivers, 1972). In order to produce healthy children, women must expend a substantial amount of energy producing each gamete (egg) and are limited to only one per month. If a child is conceived, women continue to invest heavily through extensive periods of pregnancy, birth, and breast-feeding. She can become pregnant only at particular stages of her menstrual cycle, once pregnant cannot conceive a child, and is unlikely to conceive whilst breast-feeding as this process suppresses ovulation. Therefore, the number of children that a woman can have (also known as her reproductive output) is drastically limited.

In contrast, men experience much higher rates of gamete (sperm) replenishment and can choose to make no further investment in a woman or the forthcoming child after conception. In addition, men may reproduce with another woman (given the opportunity) immediately after conception of the first child, demonstrating a much higher potential reproductive output. This sex difference has important implications for the mating behavior displayed by men and women and for the type of partner they select. Although it is difficult to understand the mating habits of an Ogre, the fact that Fiona rather than Shrek becomes pregnant and appears to be the most child-focused of the couple, perhaps indicates that the mating behavior of an Ogre mirrors that of humans.

Both men and women adopt a sexual strategy (Buss and Schmitt, 1993) influenced by the physiological and environmental pressures they face. Whilst these strategies are not necessarily conscious, they guide behavior to that which enhances a person's lifetime reproductive success. A considerable degree of within sex variation occurs with regard to both the preferred strategy and the strategy actually followed. However, there is a fundamental difference between the optimum male and female strategies that influences a range of mating behaviors such as the length of relationship (Buss and Schmitt, 1993) and type of partner (Buss and Barnes, 1986) sought.

When an Ogre Loves a Princess: Why Shrek Falls in Love with Fiona

As already mentioned, men have a much greater potential reproductive output than women. Consequently, the availability and accessibility of fertile women, rather than his own reproductive capacity, limits Shrek's reproductive success. Men that gain access to receptive fertile women are able to produce a much greater number of children than men entering a monogamous relationship with a single female, a partnership that drastically limits his potential reproductive output. Therefore, if Shrek were able to mate with a large number of fertile women, he should focus on short-term relationships with minimal investment or commitment.

However, men with a lower mate value (such as those that have few resources or are unattractive) may be unable to follow a short-term strategy. Shrek's difficulty talking to other people and the fact that other people are scared by his appearance, suggest that a short-term strategy is not feasible. For men such as Shrek that are unable to attract a large number of fertile women, a long-term relationship may be more appealing. Mating with one woman only allows a man to attract a woman that may not be interested in him for short-term relationship (Symons, 1979) and monopolize her reproductive output (Buss, 2004). When men limit the number of children that they could produce in this way, the importance of selecting an appropriate mate increases. Consequently, men are more selective when choosing a long-term compared with a short-term partner (Buss and Schmitt, 1993). Of particular importance are fertility and age.

Evolutionary theory has suggested that the physical characteristics preferred by men are not arbitrary and instead provide an indication of the individual's mate quality, in terms of health and fertility (Buss, 1987; Symons, 1979). Across a number of cultures, research has demonstrated that men place a greater importance on physical appearance than women (Buss et al., 1990), reporting a greater preference for traits such as "physically attractive" and "good looking" (Buss and Barnes, 1986). Therefore, Shrek's decision to fall in love with the beautiful Princess Fiona is consistent with other men. Although a number of aspects of physical appearance may be important, one of the most widely documented attractive features is her body shape.

Prior to puberty the distribution of body fat in men and women is remarkably similar. After puberty women develop a gynoid (hourglass) body shape and men an android (tubular) body shape. After the menopause, the female body fat distribution reverts to a more android type (Kirschner and Samojlik, 1991). Thus the distribution of body fat provides an important indication of a woman's age and reproductive status. A higher waist-to-hip ratio has been linked to difficulty conceiving and a later onset of pregnancy (Kaye et al., 1990; Zaadstra et al., 1993). The relationship between gynoid body fat distribution and fertility is further strengthened by the finding that the fat stored in the gluteofemoral region (denoting a gynoid distribution) is used almost exclusively during pregnancy and lactation (Björntorp, 1987), thus providing a clear indication of the woman's ability to sustain this energy-expensive process.

Research has consistently demonstrated that men find a ratio of 0.7 to be the most physically attractive (Singh, 1993; Furnham, Lavancy and McClelland, 2001). Whilst Fiona's waist to hip ratio is not clear, she clearly has an hourglass as opposed to a tubular shape. It is likely that this ratio contributes to Shrek's desire for Fiona, and importantly she retains the desirable body shape, even when she has transformed into an Ogre.

Putting the grr in Ogre: Why Fiona Falls in Love with Shrek

The vulnerability of a woman when pregnant or caring for a young infant and the substantial benefits afforded to the child by further investment, result in a greater preference for long-term relationships with high levels of commitment (Clark and Hatfield, 1989; Buss and Schmitt, 1993). This is reflected by the focus that Fiona (and other featured princesses) place on marriage. In a similar manner to other species, women's greater parental investment also results in greater selectivity than men when choosing a mate. There are a number of disadvantages to the selection of a poor quality partner including inadequate investment in her or her child and the poor quality genes that the child would inherit. Consequently Fiona spends a considerable amount of time thinking about the type of partner that she prefers and the traits or behavior (bravery) that a man must display in order to be suitable.

Money, Money, Money

Women prefer partners that have financial resources (Buss et al., 1990). This preference is widely recognized and displayed in a wide variety of cultures (Buss et al., 1990). Women are also attracted to the ability to obtain resources, typically displayed through traits such as ambition, status or education. The Fairy Godmother states this explicitly, advising Fiona to "find a Prince with a ton of cash." Although she mentions other traits such as physical appearance, the focus is clearly on financial resources. Fiona's decision to reject Lord Farquaad and Prince Charming is perhaps surprising given the importance of financial resources. However, a wealthy partner that is not committed to the relationship or is unkind and abusive may not actually invest the resources in his partner. Therefore, wealth alone may not be sufficient. In addition, for Fiona who is the only child of wealthy Kind Harold and Queen Lillian, resources could be obtained through other means. This reliance on parental wealth may not of course be encouraged by the King and Queen as discussed later in this chapter.

Kindness and Reliability

When Fiona realizes that Shrek is kind and considerate, her attitude toward him changes and she considers him as a potential mate. This is consistent with the importance placed on kindness and understanding by other women (Buss and Schmitt, 1993). A woman that ignores a man's kindness (or lack thereof) may become involved with a selfish or abusive partner that may monopolize resources, hurt her physical or emotionally and be unfaithful (Buss, 1991). For example it is likely that Lord Farquaad (who demonstrates his cruelty throughout the film) would have become abusive to Fiona. In contrast a partner who acts in a tender and caring manner is more likely to care for her, providing a sense of security and commitment. Kindness also indicates that Shrek will become a good parent and commit his resources to Fiona and her child without becoming selfish (Mellon, 1981; Buss, 1987). The importance Fiona places on kindness is further demonstrated by her frustration with Shrek when he becomes moody or behaves inconsistently. Women typically prefer reliable and dependable partners (Buss et al., 1990). Men who are not dependable and lack emotional stability have a greater number of affairs (Buss and Shackelford, 1997). Consequently, reliability suggests that Shrek will not abandon her for another woman and that his commitment will not change. Behavior suggesting that his feelings for her are inconsistent or that he can behave in a moody and unstable manner causes her to question her feelings for him.

Tall, Dark, and Handsome

Tall men are more attractive (Pawlowski and Jasienska, 2005), date more often (Sheppard and Strathman, 1989) and experience greater reproductive success (Pawlowski, Dunbar, and Lipowicz, 2000; Nettle, 2002) than short men. Fiona's obvious disappointment with Lord Farquaad's stature is consistent with the research in this area and the fact that women prefer to be in a relationship in which the man is taller than the woman (Swami et al., 2008). Lord Farquaad understands the manner in which his height affects his desirability, and attempts to compensate or hide this by for example pretending that he is taller when seated on his horse. The importance of male height is also clear to Shrek who uses his rival's short stature to his advantage and makes this the basis of his description to Fiona. This is consistent with previous research that finds that height is associated with the ability to intimidate potential rivals (Salska et al., 2008).

As outlined earlier, Fiona's wealth may reduce her desire for financial resources. As the availability or importance of other (particularly socioeconomic) resources decline, the importance of a man's genetic fitness that is the quality of the genes that will be passed to the child, increases (Gangestad and Simpson, 2000) and a number of indirect cues to a man's genetic fitness are available. For example, human faces become more masculinized or feminized at puberty. A considerable amount of energy is expended to develop masculine traits. For men, a surge in testosterone causes a growth of facial hair and a more prominent jaw, cheekbone, brow ridge, and the central part of the face (Enlow, 1990; Thornhill and Gangestad, 1996).

The testosterone that controls the development of these traits (Owens and Short, 1995), place the immune system under a substantial amount of stress (Zahavi, 1975; Thornhill and Gangestad, 1993). Therefore, a man displaying exaggerated sexual traits signals that his immune system has been able to cope with the elevated stress and is fairly robust (Folstad and Karter, 1992). The traits may also signal a low level of parasite load (Hamilton and Zuk, 1982) or high fertility (Symons, 1995). In fact, extreme versions of secondary sexual characteristics are preferred in a number of species including humans (Andersson, 1994; Petrie, Halliday and Sanders, 1991). Shrek has very masculinized appearance, for example, a prominent brown ridge and jaw. The definition of these features signals the presence of sex hormones and his physical masculinity and whilst not described as attractive he does demonstrate his physical and genetic fitness.

All Ogres are Equal, but Some Ogres are More Equal than Others

Status and dominance are important features of a social situation and these hierarchies form quickly. In three person groups, a dominance hierarchy forms within one minute for half of the groups and in the first five minutes in all remaining groups (Fisek and Ofshe, 1970). Whilst both men and women recognize status, the importance of obtaining a high rank differs for men and women. Nearly all women will find a mate and bear children regardless of rank. However, men's success in this arena is more variable, with dominant men holding a clear advantage. High status men are more attractive to women (Kenrick et al., 1990) and can provide the woman with greater protection and resources than low status men. In addition, dominant men may be able to successfully compete with male rivals, without fear of retaliation. Consequently, high ranking men are able to mate with younger (Grammer, 1992) and more attractive (Udry and Eckland, 1984) women. Although Shrek may not have a high status in the sense of a title or Kingdom, he is consistently recognized as dominant. For example when persecuted, the enchanted creatures turn to Shrek for leadership.

Whilst physical fighting can advertise the relative status of a competitor, it may result in serious injury for both the winner and loser. Therefore, an alternative method to identify the strongest individual or establish a dominance hierarchy would be beneficial. Behaviors that identify the strongest competitor whilst reducing the risk of injury are seen in a number of species. In humans, competitive sport may fulfill a similar role. Shrek's quest to relocate the other enchanted creatures and reclaim his swamp takes him to Duloc where there is a tournament to determine the strongest and bravest knight. As Shrek attempts to defend himself against attack, using a range of sport like skills, his physical dominance becomes clear, both to the other competitors and to the audience. The status he achieves through this competition is consistent with the recognition given to sporting champions and the fact that athletes report a greater number of sexual partners than non athletes (Faurie, Pontier and Raymond, 2004).

The Clock Is Ticking

Although Fiona's age is unclear, she has been living in a remote castle for a substantial amount of time and by the King's comment to Prince Charming ("It's not my fault you were late") we can assume that she has been waiting for her suitor to rescue (and marry her) for longer than expected. This delay may have contributed to her decision to marry the first potential partner she meets. Fiona's reluctance to spend time searching for or selecting another partner is also evidenced by the fact that when she believes Shrek does not love her, she intends to marry Lord Farquaad immediately. This sense of immediacy may reflect the manner in which her age influences her fertility and its implications for the number of children she can produce.

A women's ability to conceive and sustain a healthy pregnancy is strongly linked to her age. Whilst able to conceive much earlier, women typically avoid the risks (to both mother and child) associated with teenage pregnancy (Jolly et al., 2000; Chen et al., 2008) by giving birth to a first child in their mid to late 20s. Although delaying a first pregnancy in this manner has positive outcomes for both mother and child, women conceiving at an older age suffer increased risks of chromosomal abnormalities (Volarcik et al., 1998), and an increased risk of maternal (Callaghan and Berg, 2003) and fetal (Salihu et al., 2003) mortality. In addition, as the number of children that women can produce is constrained by the menopause, delaying the birth of the first child for too long also increases the risk of reproductive failure that is, not producing any children (Liu and Lummaa, 2009). Consequently, marrying Shrek may be a more desirable prospect than delaying reproduction further in the hope that the quality of a future mate can offset her own declining fertility.

Of course, Fiona's decision is also influenced by the spell that causes her to become an Ogre from dusk to dawn. Men place a greater importance on physical appearance than women (Buss et al., 1990). The traits preferred by men provide an indication of the individual's mate quality, with respect to her health and fertility (Buss, 1987; Symons, 1979). Fiona's reaction to her changing appearance and concern that she is ugly may therefore reflect the importance of attractiveness to her own desirability and to the likelihood that she will find a suitable partner. By ensuring that she is married before her condition is widely known, Fiona avoids the problems associated with finding (and obtaining) a suitable mate when she is undesirable.

Cuckoldry and the Patter of Not So Tiny Feet: Why Shrek Fears Fatherhood

Shrek's sexual interest in Fiona and his desire to consummate their relationship is clear. However, he becomes fearful and anxious when faced by the prospect of becoming a father. This anxiety reflects the threat of cuckoldry (raising the child of another man) and the extent to which this cuckoldry would reduce his (already limited) opportunities to father his own children. Women may cuckold their partner and mate with a partner that is more attractive than their long-term partner in order to produce children of high genetic quality whilst retaining the investment of their partner. Cuckoldry represents a substantial problem for men. Approximately 10 percent of children are believed to be the result of cuckoldry (Baker and Bellis, 1995; Platek and Shackelford, 2006).

An individual such as Shrek, who is less wealthy or attractive than Prince Charming (and other desirable alternatives), should be aware of such a risk. Men may be able to guard against the threat of cuckoldry before his partner becomes pregnant. For example, by selecting a partner with limited sexual experience (Buss and Schmitt, 1993) and increasing marital satisfaction (Shackelford and Buss, 2000), a man can substantially reduce the risk that his partner will become sexually active with another man. Shrek does seem to have reduced the risk of cuckoldry in this way by choosing a partner that has been separated from any other suitors and building a stable relationship. In addition, men can become jealous at the presence of other men, a defense which allows men to be aware of potential rivals and guard or monitor their partner. For example, before he learns of Fiona's pregnancy, Shrek's jealousy of Prince Charming is alerted when he reads her diary. He resolves to change his own appearance, thus reducing the risk that she will be attracted to another man and he will be cuckolded.

Once Fiona is pregnant, Shrek can reduce the risk of cuckoldry by ensuring that he only invests in the child/children if he is the father. The amount of resources invested is usually related to paternity confidence (Burch and Gallup, 2000) and there are a number of ways that men can assess the likelihood that they have fathered the child. In particular, men are more likely to invest in a child that they physically resemble (Platek et al., 2002). This process is actually encouraged by the mother's family, who typically comment that an infant resembles the (presumed) father (Regalski and Gaulin, 1993), which encourages him to believe that he is the father and invest in the infant. Mothers also state that their child resembles the father more than themselves, a resemblance that fathers are reluctant to see (Daly and Wilson, 1982). The greater resemblance to a father asserted by mothers cannot be verified by objective observers (McLain et al., 2000). Clearly the children Fiona bear closely resemble Shrek, this perhaps contributes to the close bonding between Shrek and the children and the investment he is willing to make. If he were to doubt the paternity of the children, he would surely be better served by obtaining the resources and status afforded by becoming ruler of the Kingdom, and its subsequent access to fertile women.

Meeting the in-laws: Why King Harold and Queen Lillian Reject Shrek

The reactions of King Harold and Queen Lillian to Shrek and his new bride are painfully clear and with little prior knowledge of their future son-in-law, the intensity of their reaction may seem difficult to explain.

However, the disgust they initially feel at their appearance may reflect an adaptive response that originally developed to promote physical health. Contagious diseases are often associated with visible cues such as lesions or discoloration (Kurzban and Leary, 2001) and species adopt a range of behaviors to reduce contact with pathogens and subsequent contamination (Hart, 1990). For example, infected individuals may be identified and avoided (Kiesecker et al., 1998). Whilst Shrek may not actually be contaminated with any noticeable illness, the avoidance of individuals with physical disabilities or in Shrek's case abnormal appearance may reflect these innate disease avoidance mechanisms in humans (Ryan, 1971; Snyder et al., 1979). In fact the King's first instinct is to avoid the meeting, a reaction that Shrek anticipated, perhaps because of similar reactions in previous encounters. The existence of the disease avoidance mechanism is supported by the fact that people with diseases that have visible symptoms attract stronger antisocial responses than less visible conditions.

Of course, the reaction of the King and Queen is more intense than the rest of the crowd who have no personal interest—or investment—in the couple. As their only child (and with it appears, a distant cousin as the only other relative) Fiona and her children represent the only opportunity for their genes to survive. Consequently, Fiona's reproductive decisions and success (including the quality of the children and ability to support them), are of the greatest importance. Her father in particular is concerned about her mating decisions and the quality of the children that she will produce. By entering a monogamous relationship with the Queen, he has drastically reduced his potential reproductive output to her level and the importance of each grandchild is of the greatest importance. As a result, his first reaction is to replace Shrek with a more suitable partner before it is too late, that is, before her mate value and reproductive success are compromised by becoming pregnant to Shrek. Whilst his choice of suitable partner is no doubt influenced by his prior debt to the Fairy Godmother, it seems likely that he would have selected a partner with similar traits (wealthy, high status family, physically attractive, etc). The importance of this decision to the King and to Fiona perhaps makes the conflict between father and daughter inevitable.

The argument about the type of partner that Fiona should marry (and have children with) represents one element of parent-offspring conflict (Trivers, 1972, 1974). Compared with other species, the human infant is particularly vulnerable after birth and requires a substantial investment from the parent in order to survive. However, whilst parental investment increases the child's chance of surviving, the investment also reduces the parent's ability to invest in other (including future) children (Trivers, 1972). This creates a pattern of conflict at times when the amount of investment can vary. For example, during pregnancy the fetus tries to obtain more resources from the mother than it is optimum for the mother to provide (Haig, 1993). This conflict appears to reach a peak during weaning (Barrett, Dunbar, and Lycett, 2002) and is most apparent when the child is young. However, the psychological mechanisms shaping the behavior of the parent and child also operate at an older age and parent-offspring conflict also occurs when the child has reached sexual maturity.

In most cultures, parents exert a degree of control over the mating decisions made by their children, including the type of partner chosen (Apostolou, 2007). Parents (as demonstrated by the King and Queen) often try to exert more control over the child than the child wishes, for example by chaperoning the child. In modern societies parents may use "cajolery, persuasion, appeals to loyalty, and threats" to influence their child's mating decisions (Sussman, 1953: p. 80). Indeed, their commitment to finding a suitable partner for Fiona is evident throughout the trilogy. By sending her to a remote castle that is guarded by a dragon, they ensure that she cannot mate with an unsuitable partner. Any suitor that successfully slays the dragon and rescues her clearly signals his commitment to Fiona and ability to resource such a daring quest; whilst being reassured that no other man has been able to mate with her. Once she has been rescued, they organize a ball to formalize the union.

There is a strong relationship between the qualities sought by parents and those favored by the child; however there is a difference in emphasis. Parents typically place a greater importance on a good family background (Apostolou, 2008; Buunk, Park, and Dubbs, 2008), one trait that may indicate his stability and ability to provide valuable resources. By encouraging their daughter to focus on these qualities, parents can reduce their own investment in the child. For example, the King and Queen favor Prince Charming, the heir to the wealthy, powerful, and socially connected Fairy Godmother. In addition, in many cultures the parents of the groom transfer a proportion of their wealth to the parents of the bride (Murdock, 1981). This payment (known as bridewealth) would clearly benefit the King and Queen and provide additional resources for the Kingdom. Although Fiona is an only child (reducing the need to conserve parental investment) evolved psychological mechanisms may continue to shape the parental preference for a particular type of partner. Indeed, Fiona seems to be aware of the importance of resources, trying to improve Shrek's apparent mate value by stating that he "has his own land."

In summary, this chapter outlines the way in which the physiological and environmental pressures faced by men and women shape the behaviors displayed within the Shrek trilogy and the expectations of the audience. In particular, these pressures influence the type of partner (with respect to both physical and personality traits) and relationship preferred by each character. The chapter also interprets behavior (such as the rejection of Prince Charming) that is inconsistent with common expectations and a character's willingness to lower their expectations in one regard if a potential partner has other desirable qualities. The assessment of this behavior from an evolutionary perspective helps identify a number of preferences and behaviors that addressed survival or reproductive problems over evolutionary history.

PART III

Instead of a Conclusion

CHAPTER 10

Potholes of Knowledge: The Politics of Studying *Shrek*

Tim Nieguth

MISS TESMAN. Well, well! To think you can write about a thing like that!
(Ibsen, 1961: "Hedda Gabler," Act I)

... ne jamais rencontrer une difficulté sans la prendre immédiatement comme sujet d'étude.
(Termier, 1908: p. 34; italics removed)

When we (the editors) conceived the idea for this volume, we hoped that a book of essays on the green ogre and his companions would attract some degree of public attention. Little did we know that an enterprising reporter from *The Sudbury Star*—a local newspaper in our hometown—would come across the call for papers that we had circulated in the usual academic venues, request an interview, and publish a front-page article on a book project that, at the time, was still in its embryonic stage. We likewise did not anticipate that the publication of this article would trigger a veritable media frenzy: for several weeks, not a day would go by without another request for an interview. All told, we fielded around a dozen interviews with local, regional, and national media.

This is obviously a rather generous application of the term "media frenzy," and one that owes much to our professional background: as social scientists, we were accustomed to the relative anonymity of academic labor and ill-prepared for the limelight of media interest (regardless of its wattage). Social science research seldom makes the news, and is deemed worthy of the front page even more rarely. While we were pleased with the public interest in our project, we could not help but be surprised. Why now, we wondered? Why, of all the projects our colleagues and ourselves had been working on, should this be the one to attract public interest? What made this project so much more "newsworthy" than our other research?

We were also surprised by the strength of feeling the book project seemed to elicit. For example, some of our colleagues were extremely supportive and seemed to consider the book project innovative and potentially insightful (or, failing that, at least original). Others clearly regarded a study on *Shrek* as an embarrassment to the profession. Similarly, while media coverage of the book project was generally positive, some of the public responses to that coverage were less than flattering. Naturally, we were more delighted with some of these responses than with others. More importantly, though, the question that increasingly puzzled us was this: Why should a book on the green ogre arouse this sort of emotional response? Especially in light of the fact that the book did not actually exist yet, that we had not received any submissions, and that we had barely begun looking for a publisher. We were, in short, at a loss to explain some of the reactions to the project.

That sense of bewilderment is what ultimately drives the present chapter. The latter is premised on the idea that analyzing the public response to our book project can shed some light on broader dynamics involved in the relationship between social science, the media, and the wider public. In particular, such an analysis can serve to illuminate some of the politics involved in knowledge creation and dissemination. It can do so in a particularly effective manner, not despite the fact that the public response to our project predated the actual book, but because of it. It is precisely because the editors could describe the project only in the most general terms that members of the public were able to use the book as a screen on which to project their own assumptions about social science, legitimate forms of knowledge, and the proper use of public resources.

The chapter will tease out some of these assumptions by examining a particular set of public responses to the book. Specifically, it will analyze online comments posted by *Sudbury Star* readers in response to the initial article on the *Shrek* project. This article was published simultaneously in print and on the *Star's* website. Most of the *Star's* online articles, including this one, allow members of the public to post comments. Opinions expressed in these comments typically tend to be divided. Opinions on the *Shrek* article were—without exception—decidedly negative. The comments revolved around two core themes: the supposedly improper use of public resources, and the perceived irrelevance of a study on *Shrek*. The chapter will briefly outline those themes, place them in a broader context, and, in doing so, offer some possible explanations for the negative responses to the *Shrek* project.

Before launching into an analysis of these criticisms, a caveat is in order. The *Sudbury Star* article attracted a grand total of a dozen online comments—hardly a sizeable sample, and one that may very well not be representative of public opinion as a whole. The analysis provided here should therefore be taken as a vignette, rather than a comprehensive portrayal and explanation of public responses to the *Shrek* project. That being said, the sort of criticisms articulated in user responses to the *Sudbury Star* article reflect common themes in public discourse around knowledge production in the social sciences, and they point to broader concerns about social science communication and the portrayal of social sciences in the media and politics. In particular, claims that certain research projects in the social sciences are irrelevant or constitute a waste of public funds are anything but rare.

By way of illustration, a political scientist at the University of Alberta recently encountered widespread criticism after one of her research projects—on the politics of *Thomas and Friends*—had been featured in the Australian, British, and Canadian media. Three-quarters of user comments posted on the websites of Canadian media outlets in response to stories covering this research project were negative. Almost half of the comments considered the project plainly irrelevant, a waste of taxpayer money, or proof of the putative disconnect between "ivory tower academics" and the "real world." A full quarter of comments were clearly gendered, ranging from suggestions that the political scientist in question ought to spend more time with her children, to overtly misogynist remarks (Nieguth and Wilton, 2010). Reader comments posted on the websites of British media outlets such as *The Daily Telegraph* or *The Daily Mail* were similarly hostile. Many of these comments lambasted the research project (which underlined the socially conservative nature of *Thomas and Friends*) as an instance of political correctness run amuck. Others insisted that the research project was irrelevant, a waste of money, or both. For example, a user by the name of Jim McWhinnie wondered "[w]ho pays for such garbage research" (2009), while another advised the political scientist in question to "stop watching kid's TV shows under the pretence of analysis, get a life, and study something important!" (Laura, 2009). Taken as a whole, these responses indicate that the kind of comments elicited by the *Sudbury Star* article may reflect widespread public sentiments.

Criticisms

Many of the online comments on the *Sudbury Star* article suggested that the commentators perceived a book project on *Shrek* as an inappropriate use of resources. For example, one user referred to the project as "a ridiculous waste of money" (Hanmerguy, 2009). Another summed up his feelings on the matter as follows: "Now here is a perfect example of waste... a study on a cartoon character... gimme a break!" (Mikey 27, 2009). Other commentators, equally unimpressed with the merits of the book project, voiced a more specific concern with the proper allocation of public funds. Thus, a user by the name of Valleyboy speculated that "[m]aybe they'll be given some government grants for this study" (2009). Another user held a similar opinion, stating that "you can probably bet they will get gov't funding" (Keno, 2009).

The first two of these comments imply that the *Shrek* project required and drew on specific research funds, whether in the form of grant money or otherwise. This suggests a broader belief on the part of the commentators that social science research typically involves funding of this nature, and that such funding is readily available for social scientists. In fact, research projects in the social sciences and humanities are commonly carried out without funding specifically allocated to those projects. Research funding, whether from the public or the private sector, is relatively scarce. By way of illustration, the National Science Foundation—a key federal funding agency for research at postsecondary institutions in the United States—allocates roughly U.S. 9 million a year to research in political science. According to the American Association for the Advancement of Science (2008), the social sciences accounted for 2 percent of federal research funds allocated during the 2007 fiscal year.

That the general public should be unfamiliar with funding structures and levels in the social sciences and humanities is, of course, no surprise: there is no reason to expect members of different professions to be familiar with processes characteristic of other occupations. In the absence of detailed information, individuals may easily tend toward projecting their own professional experience onto other contexts, despite the fact that their experience may turn out to have little relevance in these contexts.

The second set of comments speaks to concerns with the allocation of government funds more broadly. Overall, these comments seem to revolve at least as much around a generalized disaffection with government as around the *Shrek* project. They convey a palpable sense of cynicism regarding the regular use of public funds; clearly, the commentators would not have been surprised to see public funds allocated to a study they regard as unworthy of such funding. This set of comments also conveys a sense that government funding would, for whatever reason, be relatively easy to obtain for a project of this nature. We did not put this assumption to the test, so we can neither validate nor invalidate it.

In at least one instance, this sense of cynicism about the distribution of public funding involved speculation about the salary supposedly drawn by the editors of the present volume: "Seriously? I bet this guy gets paid six figures. I'll 'study' the Shrek trilogy and write you guys a report. You can pay me half of what this professor gets paid" (Jigsaw, 2009a). Interestingly, there is nothing in the *Sudbury Star* article itself that would conceivably invite such speculation. What, then, would prompt a comment of this nature? One possible explanation would seem to point, once again, to a certain level of generalized cynicism. On this reading, the comment can be read to imply that contemporary society frequently rewards individuals in a manner that is out of proportion with the value of the work they carry out. More specifically, this comment lends itself to the interpretation that academics as a class may be overpaid, especially if they choose to study phenomena such as *Shrek*.

This sentiment in turn links to wider concerns around public funding for universities in an age of constrained government spending on higher education. One user expressed these concerns as follows: "What a poor choice of stories to run. In a time when universities are trying to justify funding, why highlight this?" (Grow up Sudbury, 2009). The nature of this objection seems to be twofold: first, this user seemed to find little merit in a book project on *Shrek*. More importantly, s/he feared that drawing attention to the fact that academics pursue these sorts of study (in addition to others) may undercut public support for funding universities, thus ultimately harming other (presumably worthier) research projects.

The perception that the pursuit of studies on *Shrek* constitutes a waste of resources is predicated on the implicit assumption that *Shrek* is not an object worthy of scholarly attention. Several other comments made that assumption explicit. According to these comments, studies of *Shrek* are either outright irrelevant, or less important than a whole range of other potential research subjects. As such, these comments suggest a hierarchy of legitimate knowledge to be pursued in the social sciences. For example, a user by the name of Grow up Sudbury stated that there "are hundreds of 'meaningful' studies in mine technology or kinesiology, but the [*Sudbury Star*] chooses this one" (2009). Another user struck a similar note, suggesting that "[t]here's more important things to study in the Political Science area ... I'm sure there is" (Jigsaw, 2009a). Comments by a user called Azildian likewise stressed the importance of other areas of inquiry, questioning not only the relevance of a study on *Shrek*, but the significance of *Shrek* in the greater scheme of things:

> It's so important to study a trilogy that hasn't really changed or affected our society that much. Much more important tha[n] researching things like potholes, affordable health care, making mining efficient, reducing the cost of infrastructure, etc. (Azildian, 2009)

Unsurprisingly, many of the issues that are mentioned as examples for more important areas of study reflect local circumstances in Sudbury and Northern Ontario. For example, there is a long-standing concern with the quality of health care services in the region. Likewise, mining is a key industry in Northeastern Ontario, and many research projects at universities in the area do, indeed, revolve around the mining industry (as well as its impact on society). The reference to potholes reflects a widespread concern with the state of transport infrastructure in Sudbury and other areas of Northern Ontario, as well as a perception that governments invest insufficient resources in maintaining that infrastructure. As such, the comments reflect a desire that research conducted at public universities should address itself to improving the material life circumstances experienced by members of the public.

Arguably, few social scientists would consider this an unreasonable desire. Indeed, much research conducted in the social sciences does center on issues whose importance the commentators cited in the previous paragraph may concede more readily. To provide just one example, the editors of the current volume have pursued research on topics as varied as genocide, environmental risk assessments, and national self-government. On one possible reading, the comments by Jigsaw and

Azildian suggest that they are not aware of this fact. This is perhaps not terribly surprising, given that social science research in general seems to occupy a somewhat marginal position in public awareness (a point the chapter will return to later).

An alternative interpretation of the comments in question would suggest that the commentators are quite aware that social scientists do, indeed, pursue research on matters such as health care, mining and infrastructure (not to mention international security, human rights, globalization, immigration, gender relations, or a host of other issues that affect our lives on a daily basis and in a very immediate fashion)—they simply feel that social science research should address itself *exclusively* to such matters. That position would indicate a fairly rigid definition of "important" issues. It would point to a rather narrow construction of the benefits that can be derived from research in the social sciences. There is no room in the present chapter to revisit the long-standing debate about the role and value of liberal arts in contemporary society, but suffice it to say that many of the key contributors to this debate have construed the benefits of social science much more widely, including, for example, its potential contributions to citizenship education.

In addition, the assertion that *Shrek* "hasn't really changed or affected our society that much" (Azildian, 2009) appears problematical at best. If the previous chapters in this volume are any indication, *Shrek*—like other cultural artifacts—is an important vehicle for transporting, reflecting, or challenging societal values and collective identities. In consequence, it also provides a platform for critical engagements with prevalent values, identities, regimes, and institutions. For example, *Shrek*'s considerable success raises fundamental questions about the social predispositions and institutional arrangements that allowed the trilogy to become so successful to begin with. Moreover, the very ubiquity of *Shrek* suggests that it is a subject worth studying in its own right, simply because a significant number of individuals appear to have devoted a fair amount of time and attention to various forms of engagement with *Shrek*. Put differently, *Shrek* has changed society by the simple fact of its existence. At the most basic level, any time spent watching and discussing *Shrek* is time not spent engaging with other facets of social reality. Even in this rather minimal sense, then, society with *Shrek* is not the same as society without *Shrek*. Likewise, any societal resources invested in the production, dissemination and consumption of *Shrek* are resources not invested elsewhere. As demonstrated in the introductory chapter of this volume, *Shrek* has effected very real changes in the material circumstances of a great number of individuals and a significant redistribution of wealth. In consequence, claims that *Shrek* or similar phenomena are unworthy of scholarly attention would seem difficult to sustain.

Finally, many of the online comments on the *Sudbury Star* article convey certain notions, not only about legitimate or illegitimate areas of knowledge and social science inquiry, but also about the nature of research in the social sciences. For example, a user with the screen name Ernie Keebler (2009) offered the following comment:

> C'mon guys. I'll bet there are a whole bunch of six year olds planning their educations now. They all want to go to Laurentian to study under this idiot, sorry genius! This is marketing genius. Its called top of mind. In 10-12 years, when these kids grow up, they'll all remember that "at Laurentian, you get to watch cartoons!"

The underlying assumption here seems to be that research on a subject such as *Shrek* involves little more than simply watching the movies and (presumably) talking about them. A similar assumption is evident in the following comment by the user named Jigsaw (2009b):

> I've "studied" the Shrek trilogy. You take a drink of your beer when Shrek says the word "swamp", take a shot every time Pinocchio lies, finish your drink when someone says a sexual innuendo, etc... Man, was I wasted after that "study"...

These comments are particularly interesting for two reasons: first, they convey the idea that the value of research—whether in the social sciences or elsewhere—is constituted exclusively by its subject. On that view, it is only the "what" of research that matters. Arguably, though, the "how" and "why" of research matters as well: the kind of questions social scientists ask of their research subject, and the methods they use to answer those question, have significant implications for the purpose and meaning of their research projects. Take the following, sarcastic comment by one *Sudbury Star* reader: "I'm so proud to be a Laurentian graduate. Maybe I'll go get my Masters and do a thesis on the Smurfs!" (Ernie Keebler, 2009). There is, in fact, some intriguing research on the Smurfs, including a doctoral thesis that uses the Smurfs to develop a broader case about the meaning and implications of cultural globalization (Hubka, 1998). This example can serve as one among many others to illustrate that the point (and hence the potential value) of social science research is not necessarily located exclusively in its immediate subject matter.

Further, the comments cited in the preceding paragraphs leave little room for the possibility that social science, as a form of systematic inquiry, may follow particular routines and protocols that enjoin social scientists to approach subjects such as *Shrek* in a different fashion than a casual viewer. Consequently, there is no sense that social science research may constitute a specialized body of knowledge that can be brought to bear on a subject such as *Shrek*. Because social science research typically addresses subject matters situated within the realm of everyday experience, and because there is little public awareness of the protocols and procedures of social science research, it can be difficult to convince members of the public that research on certain subjects may have merit even if they do not consider the subject at hand intrinsically important.

Actors

To recapitulate briefly, the online comments posted by some *Sudbury Star* readers point to a perception that the pursuit of research on phenomena such as *Shrek* constitutes a waste of resources and is irrelevant. These comments rest on two implicit assumptions: first, certain objects are inherently more worthy of study and represent more legitimate types of knowledge. Second, the value of social science research is constituted exclusively by its subject (rather than its questions, methods, or implications). Commentators treated the *Shrek* project as an isolated phenomenon, divorcing it from the larger context of social science research.

These observations are troubling for a number of interrelated reasons, not least because they raise further questions regarding the role of the social sciences in a liberal democracy. Most social scientists rely on some form of public funding for their research and livelihood. In liberal democracies, this state of affairs cannot simply be taken for granted. Rather, it presupposes that the social sciences, on the whole, offer something of value to the public. Following Brady (2004: p. 1630),

> I would ask: why should public resources be used to support sociology [or the social sciences in general, TN]? If there is absolutely no connection between sociology and public well-being, sociology may

be profoundly undeserving of research grants (especially government funds), tuition dollars, administrative support, and land-grant campus space. If sociology does not maintain even a distant connection with improving society, the public has no responsibility to support our discipline. Surely, there is a better use of tax revenue than transferring it to the well-being of middle-class professionals with no concern for public society.

One need not subscribe to the tenets of public sociology (as articulated, for instance, by Burawoy, 2004; for a skeptical assessment of those tenets, see Nielsen, 2004; Tittle, 2004) in order to accept that the social sciences should provide some form of benefit to society (leaving aside the rather thorny question whom or what, exactly, we have in mind when deploying the label of "society"). Assessing the value of research requires that there be sufficient information on said research. And in fact, a good deal of information on social science research is available in public form. For instance, readers of *The Sudbury Star* can access information on the type of research pursued at Laurentian University by consulting university, departmental, and faculty websites. Likewise, a Google search will yield a considerable amount of information on social science research on a wide range of subject matters (including potholes and transport infrastructure).

What, then, explains the relative lack of public knowledge about the social sciences? Among other reasons, members of the general public may simply not be aware of the publicly available information on social science research. In addition, that information can only provide a limited picture of the social science enterprise, both because it tends to be restricted to a fairly general level where research results are concerned, and because it tends not to offer any insights into the "business" of social science—research design, research processes, funding structures, or administrative concerns. Just as importantly, a number of key actors that play crucial roles in funneling the results of social science research to a wider public—social scientists, governments, and the media—tend to do so only to a limited extent.

As a group, social scientists bear part of the responsibility for the lack of social science communication. In some ways, this may seem rather odd; after all, social scientists are trained to be communicators *par excellence*. They dedicate a rather significant share of their time— as researchers, instructors, and administrators—to communicating with various audiences. Therein, however, lies the rub. As Weiss and Singer point out, the "primary audience for social scientists is usually colleagues in the same area of specialization" (1988: p. 6). Social scientists are thus trained (and expected) to communicate their research in a highly specific format to a narrowly defined slice of the public, that is, a set of individuals who are embedded in broadly similar research problems, methods and literatures. Academic careers hinge in good measure on the publication of research results in specialized venues, such as peer-reviewed scholarly journals or recognized academic presses. Academic reward structures offer social scientists relatively few incentives to communicate their research to a wider, nonspecialist audience. Indeed, attempts to do so may occasionally be frowned upon for supposedly lacking proper scholarly rigor.

Some of the responsibility for the public image of social science rests with governments. In 2009, Canada's federal government proposed significant changes to funding for the Social Sciences and Humanities Research Council (SSHRC) and other research councils, all of which are key funding agencies for research at Canadian universities. This decision prompted little debate in Parliament. At the risk of overemphasizing the significance of this episode, the fact that elected representatives declined to enter into a comprehensive debate over public funding of the social sciences and humanities suggests that the latter rank, at best, fairly low in the consciousness of public decision makers.

Other cases involve a decidedly negative assessment of social science on the part of elected representatives. In 2009, for instance, U.S. Senator Tom Coburn proposed an amendment (SA 2631) that would have barred the American National Science Foundation from funding research in political science. A memorandum accompanying the amendment insisted that the "National Science Foundation has misspent tens of millions of dollars examining political science issues which in reality have little, if anything, to do with science" ("Coburn Amendment 2631," 2009: p. 2). The memorandum further suggested that research produced by political scientists has produced few benefits for American taxpayers. Public funding for the highly regarded American National Election Studies at the University of Michigan attracted Coburn's particular ire:

> The University of Michigan may have some interesting theories about recent elections, but Americans who have an interest in electoral politics can turn to CNN, FOX News, MSNBC, the print media, and a seemingly endless number of political commentators on the internet who pour over this data and provide a myriad of viewpoints to answer the same questions. ("Coburn Amendment 2631," 2009: p. 3)

This rationale indicates a belief that the analyses of political behavior offered by media outlets and political pundits do not differ, either in kind or orientation, from the type of analysis one might expect political scientists to produce. Overall, the views presented in the Coburn memorandum bear a striking resemblance to some of the views articulated by the *Sudbury Star* commentators discussed earlier in this chapter. The Coburn amendment was ultimately defeated, although a strong minority of Senators (36) endorsed it. While voting behavior in this as in other cases was influenced by a number of factors, the outcome of the vote at least raises the possibility that a significant proportion of key political decision makers in the United States—one of the leading global research hubs—share a profoundly skeptical attitude toward the merits of political science.

A third key party involved in shaping the public image of social science is the media. As mentioned earlier, the pronounced media interest in the *Shrek* project came as a bit of a surprise to the editors, since most social science research attracts little attention from the media. One might therefore reasonably suspect that some of the assumptions underpinning the comments posted on the *Sudbury Star* website are rooted in the particular selection of social science stories the media elects to present to the public. In particular, some commentators insisted that political science (and, presumably, other social sciences) ought to address issues of material concern to the public. This insistence may in part reflect a sense that social science research does not currently cover such issues, a sense that in turn may have been fuelled by the media's inattention to the wide range of research conducted in the social sciences.

An examination of the *Sudbury Star's* coverage of social science research conducted at Laurentian University (as Northeastern Ontario's regional university) would seem to lend some support to this explanation. A search of the Eureka database shows that about 770 articles appearing in *The Sudbury Star* mentioned Laurentian University during the one year period preceding the publication of the *Shrek* article. Typically, those articles discussed university sports, funding issues, the university's economic and cultural contributions to the local community, labor relations on campus, and similar issues. Combining a search for "Laurentian University" with "sociology" yields only two results; neither of the articles in question covered research conducted in the department of sociology. Similarly, a search for "Laurentian University" and "political science" yields a scant dozen documents; three of these covered aspects of what could loosely be labeled student life, seven contained commentaries by Laurentian political scientists on current events, one article covered a United Nations simulation organized by members of the political science department, and one document turned out to be a false positive. None of the 12 articles mentioned research projects housed in the political science department.

The paucity of social science stories in *The Sudbury Star* reflects broader patterns in media coverage of social science research. There is surprisingly little work being done on this topic, but the seminal study by Weiss and Singer (1988) offers a number of insights into the reasons why the media tend to pay relatively little attention to the social sciences, and how they tend to cover social science when they do. For example, the study points out that there is no social science "beat" in the media. Unlike crime, business, or sports, social science is not treated as a well-defined thematic area that is assigned for coverage to particular journalists. In researching the relationship between social science and the media, Weiss and Singer

> talked to a number of reporters who had just written a story which we classified as social science, and we asked them if this was the first time that they had written stories about social science. Uniformly they were taken aback; some seemed to think that we were talking gibberish. In their minds the current story was not about social science at all. They were writing about crime or business or politics or education. That they were reporting the results of *research* on the topic or citing the remarks of a *social scientist* was of little consequence. It was the *topic* of the story that provided the frame of reference for their work. Newspeople do not think about social science as a category and they do not treat it as a category. (1988: pp. 55–6; emphases in the original)

Journalists may thus make use of social scientists as commentators on certain social and political issues, or draw on research in the social sciences in the context of discussing such issues, but they typically do not cover social science research as a story in and of itself. When social science is discussed in the media, it tends to be covered not in its own right, but in relation to some other topic. Consequently, the media's selection of social science stories does not primarily have to do with the academic merits of a particular research project, but involves a number of other considerations. According to Weiss and Singer (1998: pp. 32–3), journalists cited the links of particular research to current news items, the novelty of its findings, and its ability to pique their interest as some of the key reasons for covering a social science story. In light of these observations, it is perhaps no surprise that social scientists frequently felt that media coverage of social science research tended to de-contextualize the latter by failing to place it in the context of previous and ongoing research. These findings clearly resonate with the news coverage and online comments surrounding the *Shrek* project, which suggests that the public response we received is no exception, but rather indicative of broader trends in the relationship between social science and the media.

Conclusion

When *The Sudbury Star* released a front-page article on the project that ultimately resulted in this book, other media outlets quickly followed up on this story. Over the course of a few weeks, the editors fielded a significant number of requests for interviews with print and broadcast media. While journalists were quite receptive to the *Shrek* project, the same did not prove to be true of other members of the public. For example, the online version of the initial *Sudbury Star* article attracted roughly a dozen responses, all of which were negative. The types of comments we received, as well as the apparent strength of sentiment behind some of them, suggested that the public response to the *Shrek* project would be a worthwhile subject of inquiry. Accordingly, this chapter sought to answer two questions: what sort of online responses did the *Sudbury Star* article garner, and what are some of the factors that might explain these responses?

The online comments stressed two concerns: first, many commentators felt that a study on *Shrek* amounted to a waste of resources. Second, and on a related note, many of the commentators considered such a study irrelevant, insisting that social science research ought to focus on issues that are of more immediate, material concern to the public. As such, the comments conveyed certain notions about the nature of social science, the role it ought to play within larger society, and the characteristics of "useful" knowledge. Given that the *Shrek* project was, at the time, still in its incipient stage, the commentators had no way of knowing what sort of analyses the resulting book would be able to offer. It is therefore fair to conclude that their comments reflected broader attitudes toward social science, legitimate knowledge, and the appropriate use of resources, rather than a considered engagement with the *Shrek* franchise or the book project as such. This circumstance made the comments on the *Sudbury Star* article especially interesting from a politics of knowledge perspective, because the book project presented a blank slate onto which observers could (and did) project their own assumptions.

In attempting to answer the second question, the chapter suggested that the comments in question may, at least in part, result from the kind of information on social science research that is readily available to the general public. In a nutshell, that information (perhaps unavoidably) provides only limited insight into the nature of social science research, the types of research being pursued, the processes governing the social science enterprise, and the funding structures that underpin much of the latter. Several key actors play a crucial role in shaping public information on social science research: social scientists, governments, and the media. The chapter argued that, none of these actors tend to take a particular interest in providing comprehensive information on social sciences to the wider public. In consequence, the fact that some members of the public would see little value in a study on *Shrek* is anything but surprising.

While the existence of widespread public disenchantment with research into *Shrek* or similar subjects may not be surprising, such disenchantment frequently seems to be based on a number of interrelated assumptions that are well worth considering. These assumptions can be briefly summarized as follows:

- Knowledge is not intrinsically valuable
- The value of knowledge is determined fully and exclusively by its subject matter
- We can clearly and easily distinguish between "serious" and "frivolous" knowledge
- The distinction between these two types of knowledge hinges on questions of utility
- Knowledge is "useful" if it contributes to an improvement in material life circumstances
- We can predict what kind of research will produce such results
- Research that does not do so is undeserving of public funding

All of these assumptions are highly contestable; for example, even if one accepts that there is such a thing as "frivolous" knowledge, this does not necessarily make research concerned with producing such knowledge irrelevant. On a related note, "utility" can be defined in a number of ways, not all of which revolve around the improvement of material life circumstances. Likewise, research projects may produce all sorts of unintended consequences and spin-off effects—some beneficial, some less so. This is not to say that social scientists should pay no attention to those assumptions. On the contrary, they need to take them seriously: ultimately, social scientists operating in liberal democracies must be prepared to explain why and how they consider their research beneficial if they hope to attract continued public support for their endeavors. This necessitates an engagement with assumptions that may critically inform public attitudes toward social science.

Filmography

Adamson, Andrew and Vicky Jenson (Directors). (2001). *Shrek*. The United States: DreamWorks Animation.
Adamson, Andrew, Kelly Asbury, and Vernon Conrad (Directors). (2004). *Shrek 2*. The United States: DreamWorks Animation.
Avery, Tex (Director). (1943). *Red Hot Riding Hood*. The United States: Warner Brothers.
Clampett, Robert (Director). (1934). *Coal Black and de Sebben Dwarfs*. The United States: Warner Brothers.
Darnell, Eric and Tim Johnson (Directors). (1998). *Antz*. The United States: Pacific Data Images/DreamWorks.
Demme, Jonathan (Director). (1993). *Philadelphia*. The United States: Tristar.
Docter, Pete, David Silverman, and Lee Unkrich (Directors). (2001). *Monsters, Inc*. The United States: Pixar.
Fleischer, Dave (Director). (1937). *Popeye the Sailor Meets Ali Baba's Forty Thieves*. The United States: Fleischer Studios.
Fleischer, Dave (Director). (1939). *Aladdin and His Wonderful Lamp*. The United States: Fleischer Studios.
Gillett, Burt (Producer/Director). (1933). *Three Little Pigs*. The United States: Walt Disney Productions.
Griffith, David (Director) (1915). *The Birth of a Nation*. The United States: Epoch Film.
Hand, David (Director). (1939). *Snow White and the Seven Dwarfs*. The United States: Walt Disney Productions.
Jackson, Peter (Director). (2001, 2002, 2003). *The Lords of the Rings (trilogy)*. New Zealand: Newline Cinema.
Jacobovici, Simcha (Director). (1998). *Hollywoodism: Jews, Movies and the American Dream*. Canada: Associated Productions.
Lasseter, John (Director). (1995). *Toy Story*. The United States: Pixar.
Lasseter, John and Andrew Stanton (Directors). (1998). *A Bug's Life*. The United States: Pixar.
Lee, Ang (Director). (2005). *Brokeback Mountain*. Canada and the United States: Alberta Film Entertainment and This is That Productions.

Marshall, Garry (Director). (1990). *Pretty Woman*. The United States: Touchstone Pictures.

Miller, Chris and Ramen Hui (Directors). (2007). *Shrek the Third*. The United States: DreamWorks Animation.

Mitchell, Mike (Director). (2010). *Shrek Forever After*. The United States: DreamWorks Animation.

Resnais, Alain (Director). (1955). *Night and Fog*. France: Argos Films.

Sun, Chyng Feng (Producer and Writer). (2001). *Mickey Mouse Monopoly: Disney, Childhood, and Corporate Power*. The United States: Art Media Production.

Trousdale, Gary and Kirk Wise (Directors). (1991). *Beauty and the Beast*. The United States: Walt Disney Pictures.

Van Sant, Gus (Director). (2008). *Milk*. The United States: Axon Films.

Wachoski, Andy and Larry Wachowski (Directors). (1999). *The Matrix*. Australia and the United States: Groucho II Films.

Bibliography

"About William Steig" (2000). In *Something About the Author, Volume 111*. Edited by Alan Hedblad. Gale Group. Available at http://www.williamsteig.com/williamsteig.htm [accessed January 19, 2009].
Adamson, Andrew et al. (2004). *Shrek 2—Script*. Available at http://www.script-o-rama.com/movie_scripts/s/shrek-2-script-transcript.html [accessed March 2, 2009].
Adorno, Theodor (1973). *Negative Dialectics*. New York: The Seabury Press.
Adorno, Theodor (1951/1993). *Minima Moralia: Reflections from Damaged Life*. London: Verso.
Adorno, Theodor (1991). *The Culture Industry*. Oxford: Routledge.
Adorno, Theodor (1998). "Subject and Object," in *The Essential Frankfurt School Reader*. Edited by A. Arato and E. Gebhardt. New York: Continuum Publishing.
Adorno, Theodor and Max Horkheimer (1947/1990). *The Dialectic of Enlightenment*. New York: Continuum Publishing.
Allen, Paula Gunn (1990). "The Woman I Love Is a Planet The Planet I Love Is a Tree," in *Reweaving the World: The Emergence of Ecofeminism*. Edited by I. Diamond and G. F. Orenstein. San Francisco: Sierra Club Books.
Andersson, Malte (1994). *Sexual Selection*. Princeton, NJ: Princeton University Press.
Althusser, Louis (1972). "Ideology and Ideological State Apparatus," in *Education: Structure and Society*. Edited by B. Cosin. Harmondsworth: Penguin.
Althusser, Louis (1977). *Ideologie und ideologische Staatsapparate. Aufsätze zur marxistischen Theorie*. Hamburg: VSA.
American Association for the Advancement of Science (2008). "Research in the FY 2007 Budget, by Discipline." Chart. Available at http://www.aaas.org/spp/rd/res07pie.pdf [accessed January 30, 2009].
Anzaldúa, Gloria (1987). *Borderlands/ La Frontera*. San Francisco: Spinsters/ Aunt Lute Press.
Apostolou, Menelaos (2007). "Sexual Selection under Parental Choice: The Role of Parents in the Evolution of Human Mating." *Evolution and Human Behavior*, vol.28: 403–9.

Apostolou, Menelaos (2008). "Parent-Offspring Conflict over Mating: The Case of Family Background." *Evolutionary Psychology*, vol.6: 456–68.

Apuleius, Lucius (1994). *The Golden Ass*. Translated by P. G. Walsh. New York: Oxford University Press.

Arendt, Hannah (2004). *The Origins of Totalitarianism*. New York: Schocken Books.

Azildian (2009). No title. Online post, *Sudbury Star*. Available at http://www.thesudburystar.com/ArticelDisplay.aspx?e=1469197 [accessed October 3, 2009].

Bagemihl, Bruce (1999). *Biological Exuberance: Animal Homosexuality and Natural Diversity*. New York: St. Martin's Press.

Baker, Robin and Mark Bellis (1995). *Human Sperm Competition: Copulation, Masturbation, and Infidelity*. London: Chapman and Hall.

Baring, Anne and Jules Cashford (1991). *The Myth of the Goddess: Evolution of an Image*. New York: Penguin Books.

Barrett, Louise, Robin Dunbar and John Lycett (2002). *Human Evolutionary Psychology*. Basingstoke: Palgrave.

Bateman, Angus (1948). "Intra-sexual Selection in Drosophila." *Heredity*, no.2: 349–68.

Baudrillard, Jean (1981). *A Critique of the Political Economy of the Sign*. St Louis, MO: Telos Press.

Baudrillard, Jean (1983). *Simulations*. New York: Semiotexte.

Bauman, Zygmunt (1998). *Globalization: The Human Condition*. New York: Columbia University Press.

Bayley, Harold (1912/1996). *The Lost Language of Symbolism*. 2 Vols. New York: Barnes and Noble.

Beck, Ulrich (1992). *Risk Society. Toward a New Modernity*. London: Sage.

Bell, Elizabeth, Lynda Hass and Laura Sells (eds.) (1995). *From Mouse to Mermaid: The Politics of Film, Gender and Culture*. Indianapolis: Indiana University Press.

Benhabib, Seyla (2004). *The Rights of Others: Aliens, Residents and Citizens*. Cambridge: Cambridge University Press.

Benito-Rojo, Antonio (1988). *The Repeating Island: The Caribbean and the Postmodern Perspective*. Translated by J. Maraniss. Durham: Duke University Press.

Bennett, Tony (1982). "Theories of the Media, Theories of Society," in *Culture, Society and the Media*. Edited by Michael Gurevitch, Tony Bennett, James Curran and Janet Woollacott. London: Methuen.

Bingen, Hildegard (1985). *Illuminations of Hildegard of Bingen*. Santa Fe: Bear and Co.

Björntorp, Per (1987). "Fat Cell Distribution and Metabolism," in *Human Obesity*. Edited by Richard Wurtman and Judith Wurtman. New York: New York Academy of Sciences.

Bobbio, Norberto et al. (1983). *Dicionario de Politica*. Brasilia: Editora Universidade de Brasilia.
Bordo, Susan. (1993a). *Unbearable Weight: Feminism, Western Culture, and the Body*. Berkeley: University of California Press.
Bordo, Susan (1993b). "Unbearable Weight: Feminism, Western Culture, and the Body," in *The Norton Anthology of Theory and Criticism*. Edited by Vincent Leitch et al. New York: W.W. Norton and Company.
Brabham, Daren C. (2006). "Animated Blackness in Shrek." *Rocky Mountain Communication Review*, vol.3, no.1: 64–71.
Brady, David (2004). "Why Public Sociology May Fail." *Social Forces*, vol.82, no.4: 1629–38.
Briggs, Katharine (1976). *The Encyclopedia of Fairies, Hobgoblins, Brownies, Bogies, and Other Supernatural Creatures*. New York: Pantheon.
Bryman, Alan (1999). "The Disneyization of Society". *Sociological Review*, vol.47, no.1: 25–46.
Bryman, Alan (2004). *The Disneyization of Society*. London: Sage.
Brown, Harriet (2005). "The Other Brain Also Deals With Many Woes." *The New York Times*, Aug. 23.
Burawoy, Michael (2004). "Public Sociologies: Contradictions, Dilemmas, and Possibilities." *Social Forces*, vol.82, no.4: 1603–18.
Burch, Rebecca and Gordon Gallup (2000). "Perceptions of Paternal Resemblance Predict Family Violence." *Evolution and Human Behavior*, vol.21, no.6: 429–35.
Buss, David (1987). "Sex differences in human mate selection criteria: An evolutionary perspective," in *Sociobiology and Psychology: Ideas, Issues and Applications*. Edited by Charles Crawford, Dennis Krebs and Martin Smith. Hillsdale, NJ: Erlbaum.
Buss, David (1991). "Evolutionary Personality Psychology." *Annual Review of Psychology*, no.42: 459–91.
Buss, David (2004). *Evolutionary Psychology: The New Science of the Mind*. Boston: Pearson Education.
Buss, David and M. Barnes (1986). "Preferences in Human Mate Selection." *Journal of Personality and Social Psychology*, no.50: 559–70.
Buss, David and David Schmitt (1993). "Sexual Strategies Theory: An Evolutionary Perspective on Human Mating." *Psychological Review*, no.100: 204–32.
Buss, David and Todd Shackelford (1997). "Susceptibility to Infidelity in the First Year of Marriage." *Journal of Research in Personality*, no.31: 193–221.
Buss, David et al. (1990). "International Preferences in Selecting Mates: A Study of 37 Cultures." *Journal of Cross-Cultural Psychology*, no.21: 5–47.
Buunk, Abraham, Justin Park, and Shelli Dubbs, (2008). "Parent-offspring Conflict in Mate Preferences." *Review of General Psychology*, no.2: 47–62.

Calhoun, Craig (2003). "The Class Consciousness of Frequent Travelers: Toward a Critique of Existing Cosmopolitanism," in *Debating Cosmopolitics*. Edited by Daniele Archibugi. London: Verso.

Callaghan, William and Cynthia Berg (2003). "Pregnancy-related Mortality among Women Aged 35 Years and Older, United States, 1991–1997." *Obstetrics & Gynecology*, no.102: 1015–21.

Caputi, Jane (1993). *Gossips, Gorgons, and Crones: The Fates of the Earth.* Santa Fe: Bear and Company.

Caputi, Jane (2001). "On the Lap of Necessity: A Mythic Interpretation of Teresa Brennan's Energetics Philosophy." *Hypatia: A Journal of Feminist Philosophy*, vol.16, no.2: 1–26.

Caputi, Jane (2004). *Goddesses and Monsters: Women, Myth, Power and Popular Culture*. Madison: University of Wisconsin Press.

Caputi, Jane (2005a). "Dirt," in *Encyclopedia of Religion and Nature*. Edited by Bron R. Taylor. New York: Thoemmes Continuum.

Caputi, Jane (2005b). "Sexuality and Green Consciousness," in *Encyclopedia of Religion and Nature*. Edited by Bron R. Taylor. New York: Thoemmes Continuum.

Caputi, Jane (forthcoming 2012). "Feeding Green Fire," *Journal for the Study of Religion, Nature and Cutlure.*

Carroll, David (1999). *Swampwalker's Journal: A Wetlands Year*. Boston: Houghton Mifflin.

Carson, Rachel (1998). "To Understand Biology [1960]," in *Lost Woods: The Discovered Writing of Rachel Carson*. Edited by Linda Lear. Boston: Beacon Press.

Chandler, Daniel (2000). *Marxist Media Theory*. Available at http://www.aber.ac.uk/media/Documents/marxism/marxism.html [accessed November 11, 2009].

Chen, Xi-Kuan et al. (2008). "Increased Risks of Neonatal and Postnatal Mortality Associated with Teenage Pregnancy Had Different Explanations." *Journal of Clinical Epidemiology*, no.1: 688–94.

Chevalier, Jean and Alain Gheerbrant (1994). *The Penguin Dictionary of Symbols*. Translated by John Buchanan-Brown. New York: Penguin Books.

Chomsky, Noam (2002). *Media Control. The Spectacular Achievements of Propaganda*. New York: Seven Stories Press.

Cixous, Hélène (1981). "The Laugh of the Medusa," in *New French Feminisms*. Edited by Elaine Marks and Isabelle de Courtivron. New York: Schocken Books.

Clark, Russell and Elaine Hatfield (1989). "Gender Differences in Receptivity to Sexual Offers." *Journal of Psychology and Human Sexuality*, no.2: 39–55.

"Coburn Amendment 2631" (2009). Available at http://coburn.senate.gov/public/index.cfm?FuseAction=Files.View&FileStore_id=82180b1f-a03e-4600-a2e5-846640c2c880 [accessed November 29, 2009].

Collins, Patricia Hill (1998). *Black Feminist Thought: Knowledge, Consciousness, and the Politics of Empowerment*. New York: Routledge.
Connor, Steve (2005). "The State of the World? It Is on the Brink of Disaster." *The Independent UK*, March 30. Available at http://www.commondreams.org/headlines05/0330-04.htm [accessed August 30, 2009].
Curran, James, Michael Gurevitch and Janet Woollacott (1982). "The Study of the Media: Theoretical Approaches," in *Culture, Society and the Media*. Edited by Michael Gurevitch, Tony Bennett, James Curran and Janet Woollacott. London: Methuen.
Daly, Mary (1978). *Gyn/Ecology: The Metaethics of Radical Feminism*. Boston: Beacon Press.
Daly, Mary (1984). *Pure Lust: Elemental Feminist Philosophy*. Boston: Beacon Press.
Daly, Martin and Margo Wilson (1982). "Whom Are Newborn Babies Set to Resemble?." *Ethology and Sociobiology*, no.3: 69–78.
Debord, Guy (2006). *The Society of the Spectacle*. London: Rebel Press.
Dewey, John and Arthur Bentley (1949). *Knowing and the Known*. Westport: Greenwood Press Publishers.
Dombey, Henrietta (1992). "Lessons Learnt at Bed-time," in *New Readings: Contributions to an Understanding of Literacy*. Edited by Keith Kimberley, MargaretMeek and Jane Miller. London: A & C Black.
Doucet, Marc G. (2005). "Child's Play: The Political Imaginary of International Relations and Contemporary Popular Children's Film." *Global Society*, vol.19, no.3: 289–306.
"DreamWorks' Shrek Franchise Delivers a Record-Setting $1.6 Billion in Consumer Home Entertainment Spending" (2005). *Business Wire*. FindArticles.com. Available at http://findarticles.com/p/articles/mi_m0EIN/is_2005_Jan_4/ai_n8681654 [accessed January 3, 2010].
Dundes, Lauren (2001). "Disney's Modern Heroine Pocahontas: Revealing Age-old Gender Stereotypes and Role Discontinuity under a Facade of Liberation." *Social Science Journal*, vol.38, no.3: 353–65.
Dunn, David Hastings (2006). "The Incredibles: An Ordinary Day Tale of a Superpower in the Post 9/11 World." *Millennium*, vol.34, no.2: 559–62.
Dworkin, Andrea (1987). *Intercourse*. New York: The Free Press.
Editorial (2005). "Redemption in the Bayou." *The New York Times*, September 5. Available at http://www.nytimes.com/2005/09/05/opinion/05iht-edbayou.html?_r=1 [accessed May 10, 2009].
Elias, Norbert (1978). *What is Sociology?* New York: Columbia University Press.
Elias, Norbert (1983). *The Court Society*. New York: Pantheon.
Elias, Norbert (1987). *Involvement and Detachment*. London: Blackwell.
Elias, Norbert (2000). *The Civilizing Process*. London: Blackwell Publishing.
Elias, Norbert (2001). *The Society of Individuals*. New York: Continuum.

Elias, Norbert and Eric Dunning (1986). *Quest for Excitement: Sport and Leisure in the Civilizing Process.* Oxford: Blackwell.

Elias, Norbert and John Scotson (1994). *The Established and the Outsiders: A Sociological Enquiry into Community Problems.* London: Sage.

Elliott, Ted et al. (2001). *Shrek—Script.* Available at http://www.imsdb.com/scripts/Shrek.html.

Emirbayer, Mustapha (1997). "Manifesto for a Relational Sociology." *The American Journal of Sociology,* vol.103, no.2: 281–317.

Enlow, Donald (1990). *Facial Growth.* Philadelphia: Harcourt Brace.

Ernie Keebler (2009). No title. Online post, *Sudbury Star.* Available at http://www.thesudburystar.com/ArticelDisplay.aspx?e=1469197 [accessed October 3, 2009].

Evely, Christine (2005). "'Shrek 2': Beyond the Screen." *Screen Education,* vol.38: 62–6.

Eyerman Ron and Andrew Jamieson (1998). *Music and Social Movements.* Cambridge: Cambridge University Press.

Faherty, Vincent (2001). "Is the Mouse Sensitive? A Study of Race, Gender, and Social Vulnerability in Disney Animated Films." *Studies in Media & Information Literacy Education,* vol.1, no.3: n.p.

Fairclough, Norman (1992). *Discourse and Social Change.* Cambridge: Polity Press.

Faurie, Charlotte, Dominique Pontier, and Michel Raymond (2004). "Student Athletes Claim to Have More Sexual Partners than Other Students." *Evolution and Human Behavior,* vol.25: 1–8.

Finch, Robert (2004). "Seeing the Light," in *This Sacred Earth: Religion, Nature, Environment.* Edited by Roger Gottlieb. New York: Routledge.

Fisek, Hamit and Richard Ofshe (1970). "The Process of Status Evolution." *Sociometry,* vol.33: 327–46.

Folstad, Ivar and Andrew Karter (1992). "Parasites, Bright Males, and the Immunocompetence Handicap." *American Naturalist,* vol.139: 603–22.

Freud, Sigmund (1969). *Civilization and Its Discontents.* New York: W. W. Norton and Company.

Furnham, Adrian, Meritxell Lavancy and Alastair McClelland (2001). "Waist-to-hip Ratio and Facial Attractiveness: A Pilot Study." *Personality and Individual Differences,* vol.30: 491–502.

Gabler, Neal (1987). *An Empire of Their Own: How the Jews Invented Hollywood.* Doubleday: New York.

Gangestad, Steven and Jeffry Simpson (2000). "The Evolution of Human Mating: Trade Offs and Strategic Pluralism." *Behavioural and Brain Sciences,* vol.33: 573–644.

Geffcken, J. (1926). "Eumenides, Erinyes," in *Encyclopedia of Religion and Ethics Volume 5.* Edited by J. Hastings. New York: Scribner's.

Gerbet, Thomas (2009). 'Les Shrekologues', radio documentary diffused on the 17th of April on Radio-Canada. http://www.radio-canada.ca/audio-video/pop.shtml#urlMedia=http://www.radio-canada.ca/Medianet/2009/CBF/MacadamTribus200904172106_2.asx [accessed May 10, 2009].

Giddens, Anthony (1990). *The Consequences of Modernity*. Stanford: Stanford University Press.

Gillespie, Greg (2008). "Dressed to Kilt: The Shrek Tartan and the Discourse of Highlandism," Presented to the Popular Culture Association Annual Conference, San Francisco, California.

Giroux, Henry (1995). "Animating youth: The Disneyfication of Children's Culture." *Socialist Review*, vol.24, no.3: 23–55.

Giroux, Henry (1999). *The Mouse that Roared: Disney and the End of Innocence*. Lanham: Rowman and Littlefield.

Giroux, Henry (2004). "Are Disney Films Good for Your Kids?," in *Kinderculture: The Corporate Construction of Childhood*. Edited by Shirley Steinberg and Joe Kincheloe. Boulder: Westview Press.

Gottlieb, Roger (2004a). "Religion in an Age of Environmental Crisis," in *This Sacred Earth: Religion, Nature, Environment*. Edited by Roger S. Gottlieb. New York: Routledge.

Gottlieb, Roger (ed.) (2004b). *This Sacred Earth: Religion, Nature, Environment*. New York: Routledge.

Grammer, Karl (1992). "Variations on a Theme: Age Dependent Mate Selection in Humans." *Behavioral and Brain Sciences*, vol.15: 100–2.

Graves, Robert (1966). *The White Goddess*. New York: Farrar, Straus, Giroux.

Grayson, K., M. Davies and S. Philpott (2009). "Pop Goes IR? Researching the Popular Culture—World Politics Continuum." *Politics*, vol.29, no.3: 155–63.

Greenberg, Daniel (1992). *Magic*. Niles, IL: DC Comics, Mayfair Games Inc.

Griffin, Susan (1989). "Split Culture," in *Healing the Wounds: The Promise of Ecofeminism*. Edited by Judith Plant. Philadelphia: New Society Publishers.

Grow up Sudbury (2009). No title. Online post, *Sudbury Star*. Available at http://www.thesudburystar.com/ArticleDisplay.aspx?e=1469197 [accessed October 3, 2009].

Gurevitch, Michael, Tony Bennett, James Curran and Janet Woollacott (eds.) (1982). *Culture, Society and the Media*. London: Methuen.

Habermas, Jürgen (1984). *The Theory of Communicative Action, vol. 1*. Boston: Beacon Press.

Habermas, Jürgen (1987). *The Theory of Communicative Action, vol. 2*. Boston: Beacon Press.

Haig, David (1993). "Genetic Conflicts in Human Pregnancy." *Quarterly Review of Biology*, vol.68: 495–532.

Hall, Stuart (1982). "The Rediscovery of 'Ideology': Return of the Repressed in Media Studies," in *Culture, Society and the Media*. Edited by Michael Gurevitch, Tony Bennett, James Curran and Janet Woollacott. London: Methuen.Hall, Stuart (ed.) (1997). *Representations: Cultural Representations and Signifying Practices*. London: Sage.

Hamilton, William and Marlene Zuk (1982). "Heritable True Fitness and Bright Birds: A Role for Parasites?." *Science,* vol.218: 384–7.
Hanh, Thich Nhat (1988). *The Heart of Understanding.* Berkeley: Parallax Press.
Hanmerguy (2009). No title. Online post, *Sudbury Star.* Available at http://www.thesudburystar.com/ArticelDisplay.aspx?e=1469197 [accessed October 3, 2009].
Harries, Elizabeth Wanning (2001). *Twice Upon a Time. Women Writers and the History of the Fairy Tale.* Princeton: Princeton University Press.
Hart, Benjamin (1990). "Behavioural Adaptations to Pathogens and Parasites: Five Strategies." *Neuroscience and Biobehavioral Reviews,* vol.14: 273–94.
Haynes, Roslynn (2003). "From Alchemy to Artificial Intelligence: Stereotypes of the Scientist in Western Literature." *Public Understanding of Science,* vol.12, no.3: 243–53.
Herman, Edward and Noam Chomsky (2002). *Manufacturing Consent. The Political Economy of the Mass Media.* New York: Pantheon Books.
Hinkins, Jillian (2007). "'Biting the Hand that Feeds': Consumerism, Ideology, and Recent Animated Film for Children." *Papers: Explorations into Children's Literature,* vol.17, no.1: 43–50.
Hogan, Linda (1995). *Dwellings: A Spiritual History of the Living World.* New York: Touchstone Books.
Hogan, Linda (1998). *Power.* New York: W. W. Norton.
Hopkins, John (2004). *Shrek. From the Swamp to the Screen.* New York: Harry Abrams Publishers.
Hubka, David (1998). *Globalization of Cultural Production: Children's Animated Television, 1978 to 1995.* PhD thesis. Ottawa: Carleton University.
Hurd, Barbara (2001). *Stirring the Mud: On Swamps, Bogs, and Human Imagination.* Boston: Beacon Press.
Hurston, Zora Neale (1938/1983). *Tell My Horse.* Berkeley: Turtle Island.
Ibsen, Henrik (1961). *Hedda Gabler and Other Plays.* Translated by Una Ellis-Fermor. Harmondsworth: Penguin.
Ingham, Richard (2005). "New Orleans Disaster Serves Tough Lessons" Available at http://abc.net.au/science/news/enviro/EnviroRepublish_1453141.htm [accessed September 5, 2009].
Inglehart, Ronald (1990). *Culture Shift in Advanced Industrial Society.* Princeton, N.J.: Princeton University Press.
"Interview: Jeffrey Katzenberg, DreamWorks Founder and Shrek Producer" (2007). *The Independent,* June 22. Available at http://www.independent.co.uk/arts-entertainment/films/features/interview-jeffrey-katzenberg-dreamworks-founder-and-shrek-producer-454072.html [accessed June 15, 2009].
Irigaray, Luce (1993). *Sexes and Genealogies.* New York: Columbia University Press.

"Is Shrek Bad for Kids?" (2007) *Time.com*. Available at http://www.time.com/time/magazine/article/0,9171,1619573,00.html [accessed June 14, 2009].

Jigsaw (2009a). No title. Online post, *Sudbury Star*. Available at http://www.thesudburystar.com/ArticelDisplay.aspx?e=1469197 [accessed October 3, 2009].

Jigsaw (2009b). No title. Online post, *Sudbury Star*. Available at http://www.thesudburystar.com/ArticelDisplay.aspx?e=1469197 [accessed October 3, 2009].

Jim McWhinnie (2009). No title. Online post, *Daily Mail*. Available at http://www.dailymail.co.uk/news/article-1234547/Thomas-The-Tank-Engine-branded-right-wing-conservative-demeaning-women.html [accessed April 21, 2010].

Jolly, M. C. et al. (2000). "Obstetric Risks of Pregnancy in Women less than 18 Years Old." *Obstetrics & Gynecology*, vol.96: 962–6.

Kant, Immanuel (1784/1991). "Idea for a Universal History with a Cosmopolitan Intent," in *Kant's Political Writings*. Edited by Hans Reiss. Cambridge: Cambridge University Press.

Kaye, S. A. et al. (1990). "The Association of Body Fat Distribution with Lifestyle and Reproductive Factors in a Population Study of Postmenopausal Women." *International Journal of Obesity*, vol.14: 583–91.

Kellner, Douglas (2003). "Cultural Studies, Multiculturalism, and Media Culture," in *Gender, Race and Class in Media*. Edited by G. Dines and J. M. Humez. Thousand Oaks: Sage.

Keno (2009). No title. Online post, *Sudbury Star*. Available at http://www.thesudburystar.com/ArticelDisplay.aspx?e=1469197 [accessed October 3, 2009].

Kenrick, Douglas et al. (1990). "Evolution, Traits, and the Stages of Human Courtship: Qualifying the Parental Investment Model." *Journal of Personality*, vol.58: 97–116.

Kiesecker, Joseph et al. (1998). "Behavioral Reduction of Infection Risk." *Proceedings of the National Academy of Sciences in the United States of America*, vol.96: 9165–8.

Kirschner, M. A., and E. Samojlik (1991). "Sex Hormone Metabolism in Upper and Lower Body Obesity." *International Journal of Obesity*, vol.15: 101–8.

Kurzban, Robert and Mark Leary (2001). "Evolutionary Origins of Stigmatization: The Functions of Social Exclusion." *Psychological Bulletin*, vol.127: 187–208.

Lapsley, Robert and Michael Westlake (1988). *Film Theory: An Introduction*. Manchester: Manchester University Press.

Lasswell, Harold (1948). "Structure and Function of Communication in Society," in *The Communication of Ideas*. Edited by Lyman Bryson. New York: Institute for Religious and Social Studies.

Latour, Bruno (1988). *Science in Action*. Cambridge, MA: Harvard University Press.
Latour, Bruno (2004).*Politics of Nature. How to Bring the Sciences into Democracy*. Cambridge, MA: Harvard University Press.
Latour, Bruno (2005). *Reassembling the Social. An Introduction to Actor-Network-Theory*. Oxford, UK: Oxford University Press.
Laura (2009). No title. Online post, *Daily Mail*. Available at http://www.dailymail.co.uk/news/article-1234547/Thomas-The-Tank-Engine-branded-right-wing-conservative-demeaning-women.html [accessed April 21, 2010].
Leong, Anthony (2001). "Shrek Movie Review." *Frontier,* no.22. Reproduced on http://www.mediacircus.net/shrek.html [accessed July 2, 2009].
Leopold, Aldo (1947), "The Ecological Consciousness," in *The River of the Mother of God and Other Essays by Aldo Leopold*. Edited by Susan L. Flader and J. Baird Callicott. Madison, WI: The University of Wisconsin Press, 338–46.
Leopold, Aldo (1968 (1949)). *A Sand County Almanac: With Essays on Conservation from Round River*. New York: Ballantine.
Lerner, Gerda (1986). *The Creation of Patriarchy*. New York: Oxford University Press.
Lerner, Gerda (1997). *Why History Matters: Life and Thought*. New York: Oxford University Press.
Linklater, Andrew (1990). *Men and Citizens in the Theory of International Relations*. London: Macmillan (2nd edition).
Linklater, Andrew (1998). *The Transformation of Political Community. Ethical Foundations of the post-Westphalian Era*. Cambridge: Polity Press.
Linklater, Andrew (2001). "Marxism," in *Theories of International Relations*. Edited by Scott Burchill et al. Basingstoke: Palgrave Macmillan, 129–54.
Liu, Jianghua and Virpi Lummaa (2009). "*Effects of Delaying First Reproduction on Reproductive Failure in Human Females.*" Poster session presented at the annual meeting of the European and Human Behaviour & Evolution Association, St Andrews, Scotland.
Lomer, Beverly (2005). "Hildegard of Bingen," in *The Encyclopedia of Religion and Nature*. Edited by Bron R. Taylor. New York: Thoemmes Continuum.
Lopez, Barry (1986). *Arctic Dreams*. New York: Vintage Books.
Maguire, Gregory (1995). *Wicked: The Life and Times of the Wicked Witch of the West*. New York: Regan Books.
Maltin, Leonard (1987). *Of Mice and Magic: A History of American Animated Cartoons*. New York: Plume Books.
Mann, Michael (1986). *The Sources of Social Power, vol. 1: A History of Power from the Beginning to A.D. 1760*.Cambridge: Cambridge University Press.
Marshall, Elizabeth and Özlem Sensoy (2009). "The Same Old Hocus-Pocus: Pedagogies of Gender and Sexuality in *Shrek 2*." *Discourse: Studies in the Cultural Politics of Education*, vol.30, no.2: 151–64.

Bibliography • 175

Martin, Ann (2006). *Red Riding Hood and the Wolf in Bed. Modernism's Fairy Tales*. Toronto: University of Toronto Press.
Marx, Karl (1977). *A Contribution to the Critique of Political Economy*. Moscow: Progress Publishers.
Mathijs, Ernest (ed.) (2006). *The Lord of the Rings: Popular Culture in Global Context*. London: Wallflower Press.
Mayall, Berry (2002). *Toward a Sociology of Childhood*. Maidenhead: Open University Press.
McDonald's (2007). "McDonald's® brings the Joy of Shrek® to Customers around the World." Available at http://www.prnewswire.com/cgi-bin/stories.pl?ACCT=109&STORY=/www/story/05-08-2007/0004583765& EDATE= [accessed September 15, 2009].
McKay, John (2005). "Shrek Character is target of traditional Values Religious Group." *The Canadian Press*, 22 February. Available at http://www.commondreams.org/headlines05/0222-06.htm [accessed September 25, 2009].
McLain, D. K. et al. (2000). "Ascription of Resemblance of Newborns by Parents and Nonrelatives." *Evolution and Human Behavior*, vol.21: 11–23.
Médiamétrie—TF1 (2008). "Audience: Confessions intimes et Shrek ont séduit le public de TF1," 20 February. Available at http://www.actuzap-tele.com/audiences_tele/4903-audiences-confessions-intimes-et-shrek-ont-seduit-le-public-de-tf1.html [accessed September 17, 2009].
Mellon, Sidney (1981). *The Evolution of Love*. San Francisco: W.H. Freeman.
Melucci, Alberto (1996). *Challenging Codes: Collective Action in the Information Age*. Cambridge, U.K.: Cambridge University Press.
Mikey27 (2009). No title. Online post, *Sudbury Star*. Available at http://www.thesudburystar.com/ArticelDisplay.aspx?e=1469197 [accessed October 3, 2009].
Mitchell, Elvis (2001). "So Happily Ever After: Beauty and the Beasts." *The New York Times*, May 16, p. E1.
Monaghan, Patricia (1999). *The Goddess Companion: Daily Meditations on the Feminine Spirit*. St. Paul: Llewellyn Publications.
Montaigne, Michel de (1595/1960). *Essays. Volume 1*. New York: Anchor Books (translated by Donald Frame).
Mulvey, L. (1975). "Visual Pleasure and Narrative Cinema," in *Feminisms: An Anthology of Literary Theory and Criticism*. Edited by R. R. Warhol and D. Price-Herndl. New Jersey: Rutgers University Press.
Murdock, George (1981). *Atlas of World Cultures*. Pittsburgh: University of Pittsburgh Press.
Nash Information Services (1997–2009). "Box Office History for Shrek Movies." Table, *The Numbers*. Available at http://www.the-numbers.com/movies/series/Shrek.php [accessed January 3, 2010].

Nasr, Seyyed Hossein (2004). "Ours Is Not a Dead Universe." *Parabola: Myth, Tradition, and the Search for Meaning*, vol.29, no.2: 6–13.

Negus, Keith (1999). *Music Genres and Corporate Culture*. London: Routledge.

Nettle, Daniel (2002). "Height and Reproductive Success in a Cohort of British Men." *Human Nature*, vol.13: 473–91.

Newman, Barbara (2003). *God and the Goddesses: Vision, Poetry, and Belief in the Middle Ages*. Philadelphia: University of Pennsylvania Press.

Newsday (1984). "The Magical Creatures of William Steig" Available at www.williamsteig.com/article-newsday84.htm [accessed September 4, 2009].

Nexon, Daniel H. and Iver B. Neumann (eds.) (2006). *Harry Potter and International Relations*. Lanham: Rowman and Littlefield.

Nieguth, Tim and Shauna Wilton (2010). "Popular Culture and Canadian Political Science," unpublished manuscript.

Nielsen, François (2004). "The Vacant 'We': Remarks on Public Sociology." *Social Forces*, vol.82, no.4: 1619–27.

Nisbet, Matthew C. et al. (2002). "Knowledge, Reservations, or Promise?: A Media Effects Model for Public Perceptions of Science and Technology." *Communication Research*, vol.29, no.5: 584–608.

The Numbers (2004). [chart depicting top 10 grossing movies of 2004]. Available at http://www.the-numbers.com/market/2004.php [accessed June 14, 2009].

O'Connell, Sean (2007). "Shrek the Third." May 19. http://www.filmcritic.com/reviews/2007/shrek-the-third/ [accessed July 2, 2009].

O'Neill, B. (2001). "Shrek: The Anti-Fairytale." Available at http://www.spiked-online.com/Articles/00000002D16D.htm [accessed June 14, 2009].

Owens, Ian and Roger Short (1995). "Hormonal Basis of Sexual Dimorphism in Birds: Implications for New Theories of Sexual Selection." *Trends in Ecology & Evolution*, vol.10: 44–7.

Pawlowski, Boguslaw and Grazyna Jasienska (2005). "Women's Preferences for Sexual Dimorphism in Height Depend on Menstrual Cycle Phase and Expected Duration of Relationship." *Biological Psychology*, vol.70: 38–43.

Pawlowski, Boguslaw et al. (2000). "Tall Men Have more Reproductive Success." *Nature*, vol.403: 156.

Petrie, Marion, Tim Halliday, and Carolyn Sanders (1991). "Peahens Prefer Peacocks with Elaborate Trains." *Animal Behaviour*, vol.41: 323–31.

Pilgrim, David (2000). "The Coon Caricature" Available at http://www.ferris.edu/news/jimcrow/coon/ [accessed September 4, 2009].

Pimentel, Octavio and Velázquez, Paul (2009). "*Shrek 2*: An Appraisal of Mainstream Animation's Influence on Identity." *Journal of Latinos and Education*, vol.8, no.1: 5–21.

Platek, Steven and Todd Shackelford (2006). *Female Infidelity and Paternal Uncertainty: Evolutionary Perspectives on Male Anti-cuckoldry Tactics*. Cambridge: Cambridge University Press.

Platek, Steven et al. (2002). "Children's Faces: Resemblance Affects Males but not Females." *Evolution and Human Behavior,* vol.23: 159–66.
Plumwood, Val (1993). *Feminism and the Mastery of Nature.* New York: Routledge.
Price, Jeffrey et al. (2007). *Shrek the Third—Script.* Available at http://www.joblo.com/scripts/script_shrekthethird.pdf
Prince, David (2008). *The Pixar Touch. The Making of A Company.* New York: Alfred A. Knopf.
Propp, Vladimir (1968). *Morphology of the Folktale.* Austin: University of Texas Press.
Regalski, Jeanne and Steven Gaulin, (1993). "Whom are Mexican Infants Said to Resemble? Monitoring and Fostering Paternal Confidence in the Yucatan." *Ethology and Sociobiology,* vol.14: 97–113.
Reich, Wilhelm (1970). *The Mass Psychology of Fascism.* Translated by V. Carfagno. New York: Farrar, Straus, Giroux.
Reuters (2005). "Dream Works Shares Slide On Weak Sales." *The New York Times,* May 11, p. C5.
Ritzer, George (2000). *The McDonaldization of Society.* Boston: Pine Forge Press.
Roach, Catherine (2005). "Mother Nature Imagery," in *Encyclopedia of Religion and Nature.* Edited by Bron R. Taylor. New York: Thoemmes Continuum.
Rousseau, Jean-Jacques (1754/1983). "Discourse on the Origin of Inequality," in *The Essential Rousseau.* Translated by Lowell Bair. New York: Meridian.
Rupert, Mark (2007). "Marxism and Critical Theory," in *International Relations Theories: Discipline and Diversity.* Edited by Tim Dunne, Milja Kurki and Steve Smith. Oxford: Oxford University Press, 148–65.
Ryan, William (1971). *Blaming the Victim.* New York: Pantheon.
Salihu, Hamisu et al. (2003). "Childbearing beyond Maternal Age 50 and Fetal Outcomes in the United States." *Obstetrics & Gynecology,* vol.103: 1006–14.
Salska, Irmina et al. (2008). "Conditional Mate Preferences: Factors Influencing Preferences for Height." *Personality and Individual Differences,* vol.44: 203–15.
Sandler, Kevin (ed.) (1998). *Reading the Rabbit: Explorations in Warner Bros. Animation.* New Brunswick, N.J.: Rutgers University Press.
Sardar, Ziuaddin (1998). *Postmodernism and the "Other."* London and Chicago: Pluto Press.
Shackelford, Todd and David Buss (2000). "Marital Satisfaction and Spousal Cost-infliction." *Personality and Individual Differences,* vol.28, no.5: 917–28.
Shaw, Miranda (2006). *Buddhist Goddesses of India.* Princeton: Princeton University Press.

Sheppard, James and Alan Strathman (1989). "Attractiveness and Height: The Role of Stature in Dating Preference, Frequency of Dating and Perceptions of Attractiveness." *Personality and Social Psychology Bulletin*, vol.15: 617–27.
Shiva, Vandana (1988). *Staying Alive: Women, Ecology and Survival in India*. London: Zed Books.
Shiva, Vandana (1997). *Biopiracy: The Plunder of Nature and Knowledge*. Boston, South End Press.
Sibeon, Roger (2004). *Rethinking Social Theory*. London: Sage Publications.
Singh, Devendra (1993). "Adaptive Significance of Female Physical Attractiveness: Role of Waist-to-hip Ratio." *Journal of Personality and Social Psychology*, vol.65: 283–88.
Sjöö, Monica and Barbara Mor (1991). *The Great Cosmic Mother: Rediscovering the Religion of the Earth*. San Francisco: Harper.
Smith, Steven (1984). *Reading Althusser*. Ithaca and London: Cornell University Press and Macmillan.
Smoodin, Eric (ed.) (1994) *Disney Discourse: Producing the Magic Kingdom*. London: Routledge.
Snyder, Melvin et al. (1979). "Avoidance of the Handicapped: An Attributional Ambiguity Analysis." *Journal of Personality and Social Psychology*, vol.37: 2297–306.
Spiegel, John (1983). *Transactions*. New York: Jason Aronson.
Starbuck, Edwin (1926). "The Female Principle", in *The Encyclopedia of Religion and Ethics*. Edited by J. Hastings. Boston: Beacon Press.
Steig, William (1990). *Shrek!* New York: Farrar, Straus, Giroux.
Stirner, Max (1964). "A Human Life," in *The Anarchists*. Edited by Irving Horowitz. New York: Dell.
Surber, Jere (1998). *Culture and Critique: An Introduction to the Critical Discourses of Cultural Studies*. Boulder: Westview Press.
Sussman, M. B. (1953). "Parental Participation in Mate Selection and its Effect upon Family Continuity." *Social Forces*, vol.1: 76–81.
Swami, Viren et al. (2008). "Factors Influencing Preferences for Height: A Replication and Extension." *Personality and Individual Differences*, vol.45: 395–400.
Symons, Donald (1979). *The Evolution of Human Sexuality*. New York: Oxford.
Symons, Donald (1995). "Beauty Is in the Adaptations of the Beholder: The Evolutionary Psychology of Human Female Attractiveness," in *Sexual Nature, Sexual Culture*. Edited by Paul Abramson and Steven Pinkerton. Chicago: University of Chicago Press.
Takolander, Maria and David McCooey (2005). "You Can't Say No to the Beauty and the Beast: Shrek and Ideology" Available at http://www.accessmylibrary.com/coms2/summary_0286-11409562_ITM [accessed June 14, 2009].

Termier, Pierre (1908). *Marcel Bertrand (1847–1907)*. Paris: H. Dunod et E. Pinat.
Thornham, Sue (1998). "Feminist Media and Film Theory," in *Contemporary Feminist Theories*. Edited by Stevi Jackson and Jackie Jones. Edinburgh: Edinburgh University Press.
Thornhill, Randy and Steve Gangestad (1993). "Human Facial Beauty: Averageness, Symmetry and Parasite Resistance." *Human Nature*, vol.4: 237–69.
Thornhill, Randy and Steve Gangestad (1996). "The Evolution of Human Sexuality." *Trends in Ecology & Evolution*, vol.11: 98–102.
Tilly, Charles (2002). *Stories, Identities, and Political Change*. New York: Rowman & Littlefield Publishers, Inc.
Tilly, Charles (2006). *Why? What Happens When People Give Reasons...And Why*. Princeton: Princeton University Press.
Tilly, Charles (2008). *Explaining Social Processes*. London: Paradigm Publishers.
Tittle, Charles R. (2004). "The Arrogance of Public Sociology." *Social Forces*, vol.82, no.4: 1639–43.
Topliss, Iain (2005). *The Comic Worlds of Peter Arno, William Steig, Charles Addams and Saul Steinberg*. Baltimore: The Johns Hopkins University Press.
Touraine, Alain (1977). *The self-Production of Society*. Chicago: Chicago University Press.
Touraine, Alain (1995). *Critique of Modernity*. London: Blackwell.
Traditional Values Coalition (2005a). "A Gender Identity Disorder Goes Mainstream." Available at http://www.traditionalvalues.org/pdf_files/TVCSpecialRpt Transgenders1234.PDF [accessed January 15, 2009].
Traditional Values Coalition (2005b). "Parents Beware: 'Shrek 2' Features Transgenderism and Crossdressing Themes." Available at http://www.traditional values.org/modules.php?sid=1659# [accessed January 15, 2009].
Trivers, Robert (1972). "Parental Investment and Sexual Selection," in *Sexual Selection and the Descent of Man 1871–1971*. Edited by Bernard Campbell. Chicago: Aldine.
Trivers, Robert (1974). "Parent-offspring Conflict." *American Zoologist*, vol.14: 249–64.
Tuana, Nancy (1993). *The Less Noble Sex: Scientific, Religious, and Philosophical Conceptions of Woman's Nature*. Bloomington: Indiana University Press.
Udry, Richard and Bruce Eckland (1984). "Benefits of Being Attractive: Differential Payoffs for Men and Women." *Psychological Reports*, vol.54: 47–56.
Umminger, Alison (2006). "Supersizing Bridget Jones: What's Really Eating the Women in Chick Lit," in *Chick Lit: The New Woman's Fiction*. Edited by Suzanne Ferriss and Mallory Young. New York: Routledge.
Unger, Johann Wolfgang and Jane Sunderland (2007). "Gendered Discourses in a Contemporary Animated Film: Subversion and Confirmation of Gender Stereotypes in *Shrek*," in *Discourse and Contemporary Social Change*. Edited

by Norman Fairclough, Giuseppina Cortese and Patrizia Ardizzone. Bern: Peter Lang, 459–85.
Valleyboy (2009). No title. Online post, *Sudbury Star*. Available at http://www.thesudburystar.com/ArticelDisplay.aspx?e=1469197 [accessed October 3, 2009].
Veblen, Thorsten (1925). *The Theory of the Leisure Class*. London: Allen & Unwin.
Volarcik, Kimberly et al. (1998). "The Meiotic Competence of In-vitro Human Ovocytes Is Influenced by Donor Age: Evidence that Folliculogenesis is Comprised in the Reproductively Aged Ovary." *Human Reproduction*, vol.13: 154–60.
Walker, Alice (1988). *Living by the Word: Selected Writings 1973–1987*. San Diego: Harcourt Brace Jovanovich.
Walkerdine, Valery (2009). *Children, Gender, Video Games: Towards a Relational Approach to Multimedia*. New York: Palgrave Macmillan.
Walters, Suzanna (1995). *Material Girls: Making Sense of Feminist Cultural Theory*. Berkeley: University of California Press.
Watts, Steven (1997). *The Magic Kingdom. Walt Disney and the American Way of Life*. Boston: Houghton Mifflin.
Weber, Cynthia (2006). *Imagining America at War: Morality, Politics and Film*. London: Routledge.
Weber, Cynthia (2009). *International Relations Theory: A Critical Introduction*. London: Routledge (3rd edition).
Weingart, Peter (2003). "Of Power Maniacs and Unethical Geniuses: Science and Scientists in Fiction Film." *Public Understanding of Science*, vol.12, no.3: 279–87.
Weinman, Jaime (2007). "'Shrek the Third' Will Get the Kids and Parents, but the Raunchy Jokes ar the Real Reason the Lovable Ogre's so Hot." *MacLean's*, May 21. Available at http://www.macleans.ca/article.jsp?content=20070521_105231_105231 [accessed September 20, 2009].
Weiss, Carol and Eleanor Singer (1988). *Reporting of Social Science in the National Media*. New York: Russell Sage Foundation.
Weissman, Kristin (1999). *Barbie: The Icon, the Image, the Ideal*. Boca Raton, FL: Universal Publishers.
Weldes, Jutta (2003). "Popular Culture, Science Fiction and World Politics: Exploring Intertextual Relations," in *To Seek Out New Worlds: Science Fiction and World Politics*. Edited by Jutta Weldes. New York: Palgrave Macmillan, 1–27.
Weldes, Jutta (2006). "High Politics and Low Data: Globalization Discourses and Popular Culture," in *Interpretation and Method: Empirical Research Methods and the Interpretive Turn*. Edited by Dvora Yanow and Peregrine Schwartz-Shea. Armonk: M.E. Sharpe, 176–86.

Wells, Paul (2002). "Where the Mild Things Are." *Sight and Sound*, vol.12, no.2: 27–8.

Whelehan, Imelda (2000). *Overloaded: Popular Culture and the Future of Feminism*. London: The Women's Press.

Wilkinson, Richard (1994). *Symbol and Magic in Egyptian Art*. New York: Thames and Hudson.

Wolf, Naomi (1991). *The Beauty Myth: How Images of Beauty Are Used Against Women*. London: Vintage Books.

Woollacott, Janet (1982). "Messages and Meanings," in *Culture, Society and the Media*. Edited by Michael Gurevitch, Tony Bennett, James Curran and Janet Woollacott. London: Methuen.

Wright, Charles (1959). *Mass Communication: A Sociological Perspective*. New York: Random House.

Wright, Will (1975). *Sixguns and Society*. Berkeley: University of California Press.

Zaadstra, Boukje et al. (1993). "Fat and Female Fecundity: Prospective Study of Effect of Body Fat Distribution on Conception Rates." *British Medical Journal*, vol.306: 484–7.

Zahavi, Amotz (1975). "Mate Selection—A Selection for a Handicap." *Journal of Theoretical Biology*, vol.53: 205–14.

Zavalkoff, Anne (2004). "Dis/located in Nature? A Feminist Critique of David Abram." *Ethics & the Environment*, vol.9: 121–39.

Zipes, Jack (1999). *When Dreams Came True: Classical Fairy Tales and Their Tradition*. New York: Routledge.

Zipes, Jack (2002). *Breaking the Magic Spell: Radical Theories of Folk and Fairy Tales*. Kentucky: University Press of Kentucky.

Zohar, Danah (1990). *The Quantum Self: Human Nature and Consciousness Defined by the New Physics*. New York: Quill/ William Morrow.

Index

A
Adamson, A., 6, 32, 37–8, 43, 62–4, 66–8, 71, 163, 165
Adorno, T., 88, 93–4, 96–7, 165
Avery, T., 88, 163
agency, 20, 88, 97, 105–6, 119, 126, 131, 150
American dream, 72, 85, 95, 163
anarchism/anarchist, 16, 178
 individual anarchism, 10, 16–17
 anarchist space, 16
Allen, P., 47–8, 165
Althusser, L., 65–7, 70, 92, 165, 178
Andersson, M., 138, 165
Anzaldùa, G., 53, 163
Apostolou, M., 143, 165–6
Apuleius, L., 43, 56, 166
Arendt, H., 19–22, 166

B
Bagemihl, B., 42, 166
Baker, R., 140, 166
Baring, A., 45, 56, 166
Barrett, L., 143, 166
Bateman, A., 133, 166
Baudrillard, J., 24, 89, 166
Bauman, Z., 99, 166
Bayley, H., 49, 166
beauty, 10, 23, 28–30, 32–8, 48, 51, 54, 64, 66, 78, 88, 129–30, 164, 175, 178–9, 181
 beauty myth, 29, 32–6, 181
Beck, U., 2, 11, 166
Bell, E., 59, 166
Benito-Rojo, A., 53, 166

Bennett, T., 70, 166, 171, 181
Bentley, A., 115, 169
Bingen, H., 46, 51, 166, 174
Björntorp, P., 135, 166
body, 9, 11, 17, 19, 24, 36, 40, 42–4, 47–8, 50–1, 53, 56, 58, 98, 103, 121, 135, 155, 167, 173, 181
 body appearance, 24
 body fat, 135
 body image, 29
 body shape, 36, 135–6
 female body, 10, 27–9, 36, 135
Bordo, S., 29, 42, 48, 167
Brabham, D., 59, 93, 167
Brady, D., 155, 167
Briggs, K., 46, 167
Bryman, A., 89–90, 167
Brown, H., 50, 167
Burawoy, M., 156, 167
Burch, R., 141, 167
Buss, D., 133–7, 140–1, 167, 177
Buunk, A., 143, 167

C
Callaghan, W., 140, 168
Caputi, J., 10, 39–40, 42, 44, 46, 48, 50–2, 54, 56–8, 168
capitalism, 10–11, 88–90, 93, 96–7, 131
 global capitalism, 92
 techno-capitalism, 88, 92, 98
Carroll, D., 42, 168
Carson, R., 41–2, 168
Chandler, D., 69–70, 168
Chevalier, J., 46, 50, 168

Chomsky, N., 11, 108–9, 113–14, 116, 123–5, 168, 172
Cixous, H., 54, 168
Clark, R., 136, 168
class, 15–16, 25, 57, 60–1, 65, 81–2, 93, 95–7, 99, 108, 110, 112, 151, 173
  capitalist class, 60, 63–4
  class consciousness, 168
  class distinction, 80, 96
  class emulation, 96
  class faction, 96
  class inequalities, 69
  class positions, 125
  class stratification, 100
  class struggle, 10, 60
  class revolution, 60
  class system, 82
  classless, 19, 22, 85, 112
  dominant class, 119–20, 124
  specialized class, 113
  leisure class, 180
  lower class, 94
  middle class, 78, 95, 156
  political class, 62
  ruling class, 63, 65, 69, 92
  upper class, 95
  working class, 61, 69–70, 80
  see also proletariat
Collins, P. H., 53, 169
Connor, S., 39, 169
construction (social), 103
  construction of the world, 59, 69
  constructivist scholars, 68
  corporate construction, 171
consumerism, 23, 102, 172
  anti-consumerism, 90
cosmopolitanism, 91, 93, 96–100, 102, 168
  Kantian cosmopolitanism, 87, 89, 91, 93, 95, 97–9, 101–2
countermovement, 105, 110, 117, 122
critical theory, 93, 108, 124, 177
cuckoldry, 140–1, 176
culture, 3, 15, 33, 38, 40–2, 48, 50, 53, 76–7, 90–2, 96–8, 113, 135–6, 143, 166–9, 171–3, 178, 181

American culture, 89
commodity culture, 80
corporate culture, 176
consumerist culture, 48
cultural convention, 4
cultural industry, 76, 87–8, 91, 165
culture of consumption, 90
dominant culture, 69–70
high/low culture, 95
kinderculture, 171
Islamic culture, 46
mass culture, 92, 94
master culture, 10, 42–3
media culture, 88, 92
mexica culture, 53
monoculture, 42, 49
popular culture, 1, 6, 10, 15, 36, 38–9, 42, 45, 56, 66, 76–8, 80, 85, 95, 171, 175–6, 180–1
sexual culture, 178
visual culture, 30
Western culture, 97, 167
world culture, 175
Curran, J., 69–70, 166, 169, 171

D
Daly, M., 52, 141, 169
Debord, G., 24, 169
democracy, 10, 16, 29, 112–13, 155, 174
Dewey, J., 103, 115, 169
dictator, 8, 111, 119
dictatorship, 19, 23
Disney, 51, 75–6, 79–81, 83–5, 87–91, 93, 96, 100, 113, 117, 163–4, 169–71, 178, 180
  anti-disney, 60, 72, 91
  Disneyfication, 88–91
  Disneyfied, 54
  Disneyization, 88–91, 167, 171
  Disneyland, 89
Doucet, M., 59, 69, 169
Dreamwork, 3, 11, 15, 75–6, 81, 83–5, 87–8, 91–3, 96, 116, 123, 163–4, 169, 172
  Dreamworkification, 88, 91, 93

Dunn, D., 59, 169
Dworkin, A., 48, 169

E
ecological, 39–40, 45, 55, 130, 174
Elias, N., 16, 21, 103, 110–11, 131, 169–70
elite, 41–2, 48, 57, 95–6, 98, 100, 110, 112–13, 124
Elliott, T., 22, 28–9, 32–3, 36, 120, 128, 170
emancipation, 68, 96
emancipatory, 9
Emirbayer, M., 170
Enlightenment, 78, 91–2, 96, 98, 165
Enlow, D., 138, 170
environmental crisis, 4, 171
essentialism, 127
ethnic, 50, 124
  ethnic cleansing, 40
  ethnicity, 16, 25, 40
Evely, C., 61–2, 170
evolutionary, 55, 106, 173
  evolutionary history, 11, 133, 144
  evolutionary laws, 106
  evolutionary perspective, 133, 144, 167, 176
  evolutionary problems, 133
  evolutionary psychology, 11, 133, 135, 137, 139, 141, 143, 166–7, 178
  evolutionary theory, 133, 135
Eyerman, R., 117–18, 170

F
Faherty, V., 170
Fairclough, N., 170, 180
fairy tale, 1, 5–6, 8–9, 22, 24, 27–8, 30, 37–8, 43–4, 49–50, 55–6, 60–2, 65–7, 71–2, 75–85, 87, 100, 112, 114, 117–18, 120, 172, 172, 181
fascism, 47, 177
  anti-fascist, 45
  fascist, 54
Faurie, C., 139, 170

feminism/feminist, 10, 28, 40, 52, 57, 90, 119, 121, 130, 167, 175, 177, 179, 181
  ecofeminism, 165, 171
  black feminism, 169
  critical feminist, 11
  feminist cultural theory, 180
  feminist theory, 29, 36, 179
  feminist philosophy, 40, 168–9
  French feminism, 168
  radical feminism, 57, 169
fertility, 11, 46, 135, 138–40
Finch, R., 42, 170
Fisek, H., 138, 170
Folstad, I., 138, 170
Frankfurt School, 11, 91, 96–7, 108, 165
financial resources, 136, 138
Freud, S., 110, 170
functionalism, 76
Furnham, A., 135, 170

G
Gabler, N., 94, 170
Gangestad, S., 138, 170, 179
Geffcken, J., 47, 53, 170
gender, 9, 15–16, 24–5, 40, 50, 75–6, 78–9, 81–3, 93, 101, 106, 122–3, 153, 166, 168–70, 173–4, 179–80
  gender and identity, 123
  gender and sexuality, 59
  gender conflicts, 15
  gender norms, 9, 81–2
  gender roles, 57, 76, 82
  gender studies, 39
  see also transgender
genetic, 138, 140, 171
genocide, 126, 152
genocidal, 47
Gerbet, T., 126, 128, 130, 170
Giddens, A., 98, 171
Giroux, H., 59, 76–7, 88, 171, 177–8
globalization, 98–9, 102, 153–4, 166, 172, 180
Gottlieb, R., 39, 56, 170–1
Grammar, K., 139, 171

Graves, R., 57, 171
Grayson, K., 59, 171
Greenberg, D., 45, 171
Griffin, S., 40, 171
Gurevitch, M., 70, 166, 169, 171, 181

H
Habermas, J., 121, 171
Haig, D., 143, 171
Hall, S., 15, 93, 108, 166, 171
Hamilton, W., 138, 172
Hanh, T. N., 41, 172
Harries, E., 78, 172
Hart, B., 142, 172
Herman, E., 113–14, 125, 172
Hinkins, J., 93, 172
Hitler, A., 20, 22
Hobbes, T., 109
Hogan, L., 56, 172
Holocaust, 119
Hollywood, 6, 60–1, 69–72, 76, 79, 84, 87, 95–6, 124, 163, 170
Hopkins, J., 6, 8–9, 15, 23, 62, 172, 179
Horkheimer, M., 93–4, 96–7, 165
Hubka, D., 154, 172
Hurd, B., 43, 49, 172
Hurston, Z., 53, 172

I
Ibsen, H., 147, 172
identity, 1, 9, 23–5, 59, 67, 121, 176
  gender identity, 123, 179
  identity of non-western cultures, 97
ideology, 20, 60, 65–9, 71–2, 89, 92–3, 97, 108, 165, 171–2, 178
inclusive society, 10, 24
Ingham, R., 57, 172
Inglehart, R., 121, 172
Irigaray, L., 52, 172

J
Jews, 22, 95–6, 100, 163, 170
  Jewish, 94–6
Jolly, M. C., 139, 173

K
Kant, I., 98, 173
Kantian, 25, 87, 98
  see also Kantian cosmopolitanism
Kantian cosmopolitanism, 87–102
Katzenberg, J., 23, 83–5, 87, 91, 116, 172
Kaye, S. A., 135, 173
Kellner, D., 76, 173
Kenrick, D., 138, 173
Kiesecker, J., 142, 173
Kirschner, M. A., 135, 173
Kurzban, R., 142, 173

L
Lapsley, R., 70, 173
Lasswell, H., 76–7, 173
Latour, B., 103–4, 106, 115, 174
legitimate knowledge, 152, 160
Lenin, V., 119
  Leninist, 121
Leong, A., 87, 174
Leopold, A., 39, 56, 174
Lerner, G., 52, 57, 174
liberal, 94
  imperial neoliberalism, 92, 97
  liberal arts, 153
  liberal democracy, 10, 16, 22, 155, 162
  liberal humanism, 92, 98
  liberal societies, 96
  neoliberal capitalist imperialism, 98
  neoliberal project, 102
  neoliberal understanding of globalization, 98
  neoliberalism, 11, 91
  neoliberal doxa, 11, 91, 97, 102
  neoliberal ideology, 92
Linklater, A., 16, 25, 63, 70, 174
Liu, J., 140, 174
Lomer, B., 46, 174
Lopez, B., 56, 174

M
Maguire, G., 45, 174
Mann, M., 103, 109, 111, 131, 174

Marshall, E., 59, 71, 76–7, 81, 84, 164, 174
Martin, A., 78–80, 83, 175
Marx, K., 63, 69, 112, 175
  classical Marxist, 60, 69–70
  Marxism, 63, 168, 174, 177
  Marxist, 10, 60, 62, 64, 68, 70, 97, 168, 174
  Neo-Marxist, 59–61, 63, 65, 68–71
masculinity, 138
Mathijs, E., 5, 175
Mayall, B., 126, 175
McDonaldization, 90, 102, 177
McKay, J., 126, 175
Mclain, D. K., 141, 175
media, 2, 10, 29, 36, 60, 64, 69–72, 76–7, 81, 88, 90–3, 113, 147–9, 157–61, 164, 166, 168–76, 179–81
mechanism, 70, 97, 133, 142
  psychological mechanism, 11, 143–4
Mellon, S., 137, 175
Melucci, A., 121, 124, 175
Mitchell, E., 76, 164, 175
modern, 1, 6, 66, 78, 89, 97, 143, 169
  modernism, 80, 175
  modernist, 80, 92
  modernity, 4, 97–9, 166, 171, 179
  modernization, 98
  Roman modern games, 113
monarchy, 22, 71
Monaghan, P., 51, 175
Montaigne, M. de, 17–18, 175
moral, 9, 24, 27, 62, 65, 77–8, 101, 122, 124
  immoral, 24
  Kantian moral, 25
  moral power, 92
  moral values, 124
  morally repulsing examples, 114
  morality, 64, 97, 180
  patriarchal moralistic, 49
Mulvey, L., 30, 175
Murdock, G., 143, 175

N
Nasr, S., 56, 176
Nazism, 21
National socialism, 20
Nazi, 19, 22
Negus, K., 77, 176
neoconservative, 3, 105, 122–3
Nettle, D., 137, 176
Nexon, D., 10, 59, 176
Newman, B., 51, 176
Nieguth, T., 149, 176
Nielson, F., 156, 176

O
O'Connell, S., 87, 176
O'Neil, B., 27–8, 176
Owens, I., 138, 176
otherization, 9

P
patriarchy, 40, 57, 89, 131, 174
  patriarchal, 92
  patriarchal delusion, 35
  patriarchal family, 122
  patriarchal historical period, 55
  patriarchal ideology, 93
  patriarchal moralistic, 49
  patriarchal myths, 52–4
  patriarchal social order, 108
  patriarchal social structure, 52
  patriarchal social system, 78
  patriarchal society, 10, 29, 33, 124
Pawlowski, B., 137, 176
Perrault, C., 78
Petrie, M., 138, 176
Pilgrim, D., 50, 176
Pimentel, O., 59, 176
Pixar, 84–5, 88, 90, 93, 163, 177
Platek, S., 140–1, 176–7
Plumwood, V., 40–2, 177
pogrom, 20, 119
politicization, 6
populism, 80
post-modern, 6, 92, 99, 166
  late modernity, 166
  new modernity, 166
  post-modernism, 97, 177

power, 1, 15, 40, 54, 60, 63–5, 68–9, 71, 99–101, 111, 113, 119–22, 131, 168, 172, 174, 180
  absolute power, 20
  bodily powers, 55
  centered power, 98
  corporate power, 164
  cultural power, 100
  disempowered, 71
  economic power, 60, 62–3
  empowerment, 36, 169
  girl power, 77
  greening power, 45–6
  moral power, 92
  political power, 24, 63–4, 69
  power by small elite, 57
  power elite, 98
  power of business, 63, 65
  power of capital, 63
  power of the green, 44
  power relations, 99, 109–10, 113, 122
  power (re-)production, 72
  power structure, 65, 67, 69, 75
  powerful, 23, 30, 44, 54, 62, 64–5, 103–7, 112, 119, 124–5, 143
  powerful/powerless, 6
  powerful actors, 65
  powerful circle, 51
  powerful consumerism ideology, 60
  powerful female deities, 53
  powerful God, 112
  powerful ideology, 60, 66–8
  powerful strategy, 79
  powerless, 65, 125
  power relations, 11
  powers of creation, 55
  powers of the imagination, 49, 56
  social power, 49, 65, 174
  subversive power, 92
  superpower, 169
Price, J., 31, 34, 130, 175, 177
Prince, D., 84, 177
Propp, V., 24, 177
proletariat, 60–2, 64–5, 71–2, 97
  see also class, working class
propaganda, 19, 21, 59, 92, 113, 124, 168

R
race, 15
racism, 48, 50, 57, 89, 127
Regalski, J., 141, 177
Reich, W., 47, 57, 177
reification, 91, 131
reductionist theory, 112, 131
relational, 11, 122, 124, 170, 180
revolution, 121
  class revolution, 60
  revolutionary, 6, 35, 60, 69, 71–2, 88
  revolutionary dream, 120
  revolutionary leader, 120
  revolutionary mass, 61
  revolutionary vanguard, 61
  social revolution, 38, 72
  total revolution, 119
Ritzer, G., 90, 102, 177
Roach, C., 51, 177
Rousseau, J.-J., 17–18, 177
Rupert, M., 63, 177
Ryan, W., 142, 177

S
Salihu, H., 140, 177
Salska, I., 138, 177
Sandler, K., 88, 177
Sardar, Z., 97, 177
sexism, 48, 57
sexual characteristics, 34, 138
Shackelford, T., 137, 140–1, 167, 176–7
Shaw, M., 46, 177
Sheppard, J., 137, 178
Shiva, V., 42, 51, 55, 57, 178
Sibeon, R., 131, 178
Singh, D., 135, 178
Sjöö, M., 42, 49, 55, 57, 178
Smith, S., 65, 177–8
Smoodin, E., 59, 178

social movement, 11, 24–5, 105, 108, 110–12, 117–20, 124–6, 130, 170
new social movements, 117, 119
see also countermovement
social satire, 75–6
socialism, 88, 94
socialization, 68, 70
socializing, 59–60, 69, 90
Snyder, M., 142, 178
Starbuck, E., 51, 61, 178
stalinist, 20
state, 17, 20, 33, 64, 66, 67, 92, 98, 111, 121
  bourgeois state, 60
  democratic state, 23
  ideological state apparatus, 60, 70, 165
  natural state, 34
  state legislative, 122
  state propaganda, 113
  see also totalitarianism, totalitarian state
status, 24, 43, 57, 64, 95–6, 119, 135–6, 138–9, 141, 170
Steig, W., 4–6, 9, 47, 75, 80–1, 93–4, 125, 165, 176, 178–9
stereotype, 29, 42, 50, 77, 93, 169, 172, 179
Stirner, M., 17, 178
structure, 67, 69, 77, 80, 96, 112, 157, 165, 173
  academic reward structure, 67
  capitalist structure, 71
  funding structure, 150, 156, 161
  ideological structure, 70
  infrastructure, 114, 152–3, 156
  insiduous structure, 99
  intertextual structure, 93
  modern structure, 97
  narrative structure, 4
  political structure, 83
  power structure, 65, 69, 75
  social structure, 40, 52, 65, 84, 110
  structure of a fairy tale, 6
  structure of prevailing modes of production, 69
  structure of work and property, 61
structured definition, 29
structure of domination, 96, 99
structure of oppression, 97
superstructure, 63, 69, 112
structuralist, 6, 8
Surber, J., 96, 178
Sussman, M. B., 143, 178
Swami, V., 137, 178
Symons, D., 135, 138, 140, 178

T
Takolander, M., 27–8, 35, 38, 93, 178
Termier, P., 147, 179
Thornham, S., 29, 179
Thornhill, R., 138, 179
Tilly, C., 111, 114, 179
Tittle, C., 156, 179
Topliss, I., 94, 179
totalitarianism, 10, 16, 19–22, 25, 166
totalitarian, 20–2, 119, 121
totalitarian architecture, 20
totalitarian propaganda, 21
totalitarian state, 19
Touraine, A., 119, 121, 179
transgender, 24, 100, 118, 122–3, 128, 149, 179
transaction, 122, 125–6, 128, 130–1, 178
transactional, 11, 103–4, 106–9, 111, 113–15
transactor, 103–9, 111, 113, 115–17, 119, 121–7, 129–31
Trivers, R., 133, 142–3, 179
Tuana, N., 51, 179

U
Udry, R., 139, 179
Umminger, A., 30, 33, 179
Unger, J., 59, 93, 179

V
Veblen, T., 96, 180
Volarcik, K., 140, 180

W

Walker, A., 57, 180
Walkerdine, V., 108, 180
Walters, S., 29–30, 180
Warner Brothers, 79, 84, 88, 163
Weber, C., 10, 59, 180
Weinman, J. R, 116, 180
Weiss, C., 156, 159, 180
Weissman, K., 29–30, 36, 180
Weldes, J., 59, 180
Whelehan, I., 36, 181
Wolf, N., 10, 33–8, 123, 181

Woollacott, J., 70, 166, 169, 171, 181
Wright, W., 6–9, 16, 181

Y

Yiddish, 48

Z

Zaadstra, B., 135, 181
Zahavi, A., 138, 181
Zavalkoff, A., 57, 181
Zipes, J., 49–50, 181
Zohar, D., 57, 181